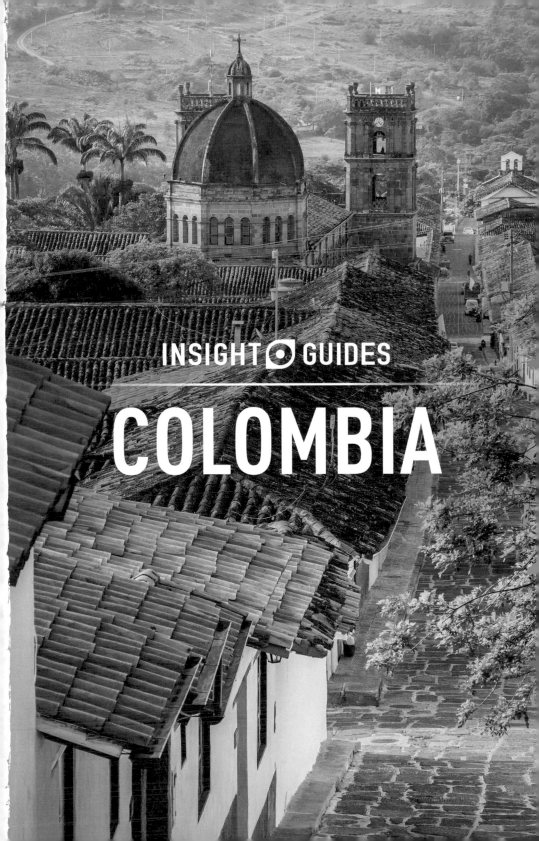

INSIGHT ● GUIDES

COLOMBIA

⦿ Walking Eye App

YOUR FREE DESTINATION CONTENT AND EBOOK AVAILABLE THROUGH THE WALKING EYE APP

Your guide now includes a free eBook and destination content for your chosen destination, all for the same great price as before. Simply download the Walking Eye App from the App Store or Google Play to access your free eBook and destination content.

HOW THE WALKING EYE APP WORKS

Through the Walking Eye App, you can purchase a range of eBooks and destination content. However, when you buy this book, you can download the corresponding eBook and destination content for free. Just see below in the grey panels where to find your free content and then scan the QR code at the bottom of this page.

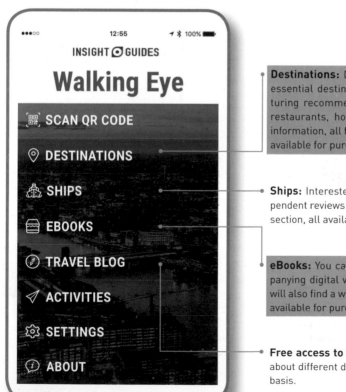

Destinations: Download your corresponding essential destination content from here, featuring recommended sights and attractions, restaurants, hotels and an A–Z of practical information, all for free. Other destinations are available for purchase.

Ships: Interested in ship reviews? Find independent reviews of river and ocean ships in this section, all available for purchase.

eBooks: You can download your free accompanying digital version of this guide here. You will also find a whole range of other eBooks, all available for purchase.

Free access to travel-related blog articles about different destinations, updated on a daily basis.

HOW THE DESTINATION CONTENT WORKS

Each destination includes a short introduction, an A–Z of practical information and recommended points of interest, split into 4 different categories:

• Highlights
• Accommodation
• Eating out
• What to do

You can view the location of every point of interest and save it by adding it to your Favourites. In the 'Around Me' section you can view all the points of interest within 5km.

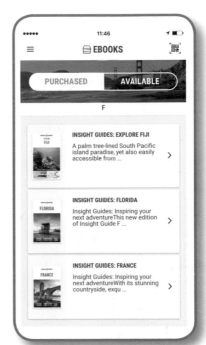

HOW THE EBOOKS WORK

The eBooks are provided in EPUB file format. Please note that you will need an eBook reader installed on your device to open the file. Many devices come with this as standard, but you may still need to install one manually from Google Play.

The eBook content is identical to the content in the printed guide.

HOW TO DOWNLOAD THE WALKING EYE APP

1. Download the Walking Eye App from the App Store or Google Play.
2. Open the app and select the scanning function from the main menu.
3. Scan the QR code on this page – you will then be asked a security question to verify ownership of the book.
4. Once this has been verified, you will see your eBook and destination content in the purchased ebook and destination sections, where you will be able to download them.

Other destination apps and eBooks are available for purchase separately or are free with the purchase of the Insight Guide book.

CONTENTS

Travel Tips

TRANSPORTATION

A – Z

Maps

LEGEND

🔎 Insight on
📷 Photo Story

THE BEST OF COLOMBIA: TOP ATTRACTIONS

From reminders of its colonial past, to fashionable trendy neighborhoods, here are the top attractions this captivating country has to offer...

△ **Cartagena's walled city**. Walk along the ancient ramparts of this dominant fortress city and you'll understand the military might once wielded by Colonial Spain. Today it's a Caribbean-colonial marvel filled with great restaurants and charming boutique hotels. See page 186.

▽ **Monserrate**. Some of the greatest panoramic views on the South American continent can be seen at Cristo Redentor in Rio de Janerio, Machu Picchu in Peru – and Cerro Monserrate in Bogotá, Colombia. See page 125.

△ **Ciudad Perdida**. Not all indigenous ruins in South America are in Peru – this ancient stone city actually pre-dates Machu Picchu by about 650 years. Take a multi-day trek through the Sierra Nevadas and discover it for yourself. See page 205.

△ **Zona Cafetera**. In the mountains south of Manizales lies Colombia's premier coffee-growing region. Pick beans right off the trees or, better yet, stay on a hacienda for a few days in a hyper-caffeinated state of bliss. See page 167.

△ **La Candelaria**. Bogotá's historic center is a hilly colonial enclave home to museums, diverse restaurants, pulsing nightlife, and a bohemian spirit unrivalled anywhere else in the city. See page 118.

△ **Río Claro**. Just outside of Jardín, one of Colombia's most idyllic towns, is the Río Claro. Picturesque crystalline waters and tempting cliffs and boulders make this a perfect day trip for zip-lining, kayaking, or just taking a swim. See page 150.

◁ **San Gil**. This northern city is ground zero for Colombia's adventure-sports scene. Take to the skies in a paragliding harness or, if high altitudes aren't your thing, try braving the rapids of Río Fonce. See page 155.

△ **Popayán**. Few Spanish-colonial towns in Colombia are as well preserved as Popayán. Located near the border with Ecuador, the whitewashed facades of the old buildings transport you back in time. See page 247.

▽ **Chocó**. For years the Chocó Department, on Colombia's Pacific Coast, was undiscovered by tourists. But word has gotten out. These days more and more people are visiting remote villages like Bahía Solano and Nuqui to take in the amazing wildlife – like the migration of humpback whales that pass through every year. See page 255.

△ **Guajira Peninsula**. Colombia's largest indigenous community, the Wayúu people, live in this arid coastal area, and the surrounding desert is rich with flamingos, salt flats, and hidden beaches. See page 219.

THE BEST OF COLOMBIA: EDITOR'S CHOICE

Fascinating museums, stunning national parks and idyllic white-sand beaches... here are our recommendations for getting the best out of your visit to Colombia.

Pygmy marmoset, Amacayacu National Park.

BEST NATIONAL PARKS & PRESERVES

Amacayacu. Located on the Amazon River, this jungle is home to a wide array of wildlife, including 500 species of birds, pink river dolphins, sloths, and boisterous squirrel monkeys. See page 273. **Macuira**. At the end of the Guajira Peninsula, where the arid desert meets the refreshing ocean, exotic birds and iguanas frolic in an incongruously located patch of tropical forest. See page 225.

Reserva Natural Cañon Río Claro. Discovered by a *campesino* tracking a jaguar that was decimating his livestock, this area of outstanding beauty now attracts people from all over the world. Find out why for yourself. See page 150. **Tayrona**. Where the foothills of the Sierra Nevadas end, stunning white-sand Caribbean beaches begin. It's also home of the famed Ciudad Perdida. See page 208.

Museo del Oro.

BEST MUSEUMS

Museo Botero. This museum, in Bogotá's La Candelaria neighborhood, houses one of the finest collections of international art on the continent. See page 120. **Museo de Antioquia**. This is perhaps the best museum in Medellín, and features the works of Colombian sculpting master Fernando Botero. See page 138. **Museo del Oro**. The Gold Museum, teeming with pre-Columbian artifacts, isn't only the best museum in Bogotá – it's the best museum in the whole of Colombia. See page 123. **Museo de la Independencia**. Housed in a charming 16th-century colonial building in Bogotá, this fascinating museum takes a unique approach to exploring Colombia's independence. See page 122.

BEST ACTIVITIES

Birdwatching. Colombia has over 1,900 confirmed bird species within its borders, making it a hotspot for bird-watching enthusiasts. See page 73.

River rafting. The country's myriad rivers make for some exceptional whitewater rafting – especially in the adventure-sports capital of San Gil. See page 159.

Hiking/trekking. National parks Los Nevados and El Cocuy offer some of the most rewarding hikes and treks on the continent. See page 175.

Dancing. You can't come to Colombia without hitting up a *salsoteca* – and those in Cali are world-renowned. See page 88.

Trekking in El Cocuy Cordillera National Park.

Carnival of Barranquilla.

BEST BEACHES

Cabo San Juan. The coastal lagoons in Parque Nacional Tayrona are jewels in the sparkling crown of Colombia's Caribbean coastline. See page 209.

Capurganá. Visit the remote Chocó Department, near the Panamanian border, and laze on a little-known, picturesque white-sand beach. See page 211.

Johnny Cay. This small coral atoll is ringed with turquoise waters that crash on the south shore, making for perfect bodysurfing conditions. See page 231.

Palomino. A small town in the Guajira region that is home to one of the most stunning beaches in the country – watch out for strong currents though. See page 222.

Playa Blanca. Probably Colombia's most famous beach, this stretch of pristine white sand is just a short hop from colonial Cartagena. See page 191.

BEST FESTIVALS

Carnival. The biggest carnival celebration outside of Brazil takes place over four days before Ash Wednesday in Barranquilla. See page 202.

Feria de Cali. This festival, held from the 25th–30th of December, in Cali, is a celebration of all things salsa that also features cultural exhibitions and *Paso Fino* horse parades. See page 286.

Feria de los Flores. Every year, during the first two weeks of August, flower growers parade through the streets of Medellín carrying elaborate displays on their backs in *silleteros* (wooden racks). See page 286.

Wayúu Festival. Uribía, dubbed the 'indigenous capital of Colombia', holds Colombia's largest indigenous festival every May. The festival celebrates the Wayúu people and their unique cultural heritage. Expect lots of eating and dancing. See page 224.

Festival de la Leyenda Vallenata. Valledupar is the birthplace of vallenato music, and at the end of April the city celebrates this fact with four days of raucous live performances heavy on the accordion and *guacharaca*. See page 214.

Fiestas de San Pacho. Catholicism meets Afro-Colombian customs in September and October in Chocó's Quibdo, with street parties, parades, and *sancocho* cookouts. See page 259.

Cabo San Juan.

The Parque de la Luz, a 300-post lighting installation in Medellín.

Palm-lined beach at sunset on the Pacific Ocean, near Nuquí.

Plaza de la Trinidad, Cartagena.

WHERE REALITY MEETS MAGIC

From the brink of disaster to comeback of the century, Colombia has recently regained its status as a must-visit gem of South America.

Island off San Andrés.

Colombia has earned its status as a must-visit travel destination for the simple reason that its diverse environments offer something for everyone. Bogotá is a fascinating metropolis with culture to spare, with the pre-Columbian treasures on show at its Gold Museum the jewel in its crown. Travelers can indulge their inner Indiana Jones by venturing deep into Amazonas and canoeing on the Amazon, alongside pink river dolphins and caimans, or making friends with the world's smallest primate, the adorably diminutive pygmy marmoset. Adrenaline junkies can head to San Gil for a paragliding trip or a raft journey down raging rivers. The Guajira Peninsula, with its arid coastal deserts, beckons those looking for a spiritual retreat rich in indigenous culture. The ramparts of Cartagena's walled city tell a story of a once great fortress that protected ignominiously appropriated treasures from invading hordes, while the white-sand Caribbean beaches and crystalline waters of Santa Marta and Isla San Andrés are the stuff of postcards. Music lovers will find their fix in the salsa clubs of Cali, or the outdoor vallenato concerts in Valledupar.

Carnival of Barranquilla.

Then there's the Colombia that wary tourists have heard about for years; the country where its citizens have had to endure rather than enjoy. From the first spasms of *La Violencia*, the 10-year civil war that tore the country apart, to the constant battles and skirmishes between the government, drug cartels and leftist insurgents, Colombia is a country that has shed more than its share of blood.

Despite the darkness of the 20th century, Colombia has turned a corner. Chubby, mustached drug kingpins no longer control the nation. The government and the rebels are ready for peace once and for all, and Colombia's citizens are ready to inhabit a country where their natural happiness can dominate once again, unchecked by the darker aspects of human nature.

In many ways Colombia's renaissance is already here; the country radiates every treasure the first inhabitants found in its soil. Its mountains are emeralds, stretching to the four corners of the country; the Caribbean sunsets are pure gold. Colombia is El Dorado, and the real gems are the people – always ready to welcome visitors with open arms, just waiting for them to discover their country's natural wonders.

El Gallineral Park, San Gil.

LAND AND ENVIRONMENT

In each of Colombia's five distinct regions you'll find varied ecological wonders boasting an array of diverse flora and fauna.

Colombia's geological origins are as fascinating as they are globally significant. This nation is one of six South American countries sharing an eco-region called the Guiana Shield, which covers some 270 million hectares (667 million acres) and encapsulates myriad ecosystems that are home to rich biodiversity. This dates back over 500 million years, and scientists now believe Colombia was part of the Pangea landmass that theoretically broke up around 125 million years ago and created the Americas.

Whatever its ancient origins, Colombia's geological makeup and geographical location make it one of the most environmentally diverse countries in the world. Desert, tropical jungle, savanna, alluvial plains, coastline – it's the only South American country with both a Pacific and Caribbean coastline – and coral islands are all present here, but that doesn't mean people have settled in all of these areas. Despite a population density of 43.07 per sq km (111.55 per sq mile),

El Cocuy Cordillera and National Park.

Colombia's northern Chocó Region, where it borders Panama's Darién Gap, gets so much precipitation that it is generally regarded as one of the wettest places on earth, if not the wettest.

Colombia's approximately 48 million inhabitants mostly live in the Andean region located in and around the capital city of Bogotá.

Despite Colombia's wide variety of terrain and ecosystems, the climate is decidedly less complex. The country's proximity to the equator results in constant tropical, isothermal temperatures. The weather changes in various regions of the country mostly depend on altitude and distance to the west and north coasts. For example, Bogotá's altitude of 2,590 meters (8,500ft) means it has a cool climate year round and warm-weather clothing is often necessary at night. Visitors will find that the hottest areas of Colombia are in the northeast Guajira Peninsula and the Maracaibo lowlands in the southwest. Still, temperatures in the Caribbean lowlands and the Amazon Basin frequently top 85°F (29°C) with humidity between 80 and 90 percent. How much rainfall various regions of the country get depends on trade-wind systems and how they're affected by the different landscapes.

It's for all of these reasons that Colombia is predominantly broken up into five natural geographic regions, each of which is covered in this book. These include the Andes, where the capital city of Bogotá is located, as well as temperate Medellín and salsa-rich Cali; the *Llanos*, or eastern plains; The Amazon, which is little developed and still home to indigenous communities; the Pacific Coast, which stretches some 1,287km (800 miles) from the border with Panama to the border with Ecuador; and the Caribbean Coast, which is home to colonial Cartagena as well as the country's best beaches. Each of these regions has its own unique characteristics and compo-

Wild horse in the Cocora Valley.

sition, and travelers will find must-visit destinations in each area.

THE ANDEAN REGION

As with Ecuador, Peru, and Chile, Colombia sits on the western end of South America, right where two formidable tectonic plates converge: the west-moving Nazca Plate and the east-moving South American Plate. The point at which they meet has resulted in the geological creation of the Andes Mountains, the spine that runs along the length of the continent. In Ecuador, the Andes are a single range teeming with 5,000-meter (16,400-ft) -high volcanic peaks. However, in southern Colombia the Andes break off into three distinct cordilleras (mountain ranges) known as

Colombia boasts 58 national parks covering over 11 percent of the country's area, offering a blinding array of sights and wildlife, including canyons, glaciers, beaches, tropical jungle, over 1,900 species of birds, and the most terrestrial mammal species in the world.

the Occidental, Central and Oriental. The first two run near each other but are separated by a natural fault line known as the Cauca Valley, home to the city of Cali. The Oriental runs eastward, away from the first two, where Bogotá is located, creating the basin valley occupied by Colombia's most majestic river, the Magdalena. From there the Oriental crosses into Venezuela and becomes the Cordillera de Mérida. The Cordillera Central crosses Antioquia Department, where Medellín is located; both it and the Occidental continue north and end at the Caribbean lowlands.

The three cordilleras have high volcanic peaks. The climate in the Andes Region is determined by the position and altitude of the mountains themselves. For example, Bogotá sits nestled in the Andes at an altitude of 2,644 meters (8,675ft) – hence the chillier weather – while Cali's position in the Valle de Cauca is at 1,001 meters (3,284ft) and enjoys warmer weather. Medellín, considered by many as the happiest medium climate-wise, is between the two and sits at 1,495 meters (4,905ft) and enjoys a perpetual spring-like climate.

THE LLANOS EASTERN PLAINS (ORINOQUÍA)

This eastern region is known colloquially by a couple different names. These Llanos (plains), run from the Cordillera Oriental, east into Venezuela and to the mouth of the Orinoco River (hence *Orinoquía*). Since the 16th century, farmers have cultivated these flat grasslands for cattle grazing, and today they are a fertile ranching region comparable to Argentina's pampas flatlands. Several important rivers flow through here, making ideal transportation routes that run south all the way to the Amazon River. It is for this reason that the Llanos and the Amazon regions are often lumped together in two parts, combining to represent about half the country's surface area.

AMAZONIA

South of the Llanos is the Amazonia Region, most notable for the Amazon River, which runs along the most populous point near the town of Leticia, at the tri-borders of Colombia, Brazil, and Peru. However, the Amazon isn't the only river that tells a story. By following the Río Guaviare (a tributary of the Orinoco River) south, it's easy to see the gradual transition from fertile grassland to thick tropical forest. Two rivers (the Guayabero and the Ariari) converge to form the Guaviare, and where they do, near the town of San José del Guaviare, is a real geological marvel: the Serrania de Macarena (part of the Serrania de Macarana National Park), a 140-km (86-mile) -wide area of sandstone rock formations home to some of the most crystal-line rivers and picturesque waterfalls in the world.

THE CARIBBEAN LOWLANDS

Like the Llanos, this region of Colombia is notable for bodies of water. The area itself begins where two cordilleras start: the Sierra Nevada de Santa Marta, and the Sierra de Perijá (an extension of the Andes straddling Colombia and Venezuela). In between these two mountain ranges is the valley city of Valledupar, and to the northeast is the Guajira Peninsula. To the west are the plains of the lower Magdalena River. The Central and Occidental Cordilleras continue along this river area and finish a few hundred kilometers south of Barranquilla. About 200km (124 miles) from the ocean the Magdalena and Cauca meet, creating vast stretches of swamps and lagoons that turn into lakes during the rainy season. Along the coast, from Santa Marta to the west, you'll find Colombia's famed Caribbean beaches and stunning coral islands.

THE PACIFIC REGION

Outside of the Amazon, the Pacific Coast of Colombia is the most inaccessible area of the country. The Serrania del Baudó Mountains run about 500km (310 miles) south from Panama, through mostly forested areas to the principal city of Buenaventura. Between here and the Cordillera Occidental is a basin drained by the Atrato, San Juan, and Baudó rivers. Another 300km (186 miles) south is the border with Ecuador. This entire area receives much rainfall, and its principal eco-region, the Chocó, is the world's wettest lowland, with a massive annual precipitation of 523.6ins (13,300mm).

Colombia's Pacific Region is slowly opening up to tourists. That said there are myriad impediments to progress. The rainfall in the north means the area is difficult to reach, and the city of Buenaventura, in the south, is still ranked as one of Colombia's most dangerous. Outside the major cities, the Afro-Colombian communities that populate the area are the poorest and most neglected in the country. Still, the coastline is peppered with idyllic beaches and the offshore waters are famed for whale watching.

Tayrona National Park.

☉ AMAZONIA'S PEOPLES

Despite fewer than 100,000 people populating an area of over 100,000 sq km (38,610 sq miles), Amazonia is home to over 70 different indigenous communities. These include the Yagua, Nukak and other tribes with historical roots in various countries in the Amazon Basin. The tribes are underrepresented politically due to many factors including geographic remoteness, lack of education, and fragmentation between communities. That said, over the past two decades a spotlight has been shone on the plight of indigenous peoples in the Amazonas. One such social program involves providing educational resources to indigenous tribes and communities for sustainable management of native trees.

DECISIVE DATES

A Tairona gold pendant.

PRE-COLUMBIAN PERIOD

4000 BC
The first people occupy Colombia's Caribbean coast.

1200 BC
The Tairona indigenous people form a group of chiefdoms in the Sierra Nevada de Santa Marta Mountains.

545 BC
The Muisca indigenous tribe establishes their first settlements in Colombia's central highlands.

SPANISH COLONIALISM

1500
Rodrigo de Bastidas establishes the first Spanish settlement on the Caribbean coast.

1535
Pedro de Heredia founds Cartagena and establishes a fortress to stockpile pilfered treasure.

1538
Gonzalo Jiménez de Quesada founds Santa Fe de Bogotá.

GRAN COLOMBIA

1808
Napoleon replaces King Ferdinand VII of Spain with his brother Joseph, resulting in riots in Bogotá.

1812
After leading a military campaign in Venezeula, Simón Bolivar joins the Independence movement in Cartagena.

1819
After leading his men on a perilous journey over the Andes, Bolivar wins the decisive victory over the Spanish at the Battle of Boyacá.

1819-1828
Bolívar serves as president of Gran Colombia.

1830
Venezuela and Ecuador break away from Colombia. Simón Bolívar dies in Santa Marta.

THE ERA OF CIVIL WAR

1885
The Conservative government drafts a new, highly centralized constitution that will last for over 100 years.

1899-1903
A Liberal revolt against the Conservative government begins *La Rebelión*, also known as the War of a Thousand Days, resulting in over 100,000 deaths before the Liberals were defeated.

1932
In a border dispute, Peruvian troops occupy the town of Leticia, in Amazonas

Department; The League of Nations hands the area back to Colombia in 1934.

1948
The socialist mayor of Bogotá, Jorge Eliécer Gaitán, is assassinated, marking the beginning of *La Violencia*, a 10-year civil war fuelled by economic deprivation, anti-Communist sentiment, and religious persecution.

1957
A political truce known as the *Frente Nacional* (National Front) ends the violence and establishes a system of shared power between the Liberal and Conservative parties.

NARCOS AND GUERRILLAS

1964
The Fuerzas Armadas Revolucionarias de Colombia (FARC) forms under leader Pedro Antonio Marín, a member of the Communist Party.

Pedro Antonio Marín of the FARC.

1970
The Movimiento 19 de Abril (M19) guerrilla group, a military arm of the leftist political party Alianza Nacional Popular (ANAPO), arises in protest at the elections.

1975
Burgeoning smuggler Pablo Escobar develops his cocaine empire in Medellín.

1977
The Rodríguez Orejuela brothers, Gilberto and Miguel, found the Cali Cartel.

1982
Colombian novelist Gabriel García Márquez wins the Nobel Prize in Literature.

1984
The FARC signs a cease-fire agreement with the government and forms a political party called the Union Patriótica (UP), seeking political reforms.

1985
M19 guerrillas storm the Colombian Supreme Court, resulting in the deaths of half the judges on the bench.

1989
Popular Liberal Party presidential candidate Luis Carlos Galán is assassinated by a hit man hired by Pablo Escobar. Avianca Flight 203 is blown up the by Medellín Cartel, killing 110 people.

THE LONG ROAD TO PEACE

1989
A peace accord is signed between the government and M19, and the following year

they surrender their weapons and convert into a political party named Alianza Democratíca (M19-AD).

1993
Colombian police kill Pablo Escobar in Medellín.

1998
President Andrés Pastrana grants the FARC 42,000sq km (16,216sq miles) of land in southern Colombia in the hope of jumpstarting the peace process.

2002
After multiple guerrilla actions, including an airline hijacking, Pastrana ends peace talks and orders his military to retake FARC controlled areas.

2006
The leaders of the Cali Cartel are extradited to Florida and sentenced to 30 years each in federal prison.

2008
Three events cripple the FARC: the Colombian army kills their spokesman, Raúl Reyes; their founder, Pedro Antonio Marín, dies of a heart attack; and FARC kidnap victim Ingrid Betancourt is rescued.

2012
The FARC officially enter peace talks with President Juan Manuel Santos' administration in Havana, Cuba.

2016
In a referendum, Colombians narrowly reject a peace deal between the government and FARC that took four years to negotiate, once again keeping national peace just out of reach.

2017
Mudslides kill over 300 people in the city of Mocoa, located in the Putumayo Department in the southwest of the country.

'No' supporters celebrate following their victory in the 2016 referendum.

PRE-COLUMBIAN HISTORY

Colombia wears its ancient history on its sleeve. Well-preserved archeological sites exist throughout the country, and the cultures of its indigenous peoples are a part of the national fabric.

Visitors to Colombia will find a country rich in indigenous heritage and ancient history. In stark contrast to many Western and European countries, much of Colombia's indigenous population still thrive in various corners of the country. Their longevity perhaps isn't so much the result of the wholesome, charitable relations between early occupiers and natives, but maybe more to do with the fact that when you exist in remote, inaccessible regions of mountainous or jungle terrain, it makes it harder for conquistadors to hunt you down and enslave or murder you.

This well-preserved history makes it easier to gain an insight into not only the indigenous people of the last millennia, but the earliest inhabitants of the region too. As for the history of the land, many geologists believe Colombia was once part of Pangea, the last supercontinent, and formed when an area now known as South America broke away from present-day Africa some 200 million years ago.

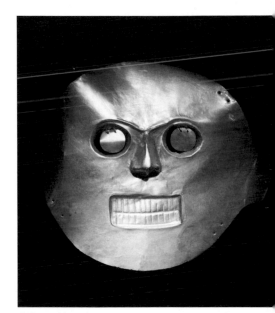

Calima gold mask.

> *Some archeologists believe that the first people arrived in Colombia around 45,000 BC, but most estimates place the timeline closer to 16,000 BC.*

HUNTER-GATHERERS

The first people arrived in Colombia during the late Pleistocene era. The archeological sites in Tibitó (located in the Andean plateaus north of Bogotá), El Totumo (in the Magadalena Valley), and Cudinamarca are generally regarded as the earliest sites of human occupation in the country. To put that into perspective, when these

early humans appeared, mastodons still roamed the land and were a principal source of food.

The aboriginal peoples migrated from the Caribbean and Mesoamerica in the north and from the southern Andes and Amazon in the south. For thousands of years, various tribes lived and subsisted off the land, establishing permanent village settlements by 2000 BC. These tribes also traded with one another, and some of the oldest-known examples of pottery formed by indigenous hands date back to around 5000 BC.

FROM TRIBES TO SOCIETIES

Between 5000 and 1000 BC the hunter-gatherers shifted to an agrarian society, establishing permanent settlements and producing pottery. By the first millennium the tribes developed sophisticated political systems and social organizations. The Tairona, for example, who existed in the coastal Sierra Nevadas, were one of the most advanced of the early societies and developed a functional economy based on agriculture, commerce, and fishing. Like other advanced indigenous communities in Latin America, they also built aqueducts, roads, stairways, and public spaces.

Other indigenous tribes include the Muisca, whose first settlements date back to around 545

The artistic legacy of the indigenous peoples of Colombia is most pronounced in their goldwork. The Muisca, for example, created elaborate gold pendants, staffs, and transformational figures combining elements of man and animal.

BC. They controlled the central Colombian Highlands. The mingling of ancient-indigenous peoples in Colombia's surrounding was facilitated by the Muisca's language, which was known as Chibcha. Linguists agree that Chibcha formed from a variety of now-extinct dialects that originated in regions as far north as Nicaragua and as far south as Ecuador. Certain Chibcha words still exist in modern Colombian Spanish, such as municipality names like Zapaquirá and Sogamoso. Even the root word of Bogotá is Chicbcha: Bacatá.

CULTURE AND CUSTOMS

A confederation of Muisca states existed in the central Andean region of Colombia, with all of them being controlled in the Bogotá area by a *zipa* (ruler in the south), and a *zaque* (ruler in the north) in modern-day Tunja. These leaders did not wield absolute power, so unlike the Incas or Aztecs, the Muisca can't be considered a kingdom or empire. Still, their leaders commanded great respect, and the *zipa* was even a de-facto intermediary between the heavens and earth. It was his responsibility to offer gifts to the Goddess Guatavita. The process involved the *zipa* covering himself with gold dust and taking a boat out to the middle of their most sacred body of water, Lake Guatavita, and throwing in gold trinkets. The lineage of individual *zipa* and *zaque* leaders can be traced back to the mid-to-late 15th century, just before the Spanish arrived in the country.

As for the economy, the Muisca's was one of the strongest on the continent. This was due in no small part to Colombia's rich abundance of gold and emeralds, which the Muisca mined copiously. They traded these precious stones and metals with one another, and this trade was the principal manner in which Muisca from different regions interacted. Their agrarian society utilized terraced farming methods in the highlands that grew, among other things, maize,

Pendant of the Tairona people, depicting a shaman.

⊘ THE ORIGINAL MELTING POT

Of all the 'immigrant nations' in the western hemisphere, Colombia might just be the first. Its early populations were comprised of indigenous groups from Mesoamerica and the Caribbean in the north, and the Andes and Amazon in the south. This created a rich diversity of cultures that benefited the country. And for the most part, these tribes co-existed peacefully and engaged in commerce, diplomacy, and redistribution with one another; lower-ranking chiefs, acting as intermediaries, would visit tribes in different regions and bring goods to exchange. This ensured indigenous groups had access to a variety of items no matter their geographical location in the country.

potatoes, quinoa, coca, and cotton, for both consumption and trade. Certain sports were part of their rituals, and one typical Colombian game, tejo, a disc-tossing sport, is said to have its roots in Muisca culture. Muisca religion revolved around worship of the sun and moon, and priests were trained from childhood to lead religious ceremonies.

NATIVE LIFE ON THE COAST

The Tairona people had their own chiefdoms back in the Sierra Nevada, Magdalena, and

around 200 BC to 1650. However, like the Muisca, they were most renowned for their distinctive goldwork, some stunning examples of which can be seen at Bogatá's Museo del Oro.

OTHER PEOPLES

The Tairona and Muisca may have been the largest of the indigenous groups, but there were other native tribes that flourished throughout the country. The Sinú, for example, established chiefdoms in the southern Caribbean Lowlands and throughout parts of Antioquia. They farmed

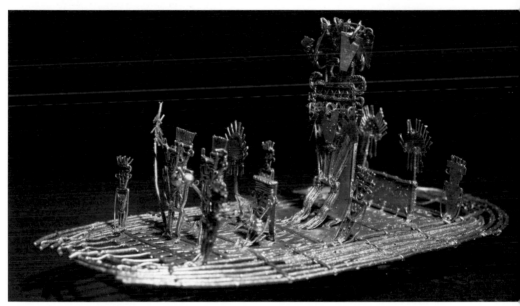

La Balsa de Eldorado (the Raft of El Dorado), from the Muisca period, on display at Bogotá's Gold Museum.

Guajira regions along the northern coast. The Tairona were the other dominant indigenous group in the country at the time, and they spoke their own version of Chibcha. Their chiefdoms date back to at least the 1st century AD, with some evidence suggesting they'd adapted to an agrarian society as far back as 1200 BC, maybe even earlier. Still, a boom in population growth turned the Tairona into a formidable society by the 11th century.

The religious beliefs of the Tairona were decidedly liberal, allowing for divorce and homosexuality, which would have been a shock for the new Catholic arrivals from Spain. The Taironas excelled at ceramics, and their craftsmanship went through various different phases from

maize and yucca in the wet marshlands, developing artificial mounds to facilitate the process. The Quimbaya people existed in certain areas of the Valle de Cauca and operated their society much the same way as the Muisca and Tairona. The Liles and Gorrones were also residents of the Valle de Cauca, and are classified as Calima, an umbrella term denoting indigenous groups who come from this region. These groups all developed economic systems based on agriculture, fishing, hunting, and trade.

All in all there are 102 indigenous groups in Colombia. Some still live in tribes to this day, living much the same as they did before Europeans arrived en masse with fever dreams of gold and a goal to conquer.

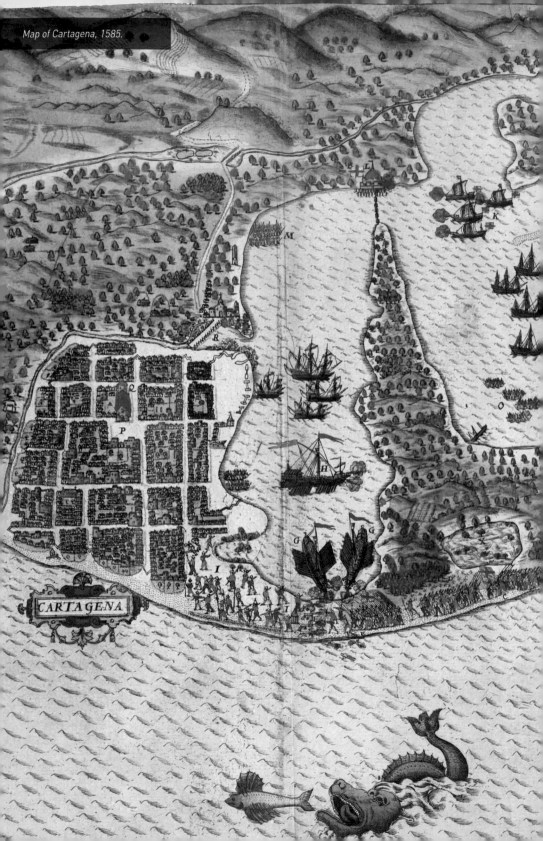

Map of Cartagena, 1585.

CARTAGENA

COLONIAL RULE

The Spanish arrived in Colombia with dreams of gold, but their legacy is of creating a nation that would one day break off from the crown and forge its own path.

THE FIRST SETTLERS

The Spanish colonization of present-day Colombia was a gradual process, with no single event bearing earth-moving significance. The first European to arrive in the land was a Spanish explorer of the Caribbean and onetime companion of Christopher Columbus named Alonso de Ojeda. He spent a brief period on Colombia's Caribbean coast, and when he returned to Spain he brought with him stories of limitless reserves of native gold, which helped give rise to the famous El Dorado legend.

Around 1500, Rodrigo de Bastidas, a conquistador with a reputation for insubordination, arrived on the northern Colombian coast. After years of delays, the Spanish Crown had finally granted him permission to form a permanent settlement, and he established Santa Marta (which is named so as it was founded on the day of St Martha's Feast). Bastidas he also named the Magdalena River.

The Spanish sacking a Caribbean village for gold, c.1602.

The city of Santa Marta was the first-ever permanent settlement in Colombia, and was founded in 1525. It is the oldest remaining city in Colombia, and the site of numerous colonial and historical landmarks, including the home where the Liberator Simón Bolívar passed away.

Baslidas' legacy is a complicated one. On the one hand certain historical records, as well as his own writings, show he had a friendly, pacifist attitude toward the natives and dealt with them peacefully. On the other hand he was a slave owner and proclaimed at the founding of Santa Marta that he would happily make war with the locals, steal their property, and sell their women and children as slaves.

During the early decades of the 16th century Europeans began bringing the first enslaved Africans to Colombia. Cartagena became the chief slave port in the country, with estimates placing the total number of African slaves arriving there at around 1 million. The supply of slaves became more frequent as the passing decades resulted in dwindling indigenous populations at the hands of the Spanish. African labor became prominent in most regions, with slaves working in the country's gold and emerald mines, cattle ranches, and textile mills.

A THIRST FOR GOLD AND LAND

While the Spanish may have never discovered El Dorado, during the early 1500s they did plunder and trade their way to accumulating vast amounts of valuable treasure, such as gold and emeralds. The bounty was so plentiful, in fact, that they needed a secure place to store it. Enter Spanish commander Pedro de Heredia, who founded Cartagena in 1533 on a site that was once an indigenous village called Calamarí. Cartagena was conceived as a fortress city, safe from pirate attacks where the Spanish could stockpile massive amounts of gold. It grew rapidly as the Spanish acquired more and more treasure, much of it plundered form the tombs of the Sinú indigenous tribes.

It soon became clear that gold from the dead would not suffice; now the Spanish wanted gold and land from the living as well. They figured most of this precious metal could be found in the largest indigenous communities, so this led to their conquest of the two main indigenous groups: the Chibcha-speaking Tairona and Muisca tribes. In 1535, a conquistador named

The city of El Dorado on the imaginary Lake Parima, c.1599.

⊘ EL DORADO: LEGEND OR TRUTH?

The Spanish conquistadors had a serious case of gold fever, and this was only exacerbated by rumors they'd heard of a city of gold located somewhere in Colombia. As with many myths and legends, part of the lore is steeped in a little truth. One ritual of the indigenous Muisca leaders involved sailing to the middle of Lake Guatavita in Colombia's central highlands and throwing gold trinkets in the water as gifts for the water goddess.

By the time word got back to Europeans, the lake had turned into a city and the trinkets vast stockpiles of gold treasure and the Spaniards pestered the locals for info regarding this mythical lost city of gold, and many locals got so irritated that they gave the obsessed foreigners false directions just to get rid of them. The fascination has continued to present times, with people searching in and around the lake for their fortune. Plans to actually drain the lake were bandied about but later quashed, and no golden utopia has ever been found.

Today the name El Dorado is a reference to any mythical place where fortunes are made in an instant. Still, despite the fiction, who knows if somewhere in the central Colombian highlands lies the site of a former great city buried under a volcanic lake, filled with gold trinkets offered up to appease the Goddess of Laguna de Guatavita.

Gonzalo Jiménez de Quesada led the principal expedition of some 800 men south from Santa Marta into the plateaus of the Andes region around Bogotá – the heart of the Muisca nation.

In 1537 the Muisca natives, led by their *zipa*, Tisquesusa, mounted a spirited resistance. However, their primitive spears and darts and were no match for the horses, attack dogs, and firearms of the Spanish. Quesada's expedition wound up dominating through sheer military superiority. This didn't seem to sway Tisquesusa though, who over the course of a month, had his subjects attack Quesada's men all over the Bogotá savanna. But it wasn't enough. Quesada knew that the majority of the indigenous peoples were loyal only to their own tribes. So with more than a little Machiavellian flare he exploited the rivalries of various native tribes and convinced the Chía and Suba people to collaborate with the Spanish Crown. Tisquesusa suffered defeat after defeat until he died in a skirmish in 1537.

REVOLTS, DEFEAT, AND EXTINCTION

After the defeat by Quesada's forces and the founding of Bogotá, the Muisca lost their strategic hold on the region. The next step by the Spanish was to control the land completely and destroy the Muisca hierarchy. They accomplished this by striking out into the central Andean plains and killing all Muisca priests as well as their *zipa* and *zaque* leaders. The remaining natives were allotted their own indigenous areas by the Nuevo Reino de Granada Government, but they were forced to work the land for the conquerors. This was a profitable labor system the Spanish implemented in various regions during the colonization of the Americas. It was known as *ecomienda*, which is a colloquial way of saying 'slave labor.'

In 1599, the Tairona revolted against the Spanish in the north, seemingly because they'd gotten fed up with Spain's economic and religious mandates. The Tairona attacked travelers and priests on high-traffic roads near Santa Marta, as well as the churches and homes of Spanish bureaucrats in the area. The Tairona chiefs were sentenced to death in 1602 and their villages were subsequently burned. By the 17th century, former Tairona villages were covered in forest. Today, their only living descendants are the Kogi tribe, whose population of around 20,500 people are located in the same area.

THE APEX OF COLONIALISM AND THE INDIGENOUS TODAY

In 1717 the Viceroyalty of New Grenada was established with Santa Fé de Bogotá as its capital. This new government body included a number of territories that now exist outside of Colombia, such as Venezuela, Ecuador, and Panama. The fact that Bogotá's central government controlled such a wide swatch of territory

The Colombian Army going into battle, c.1540.

meant that this viceroyalty became one of the principal administration centers and crown jewels of Spain's New World.

As for the legacy of the indigenous, the Tairona and Muisca tribes went from having two of the most advanced pre-Columbian societies on the continent to being all but eliminated by the Spanish. However, Muisca descendents still live in Colombia today, even in neighborhoods in Bogotá. They pass their ancestral values, such as respect for the environment and personal responsibility, down from generation to generation. Chibcha culture can be found in many places from the Caribbean coast to Cudinamarca. Many children with indigenous roots learn the language from a young age.

INDEPENDENCE FROM SPAIN

As with many South American countries, events in Europe triggered a domino effect that would see the birth of a rebellion, the end of New Grenada and the rise of the Republic of Colombia.

The Spaniards had a good run in Colombia, accumulating wealth and territory, but it was about to come to an end. Revolutionary stirrings began to take hold in the public consciousness. This was due in large part to education. As more and more people were becoming educated in the country, resentment simmered among lower classes toward the wealthy and entitled Spanish aristocracy.

This was compounded when in 1793 a Colombian journalist named Antonio Nariño published a translation of the *Rights of Man*, Thomas Paine's argument for political revolution. Nariño was imprisoned in Spain, but escaped and returned to Colombia, ready to take up the mantle once again for the independence cause. During this period it wasn't hard to see the writing on the wall. There was even a popular uprising in Ecuador in 1809, but the real fight wasn't to take place until the following year.

DECLARATION OF INDEPENDENCE

Despite the shift in mood, overall Colombians were still loyal to Spain. This was the case in 1808, when in Europe Napoleon deposed Spain's King Ferdinand VII and replaced him with his own brother Joseph. Needless to say, this inflammatory move sent shockwaves across the New World that became the spark that ignited the powder keg.

On July 20, 1810, the inhabitants of Bogotá revolted and overthrew the Spanish. They set up local administrations, or juntas, in Bogotá and Tunja and declared loyalty to the former King, Ferdinand VII. Cartagena followed suit and aligned with Tunja. Despite these revolts, full independence from Spain was a goal that would evolve from this act over the course of almost a decade.

Simón Bolívar at the Battle of Carabobo, 1821.

THE LIBERATOR

Around this time a young, charismatic, European-educated revolutionary was making noise in Venezuela. Simón Bolívar (1783–1830) was a Venezuelan creole (Spanish American) by birth but he would go on to lead armies of pro-independence patriots, many of whom were black slaves or former slaves, and eventually liberate six countries on the continent. Just three months before the 1810 revolt in Bogotá, Bolívar colluded in a conspiracy that saw a junta overthrow a provincial Spanish governor in Venezuela. In 1811, a convention in Caracas formally declared Venezuela's independence from the crown, marking the first clear declaration of full independence in New Granada.

Of course the Spanish Crown had no intention of making it easy for the rebels. By mid-1812 the Spanish had retaken the whole of the Venezuelan province and Bolívar was forced to flee to Cartagena. A skilled military tactician, Bolívar realized that he'd lost the battle but he was certainly not about to cede the war. In Cartagena he found a fortress city already in rebel hands – the perfect place to pen a manifesto with which to galvanize the populous of New Grenada. The political pamphlet Bolívar wrote is called the *Manifesto de Cartagena*, and

Simón Bolívar freeing slaves in 1816.

reflects on what led to the patriots' defeat, and how to succeed moving forward. Shortly after its publication, Bolívar adopted his famous hard line stance against the Spaniards: total unity of the Republicans and a full-on decree of 'war to the death.'

VICTORIES AND REVERSALS

Bolívar accepted a commission in Cartagena in 1812 and had some success in the Magdalena Campaign, which lasted a year. During its course, revolutionary forces took control of the Magdalena River and marched back into Caracas, where Bolívar proclaimed a 2nd Republic and appointed himself as head of state. During this time the Colombian journalist Antonio Nariño also led a military operation in the south, but was captured and imprisoned by the Spanish. Another blow occurred when the Venezuelan *caudillos* (regional leaders) retook their territory, and the Spanish once again regained power in Caracas, forcing Bolívar back into Colombia.

After Napoleon was defeated at the Battle of Waterloo in 1815, the Spanish set their sights on retaking all of the territories of New Grenada. For this purpose they relied on the ruthless military acumen of royalist General Pablo Morillo, known as The Pacifier, who launched his Spanish re-conquest around this time. A degraded Bolívar, possessing no real army with which to impede Morillo, was forced to flee to the West Indies. From 1816–1819 Morillo executed over 300 patriot sympathizers and had a hand in reintroducing the Inquisition to New Grenada.

⊘ AFRO-LATIN AMERICANS IN THE FIGHT FOR INDEPENDENCE

Simón Bolívar was an abolitionist through and through, and he possessed ideas about slavery that were far more progressive than other revolutionary countries of the time. This is perhaps best illustrated by one of his fundamental beliefs, that it was "madness that a revolution for liberty should try to maintain slavery." When this view is combined with the inescapable fact Bolívar had armies to raise and maintain, you begin to see from where he got much of his fighting force from.

Some 50 years before President of the United States Abraham Lincoln drafted his famous proclamation, Bolívar was busy issuing emancipation to slaves willing to fight for the liberation of New

Grenada. Unsurprisingly, Bolívar easily won the support of the slave and indigenous populations in the War for Independence, with much of Venezuela's African population joining him in the fight against the Spanish colonists. One such black Venezuelan, who was called Pedro Camejo, became known as the 'First Black', due to his fearless habit of riding into battle first. Camejo eventually rose through the ranks to become one of Bolívar's most famous and trusted lieutenants. The bottom line is this: the revolution simply would not have been happened without the support and fighting spirit of the region's slaves and Afro-Latinos.

One enduring legacy of Spanish Colonial rule is its universities. The oldest such university in the country, Saint Thomas, was founded in Bogotá in 1580 by the Dominican order of Roman Catholics.

But the pugnacious Bolívar wasn't done. He returned to Venezuela in 1816 and raised a new Republican army, comprised of a wide variety of soldiers, from creoles to slaves. He decided to adjust his tactics, forgoing another assault on Caracas in favor of a surprise march into the very heart of New Grenada: Bogotá. In 1819 Bolívar led a small but formidable force of around 2,500 men in a perilous journey over the Andes in order to mount their attack on the capital region. They linked up with Francisco de Paula Santander (1792–1840) and the New Grenada Army and surprised the Spanish in July of 1819, issuing the final crushing blow at the Battle of Boyacá.

Bolívar assumed the Presidency of Gran Colombia, the name given to the new union of countries, which included Colombia, Venezuela, Ecuador, and Panama, and served from 1819–1828. Bolívar lived a short, comprehensive, and complex life. He achieved much in a relatively brief time, and he did so while fighting to reconcile the dual personalities of his nature: the sober realist hoping for incremental change, and the idealistic dreamer fighting for nothing less than liberty and full equality for men. The fact that these differing notions were always a constant in him, always pulling him in different directions, is part of the key to his overall success.

THE REPUBLIC OF COLOMBIA

It was in present-day Ciudad Bolívar, in Venezuela, that La Republica de Gran Colombia was established on December 17 1819. Like in many a nascent republic, the founders didn't always agree. Bolívar and Nariño, for example, were in favor of a centralized government, while Santander envisioned a federation of sovereign states. In 1821 a constitution was drafted with Bolívar succeeding in codifying centralization into the document, officially dividing Colombia into 26 provinces within 12 departments. The slave trade was abolished, as was the Inquisition, and lands were redistributed to the indigenous.

Even with such great gains, Santander was not happy at being overlooked. Despite fighting alongside Bolívar in the revolution, he led a campaign of dissent against his old friend and in 1828 and attempted to have him killed. Santander earned a year in exile for this crime; he was originally sentenced to death, but was pardoned by Bolívar himself. Santander eventually returned to Colombia and in 1832 became the second president of the country. By this point, however, Bolívar's vision was starting to fall apart; the Liberator died in exile in Santa

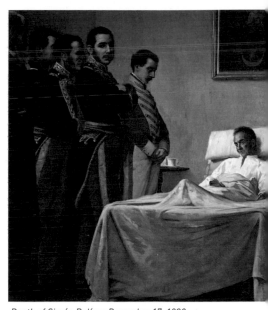

Death of Simón Bolívar, December 17, 1830.

Marta in 1830, the same year that Venezuela and Ecuador broke away. His dream of a united Latin America had died with him.

In 1863 officials changed the name of the Republic to The United States of Colombia, and in 1886 the nation adopted the name it is known as today: the Republic of Colombia. The legacy of the Spanish is a complicated one. On the one hand they arrived in the New World with the firm intention of enriching themselves and the crown at the expense of the indigenous. On the other, they brought rich culture and powerful institutions to the continent, not least of which were the universities. In Colombia, examples of rich Spanish architecture first built 500 years ago still exist today.

MODERN HISTORY

The 20th century saw Colombia descend into one of its darkest chapters of prolonged violence, but the country's commitment to its democratic institutions won out in the end.

To understand how the culture of violence took hold in Colombia, it's necessary to understand the earliest history of the sovereign nation. Almost from the moment the constitution was drafted in 1821, rival political factions fought over the direction of the country. The differing ideologies had their roots in Bolívar's conservative notions of a centralized government, and Santander's support of decentralization. These opposing forces evolved over the 19th century to become two parties: pro-clerical conservatives in favor of a centralized government, and anti-clerical liberals in favor of federalization and state autonomy.

Despite the infighting, liberals hung onto power for over 30 years from 1849. Throughout this era a number of civil wars broke out, and in 1885 the conservatives succeeded in drafting a new constitution representing their platform of centralization. This constitution also gave the nation its final name: The Republic of Colombia. The same year saw a crippling currency devaluation, which came as the result of years of civil war and internal strife. Colombia would switch to the gold standard in 1903.

THE THOUSAND DAYS WAR

Not surprisingly, the fight between Colombian political parties to impose their views on one another other didn't let up. On October 20, 1899, amid a depressed economy and accusations of fraudulent elections, the liberals staged a revolt at Socorro, in the Santander Department. The war, *La Rebelión*, was also known as the Thousand Days War. The conservatives enjoyed an early victory in October 1899 when they defeated liberal forces at the battle of the Magdalena River. However, in December rebel

Jorge Eliecer Gaitan on a banknote.

General Benjamín Herrera handed government troops a crushing defeat in Norte de Santander. This would be the liberals' only significant victory of *La Rebelión*.

In May 1900, conservative forces, led by General Próspero Pinzón, halted the advance of liberal soldiers at the Battle of Palonegro, one of the more violent encounters of the war, resulting in around 2,500 deaths on both sides. It would prove to be the decisive victory the conservatives needed, and despite the war dragging on into 1903, the liberals were never in the fight after that point. Roughly 100,000 lives were lost over the course of the conflict, and the two political parties that waged the war became fractured as a result of infighting.

PANAMA, PERU, AND CONFLICT IN THE NEW CENTURY

Despite officially being part of Nueva Grenada, Panama was mostly a self-governing territory until the Colombian constitution of 1886 relegated it to a department. Despite this downgrading, Panama remained a part of Colombia through the turn of the 20th century. However, a 1903 bid for independence caught the attention of the United States, who wanted to build a shipping canal in the region's narrow isthmus. The US lent their support and Panama rose up, with

Colombian infantry in Leticia in 1933.

the official revolution lasting from just the 3–6 of November 1903. By the time it was over Colombia was a single country, and Panamanian and US officials were happily in bed together. Work on the Panama Canal began in 1904 and it was officially opened in 1914.

From 1904–1909 Colombia had a dictator in the presidency in the form of General Rafael Reyes. A former Chief of Staff in the Colombian Army, his authoritarian government was known as the *Quinquenio* (five-year) dictatorship. Reyes had been a key player in the Panama conflict and much of the population didn't like that Colombia had failed to retain the region. Combined with continued economic fallout from the *La Rebelión* and his own extra-legal national assembly,

it didn't take long for the public to turn against him. In fact, his unpopularity led to an assassination attempt in 1906.

Reyes survived his time in office and was succeeded by Carlos Eugenio Restrepo in 1910, who restored a legal form of government. He also entered negotiations with the United States regarding their role in the Panamanian Revolution. This resulted in a US$25 million indemnity payment to Colombia, which was seen as a victory for the administration.

Just when Colombia began to get some closure with their neighbor to the north, their neighbor to the south began to start making noise. In 1922, after various disputes over the Amazon Region, Colombia and Peru had signed the Salomón-Lozano Treaty and hoped to settle the border issue once and for all. The treaty set the border between the two nations at the Río Putumayo, with the small town of Leticia to be controlled by Colombia, giving them direct access to the Amazon River. The agreement seemed to have the desired effect, that is, until Peru occupied Leticia in 1933. An official dispute was submitted by Colombia to the League of Nations, who found Peru to be in violation. They handed Leticia back to Colombia in 1934.

LA VIOLENCIA

During the 1940s and 50s, Colombia's bloodiest civil war, *La Violencia*, took place. It was fought principally between the conservative and liberal political parties, but many of the fighters and victims were poorer *campesinos*, poor people who lived and toiled in the country, far away from the halls of power in Bogotá.

As with many conflicts that spiral out of control, this particular civil war started with a single incident that led to quick escalation of hostilities. In 1948 the popular socialist mayor of Bogotá and Liberal Party candidate for president, Jorge Eliécer Gaitán, was assassinated by a lone gunman. This led to El Bogotazo, a 10-hour period of massive rioting in Bogotá that burned destroyed a huge portion of the city and resulted in some 5,000 deaths.

The ripple effect of the riots spread beyond Bogotá and into the countryside, where Gaitán enjoyed much support among the *campesinos*. The two parties waged civil war against one another through proxy combatants in the form of the *campesinos*. This, combined with the fragmentation of the political parties, led to the rise of armed entities such as paramilitary forces and guerrilla groups. Extremist police and politicians on both sides were appealing to peasants to seize agricultural lands from one another depending on their political leanings. The conservative-supporting poor stole from the liberals, and vice versa.

This all led to protracted violence among the lower economic classes for years. Not only

supremacy that would only abate in 1957 with the declaration of a fragile coalition.

THE NATIONAL FRONT

A decade of bloodshed had taken its toll. After 10 years of civil war, proxy war, rioting, internal strife, millions of displaced citizens, lack of civil authority, media blackouts, and the occasional military coup in the absence of elected leadership, the two major political parties decided enough was enough. In July 1957 the former conservative and liberal Presidents

Violence during El Bogotazo in 1948.

The Violence, as the name translates to in English, was a chillingly apt name for the conflict: over the course of a decade some 200,000 people lost their lives.

were these self-defense groups and guerrillas fighting one another, they were also forced to contend with the paramilitary forces of the Colombian Communist Party. Moreover, the Catholic Church allegedly had aligned with the conservatives and religious persecution was taking place in the form of the murder of Protestants. It was a violent battle for power and

Laureano Gómez and Alberto Lleras declared a *Frente Nacional* (National Front), or a joint-government comprised equally of conservatives and liberals. Under this system, power would be shared at the top levels, with conservative and liberal presidents alternating every four years for a period of 16 years. To the two parties, it seemed like the only way to end *La Violencia*.

The gamble paid off, ending the civil war and ushering in an era of tenuous cooperation. Liberal presidents instituted agrarian reform policies, conservative presidents further expanded upon these land entitlements. For a time it seemed like the country could function – until the Conservative Party gained more power than the liberals, and outside opposition threatened to upend the entire agreement.

M-19 AND THE FARC

During the middle of *La Violencia*, a leftist dictator general named Gustavo Rojas Pinilla had served as president. His reign came to an ignominious end when his Peronist tactics finally resulted in his trial by national tribunal and subsequent ousting. However, Pinilla did have his fans, and with his base of supporters he went on to found the Alianza Nacional Popular

Soldiers discover a stockpile of cocaine in the 1980s.

(ANAPO), which opposed both the liberals and the conservatives, in 1961.

In the period after World War I, through to the 1960s, Communism had taken root in certain areas of the country. The Partido Comunista Colombiano, or PPC (the Colombian Communist Party), had fostered popular fronts in urban regions as well as indoctrinated peasants in rural areas with the stated goal of improving education and living and working conditions. Protests and strikes were many, and land seizures were common. State military forces took notice, as did the US, who sent counter-insurgency experts to help train the Colombian Army.

In 1961 a PCC organizer named Pedro Antonio Marín, better known as Manuel Marulanda

Vélez, declared the town of Marquetalia, a poor rural area in the Caldas Department, independent. In 1964, the military carried out an attack on the town, which further galvanized Vélez and his group of Marxist-Leninists, thus leading to the creation of the Fuerzas Armadas Revolucionarias de Colombia, or the FARC.

Insurgent notions were being stoked in other areas as well. On April 19 1970, presidential elections, in which Pinilla was a candidate, were held, and conservative candidate Misael Pastrana won.

These guerrilla groups, along with others like the National Liberation Army (ELN) pressed forward for years, with each claiming to represent the interests of the workers and the poor, and each claiming the path to utopia. Starting in 1974, in response to mass kidnappings, executions, and attacks, subsequent presidential administrations made combating guerrilla insurgent groups a key focus of their party platform.

> *Supporters of Pinilla accused the conservatives of rigging the election and rose up to form one of Colombia's most famous guerrilla organizations: Movimiento 19 de Abril, or M19.*

NARCOS AND CARTELS

During the 1970s, the global cocaine market exploded. Since Colombia was – and still is – the world's biggest producer of the coca leaf, that spelled opportunity for those ruthless and industrious enough to smuggle the crop. Enter the cartels. During the mid-1970s, two dominant forces in the drug trade were established: the Medellín Cartel, headed by Pablo Emilio Escobar Gaviria and Carlos Lehder, and the Cali Cartel, formed by brothers Gilberto and Miguel Rodríguez Orejuela. Despite being competitors, they worked towards a common goal, often in concert. Both cartels warred with the government as well as guerrilla groups, who took to kidnapping family members of wealthy narcos in retaliation. However, there was a major difference: Escobar and his Medellín Cartel were the more violent and ostentatious of the two cartels. As the money rolled in, Escobar and the cartel began to live more and more extravagant lifestyles: Escobar bought a 20 sq km (8 sq mile) plot of land in Antioquia, and built a luxury home, Hacienda Nápoles, which had its own private lake, zoo, and bullring.

In 1982 Escobar, under the misapprehension he'd make a good politician, won a seat in Colombia's Chamber of Representatives as a liberal candidate. Unfortunately for him, he entered government at a time when law enforcement were first starting to openly crack down on the narco cartels. Rather than reaching across the aisle to find common ground with his political opponents, Pablo took the decidedly more hard line approach of murdering them: in 1984, he had pro-extradition Justice Minister Rodrigo Lara Bonilla, who had forced Pablo out of government, killed. In 1985 members of M19 stormed the Colombian Supreme Court in a terrorist act denouncing pro-extradition judicial findings. M19 guerrillas executed half the judges on the court in an event that would become known as the Siege of the Palace of Justice, an operation allegedly backed and funded by Escobar.

As time wore on, however, the walls began to close in as Escobar warred with anyone and everyone in a desperate attempt to protect his freedom and his business. He kidnapped and murdered police, politicians, and journalists, part of his 'silver or lead' approach to negotiating with perceived threats. The odds eventually caught up though, and Escobar went on the run. This degraded not only Escobar's drug operation, but the man himself and on December 2 1993 Pablo was discovered via radio triangulation in a safe house in the Los Olivos neighborhood of Medellín. He and his bodyguard tried to escape on the rooftops but were shot dead by the Colombian National Police, who took smiling photos kneeling over Escobar's dead body. In 2006, Cali Cartel leaders, the Rodríguez brothers, were extradited to Florida where they pleaded guilty to smuggling and were sentenced to 30 years each in federal prison.

A VIOLENT DENOUEMENT

The first cessation of violence occurred in 1984 when President Belisario Betancur's administration and FARC leaders negotiated a cease-fire. The guerrilla group then formed a political party called the Union Patriótica (UP), seeking political reforms such as land redistribution and constitutional reform. The UP was made up mostly of regular people – labor union representatives and socialist party members as opposed to soldiers. In 1986 the party enjoyed some political success, winning nine House seats and six Senate seats. However, the following year, amid amped-up violence, including the murder of UP party president Jaime Pardo, the cease-fire ended.

Employees leave the Palace of Justice during the siege.

⊘ PLATA O PLOMO

Pablo Escobar's fortunes in the drug trade were tied inexorably to violence. His official policy of dealing with law enforcement, known as *plata o plomo* (silver or lead), was as infamous as it was unambiguous. Those whom Escobar could not bribe with *plata* (silver) were dealt with by *plomo* (lead). In essence, it was a choice between the dollar or the bullet. Hundreds, if not thousands, of police officers were killed for no other reason than refusing to be corrupted. Escobar's empire was built on such ruthlessness; it is also what turned him into public enemy number one, eventually leading to his demise.

The government also still had M19 to contend with. After various kidnappings and murders throughout the 1970s and 80s and the Palace of Justice Siege, the administration of President Virgilio Barco Vargas was able to negotiate a peace accord with M19. The guerrilla group also laid down their weapons and founded a legitimate political party, the Alianza Democrática, also known as M19 EP. They had some success in the 1990 elections. However, their presidential candidate, the former guerrilla commander Carlos Pizarro Leongómez was murdered on an airline flight, allegedly on the orders of cartel members.

The FARC proved to be a much more elusive target in the peace process. By 1990 they were a member of a coalition of guerrilla groups called the Simón Bolívar Guerrilla Coordinating Board (CGSB), who were operating mostly out of Antioquia and the Cauca River Valley. Despite some initial negotiation successes between government officials and the FARC during the early 1990s, talks ultimately broke down in 1993 amid violent acts on both sides.

President Alvaro Uribe greets Colombian armed forces officials after his inauguration ceremony in 2002.

⊙ PABLO'S MYSTERY MILLIONS

During the height of its power, the Medellín Cartel supplied around 80 percent of the world's cocaine, smuggling up to 15 tons into the United States each day. Consequently, they made $70 million dollars profit every day, which worked out at a staggering $22 billion each year. They even had to spend $1,000 each week on elastic bands just to wrap up the bundles of bills. In a 2009 interview, Escobar's son claimed that his father once burned $2 million in cash just to keep his family warm whilst on the run.

Needless to say, Pablo and the cartel couldn't keep all their cash in the banks and they were earning it much faster than they could ever spend it. This soon became a major headache for Pablo, so they started storing it, mostly burying it, in various locations across the country: warehouses, farms, his own *estancia* – it was said that Escobar had buried money everywhere. The cartel wrote off 10 percent of their annual profits due to 'spoilage,' either the buried money was being nibbled by rats, getting damp and rotting or it was simply lost in transit. This 10 percent equated to over $2 billion each year. However, millions and millions of dollars are still said to still be out there, buried in the Colombian countryside. Whether or not this is true is anyone's guess. Put on your treasure-hunting hat and find out.

Successive presidents in the 1990s, like the liberal Ernest Samper, continued to try and bring the rebels to the negotiating table, but these overtures were often undermined by violence or political impropriety, including accusations that Samper financed his presidential campaign with a US$6 million donation from the Cali Cartel. These accusations were as unthinkable as they were likely, especially considering the Cali Cartel had been continuing to manage their smuggling operation from inside a Colombian prison, where they had been given light sentences.

THE 21ST CENTURY AND A DREAM OF PEACE

Liberal President Alvaro Uribe was sworn in as president in May 2002. After so much violence, so many stalled negotiations and failed peace talks, few were holding out hope that the Harvard and Oxford-educated lawyer could deliver on a campaign promise to successfully confront the FARC. However, over the course of two terms, Uribe probably did more to bring Colombia's most formidable and long-lasting rebel group to its knees than any president before him. Before Uribe took office, the FARC controlled many urban areas, including territory just one hour from Bogatá. By 2010 the rebels had been pushed to the most remote corners of the country, in the jungles near Venezuela, Ecuador, and Panama.

The process wasn't quick or easy. To succeed, Uribe had to beef up his military operation, and he did so with economic help from Plan Colombia, a joint-US/Colombian aid scheme aiming to stem the flow of cocaine to the United States, with CIA assistance. Diplomacy and triangulation were also factors, and his administration entered peace talks with other groups, such as right-wing paramilitaries.

In 2008, three events crippled the FARC's power considerably. In March the Colombian Army made an incursion into Ecuador and killed key FARC spokesman, Raúl Reyes. In May, the FARC's founder, Pedro Antonio Marín, died of a heart attack. Then in July FARC kidnap victim and former presidential candidate Ingrid Betancourt was rescued after six years in captivity. She had been one of the rebel group's highest-profile victims, and her captivity symbolized the FARC's violent effectiveness. With her rescue came the sense that the FARC was now beatable.

Since then the FARC has been on the defensive, playing a solely reactionary game as their numbers and power continue to dwindle. It was no surprise that they were willing to enter peace talks with liberal-conservative coalition President Juan Manuel Santos in Havana, Cuba in 2012. By the end the two sides had come to terms, a staggering accomplishment considering their long history of violent conflict. The

Boy's hand with the word 'yes' during the referendum.

Colombian people had the opportunity to vote on the peace deal in October 2016, and they narrowly voted it down. This can be attributed to the fact that many wounds are still open, and at least half the populous isn't ready to offer concessions to rebel group members. At least not yet anyway.

In the end, Santos may have won the 2016 Nobel Peace prize for the impressive feat of doing what no Colombian president before him could do, negotiating a deal guaranteeing lasting peace between the Colombia and the FARC. However, Scandinavian medals aside, no victory can be claimed until Colombia is at peace, and Colombians finally get to live free of violence, in the country they deserve.

KING OF THE CARTELS

For years Pablo Escobar was Colombia's most infamous citizen, but by the end he was nothing more than an example of how ruthlessness, greed and excess can bring down anyone, even the world's richest and most powerful drug lord.

Pablo Escobar.

Colombia is blessed (or cursed) with an abundant and much-sought-after natural crop in the coca leaf. This nation is still the world's principal cocaine producer, and it cultivates over 100,000 hectares of coca each year. The finished product, cocaine, is produced from the coca leaf by a relatively simple and straightforward process. Back in the 1970s the global market for cocaine drug exploded, making billionaires of a select few men – those with a head for business and a heart for ruthlessness. These were new kinds of insurgents, ones who traded Marx and military fatigue for US dollars and private jets.

MAKING A NAME FOR HIMSELF

In the mid-1970s one soon-to-be-famous smuggler was just coming into his own. A Medellín resident by the name of Pablo Emilio Escobar Gaviria had been known merely as a small-timer, but all that was about to change. He enlisted the help of his friend, Jorge Luis Ochoa Vásquez, and the two founded the Medellín Cartel, along with Carlos Lehder. By the mid-1980s the Medellín Cartel controlled 80 percent of the cocaine exports to the United States. *Forbes* listed Pablo and Jorge as billionaires.

During the 1970s and 80s, Escobar would establish a reputation for ruthless violence and over-the-top ostentatiousness. He bought property all over Colombia, including his primary residence, the sprawling Hacienda Nápoles just outside Medellín in Antioquia. He built a zoo on the grounds featuring a host of exotic animals including rhinos and hippos. He financed social redevelopment programs and was regarded as a benevolent folk hero in many of the poorer neighborhoods of Medellín. This was a calculated move on the part of Escobar that had the intended effect.

PABLO THE POLITICIAN

The earliest major tactical error by Escobar, one that would compromise the security of his empire and hasten the demise of his once-powerful cocaine operation, occurred when he decided to enter politics in 1982, winning a seat in Colombia's Chamber of Representatives as a liberal candidate. Until then, Escobar had been savvy in cultivating a Robin Hood persona among the poor and working class, especially in and around Medellín. He built soccer stadiums and many people loved him. There is little doubt that this contributed to an over-inflated ego that considered a congressional seat was the most logical next step on the road to becoming the most beloved public figure in Colombia.

Unsurprisingly, Escobar's fellow political representatives didn't welcome him with open arms. They knew his game and regarded the narco-turned-congressman with open contempt. As his profile in the drug-smuggling world increased, it became impossible for them to feign ignorance of how he paid the rent. In 1984, pro-extradition Justice Minister Rodrigo

Lara Bonilla, who had declared war on the drug cartels, forced Pablo out of the Chamber of Representatives. As you can probably guess, Pablo responded with *plomo* (lead): later that year, whilst driving in Medellín, Bonilla was shot dead by an assassin sent by Escobar.

In 1985, after representatives introduced legislation relaxing laws regarding extradition of drug smugglers from Colombia to the US, members of M19 stormed the Colombian Supreme Court. The Supreme Court had been studying the constitutionality of Colombian extradition laws, and in retaliation, M19 guerrillas, who were passionately opposed to the prospect extradition on nationalist grounds, executed half the judges on the court. All in all, 48 Colombian soldiers and 11 Supreme Court Justices were killed, along with 35 members of M19. This event would become known as the Palace of Justice Siege; it is widely believed to have been ordered and funded by Escobar, with the aim of disrupting the extradition process.

THE BIGGER THEY ARE...

From 1985 onward Escobar began to lose control, indiscriminately blowing up or killing anything or anyone that stood in his way. Much of his and the cartel's resources were consumed by fighting rival cartels and the police. Escobar's public support began to dwindle as he committed atrocity after atrocity.

In 1989, Escobar ordered the bombing of Avianca Airlines flight 203. The plane was supposed to be carrying the pro-extradition, anti-cartel politician and future Colombian President César Augusto Gaviria Trujillo. However, he ended up missing the flight for security reasons. A bomb was placed on the plane, which detonated shortly after take-off killing all 107 people on board, along with a further three victims on the ground, who were killed by falling debris. Two Americans were among the dead, which prompted the Bush Administration to join the line for those wanting to see Escobar tried and convicted for his crimes.

1989 was also the year Escobar's men gunned down Luis Carlos Galán, a popular former journalist and Liberal Party presidential candidate who had been crusading against the drug cartels. By now the murders had taken their toll and brought the Colombian government to its knees.

In 1991 the government negotiated a surrender (of sorts) with Escobar. However, it was a deal in which Pablo called all the shots. He would stay in Colombia with no threat of US extradition, in a mansion 'prison' known as *La Catedral* that had been

built to the cartel's specifications. Among other amenities, *La Catedral* had a nightclub, a football pitch, and a Jacuzzi. In 1992, when the joke became apparent to the Colombian government, they planned to have Escobar transferred to a real prison. However, Escobar and his associates caught wind of the plan, and he simply walked out the front gates of *La Catedral* and escaped.

DOWNFALL

Escobar would spend the rest of this life on the run. By this time, the US had also entered the manhunt, and Pablo's operation was severely decimated. To

Escobar's body is removed from the safe house.

make matters worse, a brutal vigilante group called *Los Pepes* (Los Perseguidos por Pablo Escobar or 'People Persecuted by Pablo Escobar), had formed, with the sole aim of destroying the Medellín Cartel. In a violent campaign, *Los Pepes* killed over 300 of Pablo's men, including his lawyers, and destroyed many of their labs and safe houses.

On December 2 1993, Escobar and his bodyguard were discovered hiding in a Medellín safe house by radio triangulation. After a brief firefight with the Colombian police, Escobar was shot dead. Afterward, elated officers posed for pictures over his dead body.

The Buen Comienzo Program for disadvantaged children in Medellín.

A woman in traditional dress carries fruit on her head in Cartagena.

COLOMBIANOS

The Colombianos of today are a representation of various heritages from the past, all of which is evidenced in the food, music, art, and culture found in Colombia's various regions.

Colombia boasts a population of around 48 million people, making it the third most populous country in Latin America, outside Mexico and Brazil, and they're a diverse bunch. Visit any one region and you'll see a demographic make-up and ethnic heritage that differs slightly – on occasion greatly – from one area to the next. Head to the north coast and you'll find a region dominated by Afro-Caribbean residents; go to Chocó and Cauca and there are majority-black populations descended from slaves who were brought to the country to work the gold mines and cane fields. And of course, indigenous communities still remain and can be found in many areas, including the Nariño and Amazonas Departments.

This isn't to suggest that Colombia is a segregated country, although racial tensions and prejudices do exist. The largest urban areas are melting pots where the country's various demographics live side-by-side and often co-mingle as one. In Bogotá, for example, the population make-up is predominantly white and *mestizo* (those with mixed white and Native American heritage). However, there's also a diverse cultural make-up comprised of those who migrated from Chocó, Costeños from the Caribbean region and descendants of 20th-century immigrants from Europe and the Middle East.

This heritage can be traced back to the beginning of the 16th century when the Spanish conquistadors arrived, the slave ships landed in Cartagena and Panama, and the natives first set eyes on new visitors with dubious intentions. It's no small thing that whole indigenous populations survived to this day in the face of Spanish colonialists and post-independence politicians. Its proof that, although Colombian race relations far from perfect, the country's commitment to

Locals in Jardín.

the preservation of their cultural and ethnic heritage is tangible.

INDIGENOUS GROUPS

Colombia is home to some 87 native tribes, which make up just over 3 percent of the country's population. The total number of indigenous peoples comprising these tribes is roughly 800,000, and they occupy nearly 31 million hectares of government *resguardos* (reserves). These autonomous territories make up about one-third of the country's total landmass, and can be found in virtually every corner of the country.

Despite this abundance of native groups, about 80 percent of the total indigenous population (70 tribes) live in the Cauca Department

on the Guajira Peninsula. These are mostly descendants of the Wayúu people, the country's largest indigenous group, whose number almost 150,000 in Colombia today. That said, the origins of all indigenous peoples in Colombia can be traced back to three main groups: the Quimbaya of the Cordillera Central, the Chibchas and the Kalina. The two most advanced tribes of the pre-colonial era were the Chibcha-speaking Tairona and Muisca. The Chibcha are still the largest ethno-linguistic group in the country, with around 150,000 native speakers.

Beauty queen at Wayúu Cultural Festival, Uribia.

> *The Wayúu are the largest indigenous group living in Colombia and they represent about 20 percent of the country's Native American population. They live mostly on the Guajira Peninsula and adhere to time-honored traditions, such as respecting the land and promoting sustainable lifestyles.*

Protection of indigenous culture and promotion of native rights has been a slow and sometimes frustrating process, although not one without its successes. A 1991 constitutional reform recognized indigenous rights by granting

natives two senate seats and the ONIC (National Colombian Indian Organization) won a third seat that same year. However, there's progress yet to be made, as many indigenous who reside in remoter areas, like Amazonia, are still under-represented politically and economically. For more details, visit www.amazonteam.com.

IMMIGRATION IN THE 19TH AND 20TH CENTURIES

Colombian immigration policy under Spanish rule was restrictive, and despite loosening restrictions once the nation became a republic, the violent unrest during the middle and later half of the 20th century made Colombia a less-than-attractive destination for immigrants.

However, in the 16th century Colombia was a very attractive landing spot for Basque immigrants. Estimates place the Basque population around this time as being nearly 10 percent of the total population, with many settling in the region of Antioquia and becoming some of the first entrepreneurs in the country. A small number also arrived toward the middle of the 20th century due to the Spanish Civil War. Germans also arrived in Colombia around this time, and estimates suggest there were 10,000 Germans living in Colombia by 1941.

People from the Middle East would continue to immigrate to the country throughout the early part of the 20th century, mostly as a result of the fallout regarding territories colonized by the Ottoman Empire. By 1945, large numbers of émigrés from the Arab-speaking world were settled in Barranquilla, Cartagena, Bogotá, and Cali, with the Sunni Muslim population settling primarily in the Maicao region. Figures place the total number of Middle-Eastern immigrants to Colombia between 40,000 and 50,000 people from 1880–1930, making them the largest immigrant group in Colombia after the Spanish.

Colombia also has a small Chinese population, mostly settled in the Cali area. Some 3,000 immigrants from North America arrived in Barranquilla in the late 19th century, and there was also an influx of African immigrants during the 19th and 20th centuries due to Colombia's constitution offering full rights to those of African descent. As economic unrest in neighboring Venezuela continues, many Venezuelans continue to cross the border en masse and settle in the capital and border cities like Cúcuta.

MINORITIES AND RACIAL HIERARCHIES

It's difficult to glean exact figures on racial demographics in Colombia, since the national census stopped referring to race in 1818 as a way to avoid non-objective classification. They now use a more general system to classify ethnic groups. General estimates suggest Colombia is 37 percent white (European descent), 49 percent *mestizo* (white/ Native American descent), 10.5 percent Afro-Colombian, and 3.4 percent Indigenous. Despite no official lines of demarcation between social categories, most Colombians still identify themselves according to a few ethnic factors, including ancestry, socio-cultural status, and physical appearance. These factors often determine social interactions and define social categories – a racial hierarchy that has its roots in the colonial social system.

Various racial groups can still be found in different concentrations in Colombia, just as they were in the 16th century. The white population was mostly concentrated in large urban centers, like Bogotá, and the *mestizo* population emerged when Spanish conquerors entered the highland areas and mixed with the female members of indigenous tribes. For centuries the *mestizo* group was a peasant class, living outside urban areas, but by the 1940s they had moved into the big cities, becoming part of the working poor. Certain indigenous groups were able to survive the Spanish conquest and subsequent co-mingling due to the fact they existed in remote areas like the arid Guajira Peninsula or the inaccessible jungles of the Amazon Region. Many of these groups retained their indigenous language and still speak it today.

Still, the hierarchal society created by the Spanish in Colombia was one where white skin was synonymous with high status and brown or black skin was associated with the lower classes. Despite outnumbering whites and those of mixed blood in certain regions, Afro-Colombians and indigenous peoples had no shared identity on a national level, which further cemented their status as minorities. An example of this can be seen in the fact that, although Colombia was the first country in the Americas to grant full rights to black population post-slavery, they were still viewed as little more than slaves for years afterward and relegated to remote coastal areas.

These factors, combined with a lack of mass immigration and fervent regionalism made it

> In 1880 Colombia saw the first wave of Syrian, Lebanese, and Palestinian immigrants arrive. They were mostly Maronite Christians but there were some Sunni Muslims as well.

Arhuaco man in Nabusimake.

easier for the Spanish to retain their traditional institutions, such as Roman Catholicism, and thus preserve their white European identity. Today there is more integration in Colombian society, particularly as historically marginalized ethnic groups continue to move into major urban centers and mix with various socioethnic classes. Still, the ugliest aspects of the old racial hierarchal system continue to exist. Indigenous tribes are still underrepresented politically, and Afro-Colombians still face economic discrimination. According to a 2005 census, 74 percent of black Colombians earn less than the minimum wage. And the Chocó, home to the majority of Afro-Colombians, is economically destitute, with little resources for education and little hope for upward mobility.

COLOMBIAN FAMILY STRUCTURE

The family structure in Colombia, as with many Latin American countries, is a highly valued aspect of society. This nation is also more traditional than other modern democracies. For example, in Colombia it is not uncommon – and often it's expected – for men and women to continue to live at home with their parents until they are married, often well into their 30s. When parents reach retirement, the responsibility then falls to the children to care for them, with the parents often living in the same house as their children and grandchildren.

As for matrimony, the Roman Catholic Church, not surprisingly, plays a significant role. Weddings are often expensive, lavish affairs that take place in colonial churches. These occasions are often marked by the bride and groom taking part in the candle ceremony, where the bride and groom light two candles and then use the two flames to light a single candle, symbolizing unity. Another matrimonial tradition is the pre-wedding *serenata* (serenade) in which the groom-to-be surprises his lady (usually while she's sleeping)

Residents of the Guajira Peninsula.

⊘ THE FORGOTTEN REFUGEES

Humanitarian crises exist throughout the world, and today there is a crisis of dire proportions in the South American country of Colombia. This is a place most outsiders now view as enjoying a peaceful renaissance, yet millions of its own citizens have been left without a home.

Colombians from the poorest parts of the country, particularly the Chocó Department, as well as *campesinos* from more remote areas, have been displaced by guerrilla groups. This occurs when the guerrillas move into rural areas that are attractive propositions for their remoteness and jungle cover, forcing the locals out or simply murdering them in the process. The Colombian government places the number internally displaced peoples due to this kind of conflict in the country at around 3.2 million people, while human rights groups have it much higher, at around 5 million.

Refugees within Colombia often live outside the major cities, like Bogotá, in the poorest and most unsafe environments. The crisis has spilled over into Ecuador, with thousands of asylum seekers looking to cross the border. Doctors Without Borders has labeled this tragic occurrence one of the world's 'forgotten crises.' However, there are things that can be done. To find out how you can help, check out The Colombian Refugee Project (www.colombian-refugeeproject.wordpress.com) and the UN Refugee Agency (www.unhcr.org/colombia.html).

in her family home with a few songs, usually accompanied by a live band. Liquor is ever present and the event often goes on for hours.

The post-marriage familial household is a patriarchal one, with clearly defined roles for the husband as the provider and wife as the caregiver. This dynamic is a result of tradition, but equal civil and property rights mean these roles aren't legally defined. Women and men are free to adjust their responsibilities to the household, and as the times progress they often do, although tradition often wins out in most Colombian families. Also, in another sign of Colombia's legal progressiveness, this traditionally Roman Catholic country legalized same-sex marriage in 2016.

WOMEN'S ROLES IN COLOMBIA

The typical household in Colombia may have patriarchal roots, but that isn't to say the country is a cultural throwback. Women often choose to have a career, and many middle and upper-income households do indeed have dual breadwinners. Still, these two cultures – the old and the modern – do clash at times. It can lead to some head-scratching moments for first-timers to Colombia, like when you meet a 30-something woman who went to medical school to become a doctor, who's still living at home, waiting to be married. There are still plenty of households where the man circumscribes the role of the woman, relegating her to domestic responsibilities and childbearing.

With the lower income classes it's a different story, as tradition takes a backseat to doing what needs to get done. As with many poorer households across the globe where the father is absent, the woman assumes all roles, from sole breadwinner to head of the family, often working two or three jobs just to survive. Regardless, women throughout the country are continuing to break down barriers, entering politics (a traditionally male-dominated arena) on the local and national levels, and pushing toward the finish line for Colombia's first-ever female president.

POVERTY AND RURAL DISPLACEMENT

Colombia's classification as an Upper Middle Income country by the World Bank is something of a misnomer. Poverty and wealth disparity continue to be big problems, and are perhaps most evident in the dilapidated shanties on the outskirts of most major cities, as well as in the horse-pulled wooden carts meandering just outside the capital's wealthiest neighborhoods.

The poverty gap disproportionally affects the most vulnerable groups in Colombia: 45 percent of the Afro-Colombians, indigenous, and *campesinos* (peasant farmers) live below the breadline. Principally, this is due to the fact that they live in remote rural areas desired by guerrilla groups. For instance, land seized in the Chocó, as well as violence and theft perpetrated against *campesinos* by these groups has led to mass dis-

Fashion journalists in Medellín.

placement, forcing thousands of people out of the country and into the poorest shanty towns outside major metropolitan centers.

Still, poverty rates have dropped significantly over the years. The National Administrative Department of Statistics (DANE) put those living below the poverty line at 47 percent in 2004. By 2015, this had significantly decreased to about 28 percent. Despite these laudable gains, a true middle-class existence remains elusive for many Colombians. That's because in 2013, DANE set the poverty line at a salary of just US$3.80 per day. And, of course, a real solution to seriously decrease poverty in Colombia will never be a reality until there is total peace between the government and the rebels.

Statue of Christ, Bogotá.

RELIGION

Like many countries in Latin America, Colombia is predominantly a Roman Catholic country – but other religions are growing fast.

For such an ethnically diverse country, Colombia is pretty homogenized when it comes to religion. This is due to a number of factors, with the most important being when the Spanish first arrived in the 16th century. This new population settled in various areas, including the Caribbean coast and the Andean Highlands. However, the rough topography of the land, as well as the remoteness of the Spanish colonial cities and outposts made it problematic for them to co-mingle with the various indigenous groups and black population. Therefore the Spanish were able to better preserve the institutions they brought with them from the Old World, such as the Roman Catholic religion, which is still the dominant religion today.

But the Spanish weren't the only ones with ideas on religion. The spiritual roots of the first slave populations had their roots in African customs, and Colombia's indigenous adhered to their religious practices. These may have fallen

Ash Wednesday Mass at a church in Cali.

Despite the relatively small numbers of Muslims in Colombia, the nation boasts the South American continent's third-largest mosque, the Mosque of Omar Ibn Al-Khattab, which is located in Maicao, La Guajira.

by the wayside in favor of Catholic conversion, but immigrants to the country in the 19th and 20th centuries brought their own religions with them. While these only represent a tiny minority in Colombia's religious landscape today, they serve to illustrate that the country is indeed a melting pot where all faiths are welcome.

INDIGENOUS RELIGIONS

Before the Spanish arrived, Colombia's various indigenous groups had their own spirituality. The highland Muisca people worshipped the sun and the moon, while the coastal Taironas had a liberal gender-based religion that was tolerant of divorce and homosexuality. Sadly the traditional customs of most indigenous tribes have been lost to time and the conquistadors' habit of converting the locals they didn't eradicate altogether.

One group that has retained some semblance of their earliest spiritual beliefs is the Kogis. These Chibcha-speaking people come from the Sierra Nevada area around Santa Marta and are descendants of the Taironas. As they still have a measurable population of some 20,000 people in the country, we have an insight into their religious practices. This group's spirituality is earth based, and they worship Aluna, a Great Mother, or Mother Nature. They believe humans to be the children of the earth, and therefore any hostile act against it, such as devastation or exploitation, is sacrilege.

Examples such as the Kogi people are few and far between, as most indigenous groups that survived the colonists were converted to Catholicism over the intervening centuries. That said, some of the most remote tribes, such as those in the Amazon, have retained their shaman-based

Inside Our Lady of Poverty Cathedral, Pereira.

spiritual practices that revolve around plants and nature. Moreover, the Nukak people of the Amazon allow for polygamy, which, depending on your point of view, is either a spiritual act or a dubious tenet of a patriarchal society.

ROMAN CATHOLICISM

From the time the first Spanish arrived, up until 1991, Roman Catholicism was the official religion of the country. Even today the religion dominates Colombia, with some 75 percent of the national population identifying as Catholic, although only about 25 percent are practicing Catholics. The transition from a national religion to a popular one came during the constitutional reforms assembly of 1991, which amended Colombia's constitution

About 2 percent of Colombians adhere to another form of religion, including Judaism, Buddhism, Mormonism, and Hinduism.

to abolish the Roman Catholic Church as a state institution and allow for total freedom of religion.

During colonial times the church was responsible for all institutions, including universities, hospitals, and prisons. This heritage is partly what makes Colombia such an alluring destination for architecture buffs: the colonial landmarks that still exist throughout the country, like the grand old Spanish cathedrals found in almost every city and town, are very well preserved. As the heritage of Roman Catholicism is so ingrained in the cultural landscape and psyche, it's likely that it will remain a strong force in Colombian culture for some time.

Despite estimates suggesting that almost two-thirds of Colombia's Roman Catholics aren't regular practitioners of their faith, the tradition of this religion and its societal underpinnings are ever-present. The majority of Colombians take part in religious ceremonies, such as baptisms and first communions; religious holidays are observed – and religious festivities boisterously celebrated – among the populous. Even though the trend of strict observance of Catholicism is a declining one, Colombia still remains a very pious country.

THE PROTESTANTS

Colombia also has a small but conspicuous Protestant community. This religious demographic has its roots in the missionaries who came here to preach the good word in the 1930s. As in many places where Protestants and Catholics co-existed in close proximity, relations between the two factions weren't always cordial. History suggests certain factions of the church oppressed the Protestants, and the Catholic Church was even accused of inciting violence against them in what would result in the murder of over 100 Protestants during *La Violencia*, in the 1940s and 50s.

Today things are different. Some estimates place modern *Evangelico* (Protestants) numbers around 1.5 million, making up somewhere between three and four percent of Colombia's total population. There are many Protestant denominations in existence in Colombia today. Official estimates suggest that Protestantism membership is actually increasing faster than the national growth rate.

ISLAM IN COLOMBIA

According to the Pew Research Center, there are some 14,000 practicing Muslims in Colombia, making up less than 1 percent of the total population. Practitioners of Islam can mostly be found in the larger cities, like Bogotá, or coastal areas where people from the Arab-speaking countries in the Middle East relocated to during the 19th and 20th centuries.

OTHER RELIGIONS

Because Roman Catholicism dominates the spiritual landscape in Colombia, it's easy to overlook other religions, of which there are many. True, taken together the numbers of these religions represent just a few percent of the total population, but the statistics serve to illustrate that there is, in fact, religious diversity in Colombia. These groups can be found everywhere, from the big cities to the poor mountain towns.

There is a slowly growing Taoist movement in Colombia, which has unfortunately been tainted with violence and scandal. Taoists continue to stage peaceful protests in Bogotá, in response to what they believe are massacres by paramilitary groups to stifle religious freedom. However, a team of government prosecutors and investigators raided a Taoist commune in rural Santander in 2004 and captured one of its leaders, Diego

Leon Agudelo. They claim Agudelo was operating with paramilitaries to create illegal armed groups who took orders from Taoism community founder Luis Gustavo Morales Sierra. Supposedly this group was responsible for a number of killings between 1989 and 2004.

Out of all Colombians who identify as religious, some 36 percent do not actively practice their faith. This relatively high percentage might help explain the presence of another marginal demographic: Atheists and Agnostics, who make up about 3 percent of the total population.

Stone phallus at El Infiernito.

⊘ FERILITY RITES AT EL INFIERNITO

Even today, a large part of the Colombian culture – at least where men are concerned – is obsessed with sexual stamina. Many foods, including *caldo de raíz*, are said to possess aphrodisiac qualities that will make a man 'strong like a bull.' However this isn't a new concept, far from it in fact: if Colombian history teaches us anything, it's that prowess in the fertility department was a significant preoccupation – even a religious concern – back in indigenous times.

This preoccupation is apparent in the fertility sculptures that can be seen at the Museo del Oro in Bogotá. However, the most well-endowed examples can be found at the archeological site of El

Infiernito, which is located just outside of Villa de Leyva. Here sits a veritable Easter Island of giant stone penises, erected, so to speak, by the Muisca people. The site was dubbed 'Little Hell' – probably by pious Spaniards who took a break from pillaging gold and exploiting the locals to vent their righteous indignation at such immodesty. Interestingly, experts now believe the figures to have served some kind of astrological purpose as well, as they seem to align directly with the moon, sun, and particular constellations. You can book an excursion to El Infiernito in Villa de Leyva at Colombian Highlands via Hostel Renacer.

Mujer vestida
1989. Bronce

ART AND LITERATURE

Colombia is known for its beauty, culture, and mysticism –
a combination that has allowed it to produce some of the
most formidable writers and artists of the last two centuries.

It's no surprise that during the first centuries of Spanish colonization, Colombian artwork was heavily steeped in religion. Church commissions from Spain and the Netherlands are responsible for most of the art of this time period, with many paintings depicting the Virgin Mary. Examples of these can be seen in the churches of Bogotá. In Tunja, there are some famous wall murals from the 17th century in the homes of the town's elite residents. These murals feature decidedly secular themes, loaded with mythological figures and exotic animals.

During the early colonial times, religious sculptures were also imported to the New World from workshops in Andalusia. However, local artisans soon began producing the carved polychrome altarpieces that you still see in Colombia's colonial churches today. Both painting and sculptures would evolve heavily over time, with Colombian art coming into its own during the 19th and 20th centuries.

Public art praising Gabriel García Márquez in Cartagena.

THE 19TH CENTURY AND ORIGINS OF COLOMBIAN ART

Colonial art continued to dominate the cultural landscape from the 17th century until the early 19th century. These were the formative years when Colombia was fighting for independence, and many works of this time featured heroic depictions of Simón Bolívar. One such work by Pedro José Figueroa, on display at the Casa Quinta de Bolívar in Bogotá, presents the Liberator as father of the nation as he stands with an arm around a small girl who represents the new Republic of Colombia.

The Museo Nacional in Bogotá is also a good place to see art from the post-independence era of the 19th century. One painting by artist Luis García (1816–1887) depicts a sentimental scene during the death of General Santander, surrounded by weeping supporters. The Museo Nacional also has two representations of the country's most famous heroine martyr, Policarpa Salavarrieta, also known as La Pola, the former slave who fought for Colombian independence before being executed by the Spanish in 1817. Both paintings are from a period of time just before her execution but contrast each other in tone and mood, with one depicting her being led to her death, while the other, attributed to artist Epifanio Garay (1849–1903), shows her sitting calmly, waiting defiantly to die. The Biblioteca Nacional in Bogotá displays some drawings by journalist and master caricature artist Alberto Urdaneta (1845–1887), who studied in France alongside Meissonier.

ARTISTS IN THE 20TH CENTURY

While the European art scene was experiencing a revolution during the early part of the 20th century, most Colombian artists were happy with their academic aesthetics in landscapes and figures. If there was a sole pioneer in the Colombian art scene during this time it was most certainly Andrés de Santa Maria (1860–1945), a European-educated painter specialising in mod-

Regreso del Mercado by Andrés de Santa María.

ern art. Santa Maria's use of thick textures and personal subject matter combined to create a truly unique artistic voice, although it's clear that Paul Cezanne is a heavy influence. His works can be seen at the Museo Nacional in Bogotá.

The 1930s saw the rise of Mexican muralists on the continent's art scene, and this trend found its way to Colombia. What appealed to young Colombian artists about the murals – as opposed to European Cubism and Futurism – was that it continued a figurative tradition in art whilst allowing for a social conscience. Liberal moods were beginning to awaken in the Colombian psyche during this period, and social movements were arising throughout the country. Pedro Nel Gómez (1899–1984), an artist from

Medellín, was the first to paint murals inside public buildings in Colombia, and his work often depicted indigenous tribes and, as with many other muralists of the time, the plight of the poor and working class. His murals can be seen at the Central Library of the University of Medellín, and his paintings and other works are on display at the Casa Museo Pedro Nel Gómez, also in Medellín. Some notable muralists who followed Gómez include Alipio Jaramillo (1913–1999), whose depictions of violence and struggle are vivid and haunting, and Carlos Correa

> *Today Colombia's art scene is as thriving as ever, with a host of galleries throughout the country. It's in many of these venues that young artists have a platform to showcase their work, each doing their part to shape Colombian artistic expression and legacy for now and into the future.*

(1912–1985), whose works were softer in tone but just as striking.

Abstractionism arrived in Colombia during the 1950s, courtesy of a German-born Colombian called Guillermo Wiedemann (1905–1969). His love of the tropics imbued his works with an explosion of Expressionist color and light. Alejandro Obregón (1920–1992) was a figurative artist of the time who preferred nationalistic themes done in colors so bright they assault the senses. This contrasts with another progressive artist, Beatriz Gonzalez (1938–), whose pop art often presents bold and colorful depictions of military and family subjects in an off-kilter way, rendering them empty.

SCULPTURE IN COLOMBIA

Sculpture has a firm place on Colombia's art scene, with many versatile practitioners famous as much for their sculptures as they are for their paintings. Fernando Botero (1932–), for example, works in both mediums but his national – and international – fame derives from his sculpted works, and they are a sight to behold – and touch. Botero touches on national themes, rendering Colombian archetypes – dictators, narcos, matrons, prostitutes, and more – in exaggerated, corpulent dimensions.

Rodrigo Arenas Betancourt (1919–1995) took a more fantastic approach to his art than Botero. His figures are many things at once: heroic, melodramatic, and boundary-pushing – all of which can be seen in his *Bolívar Desnudo*, a bronze equestrian sculpture of a naked Liberator astride is horse, which can be found in Pereira. Edgar Negret (1920–2012) was a constructionist, primarily working in metal, whose works are some of the most iconic in the country. Some can be found at the Casa Museo Negret in Popayán.

has been lost to time. During the colonial period most of the literature was produced by the upper classes in concert with the Catholic Church. Writers of this period, such as Gonzalo Jiménez de Quesada, the founder of Bogotá, tended to be conquistadors, and their literary output served little purpose other than to defend Spain's behavior during the conquest of the New World.

It was just after independence when Colombia not only began to develop its national identity but also started to find its literary voice. José Nieto (1805–1866) was the most famous

Paintings by Fernando Botero, on display in Medellín's Antioquia Museum.

Out of all the sculpted bronze representations of the great Símon Bolívar, none is as eye-catching as Bolívar Desnudo, a sculpture of the Liberator in the nude and astride his horse. It's located in the Plaza de Bolívar in Pereira, in the Zona Cafetera, and is the work of Rodrigo Arenas Betancourt.

THE COLOMBIAN LITERARY SCENE

Unfortunately the poetic tradition of the indigenous peoples of Colombia was oral, as opposed to written, meaning there is little documentation of their history, and most of their heritage

of the first true Colombian writers, in the sense that he was a citizen of a new Republic writing about that nation's history. *Ingermina, o la hija de Calamar* (Ingermina, or the child of Calamar), is Nieto's historical novel about the conquest of the indigenous Calamar people.

The 19th century was defined by romantic poetry and a narrative trend known as *costumbrista*, a realistic style popular in Bogotá that depicted local life. One such example is *Manuela* by Eugenio Diaz (1803–1865). Literary reviews began to take off around this time too, and the first movement of writers who weren't members of the elite upper classes emerged in Antioquia, particularly in Medellín. Tomás Carrasquilla (1858–1940) famously recounted his middle-class upbringing in novels that were notable for characters that spoke in natural, colloquial style typical of real-life *paisas*.

As with other artists, the social conscience of Colombian writers began to develop during this period and was only exacerbated by *La Violencia*. During the civil war and dictatorship of Rojas Pinilla, a poetic movement of free expression emerged called Mito. A literary magazine of the same name was one of the few outlets were poets could publish their work without fear of reprisal. The content reflected the political concerns of the time, and the writers of the movement were influenced heavily by French contemporaries like Sartre, as well as fellow latinos like Borges. Then, in the late 1960s, an unknown Colombian author named Gabriel García Márquez published his masterwork *Cien Anos de Soledad*, and changed the Colombian, and global, literary landscape forever. Márquez went on to win the Nobel Prize for Literature in 1982 (see panel).

The 1970s and 80s saw other writers rise in stature, like Fanny Buirago (1943–) and Manuel

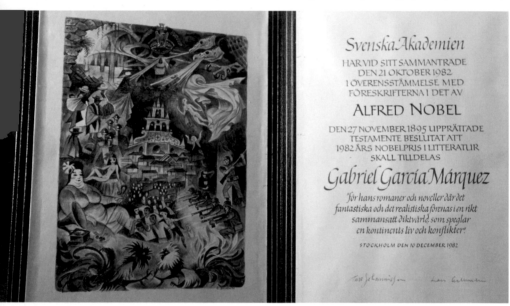

The Nobel Prize diploma of Gabriel García Márquez.

⊘ 100 YEARS OF SOLITUDE

In 1967, a real literary upheaval occurred in Colombia, one that would send shockwaves across the world. That's when a former journalist named Gabriel García Márquez (1927–2014) published his masterpiece, *Cien Anos de Soledad* (One Hundred Years of Solitude). It didn't merely arrive on the scene, but rather exploded onto it. The novel was notable for its straightforward, realistic style that blended wild fantasy with mundane reality. Real-world residents of the fictional town of Macondo mixed with ghosts, and otherwise regular people levitated into the sky without warning. The style that was formed in these pages became known as *lo real maravilloso*, or Magical Realism.

Zapata Olivella (1920–2004), whose novels pit the classic heritage of the Caribbean Coast against the encroaching North American culture. Other notable writers of more recent times include Juan Gabriel (1973–) and Laura Restrepo (1950–). Today's Colombian postmodernists often live and work in Europe, and they make a concerted effort to distance themselves from the Magical Realism that defined their country. This attitude is especially true with the younger generations of literary students and author-groups, who typically want to forge their own path. But no doubt all the culture, superstition and heritage that García Márquez mined for his masterwork will at least partially inform Colombian – and indeed Latin-American – literature for eras to come.

GABO AND THE BIRTH OF MAGICAL REALISM

Flying carpets, levitating priests, pig-tailed babies – up until the mid-20th century this was the stuff of fantasy fiction, but in 1967 that all changed.

Most writers work within the bounds of literary genres, but when *Cien Anos de Soledad* (*100 Years of Solitude*) was published in the late 1960s, it seemed that a type of storytelling that didn't exist before was now right in front of the Western literary world's face.

BEFORE THE AUTHOR BECAME THE AUTHOR

The man responsible for this literary sea change, Gabriel García Márquez (1927–2014) was born in Aracataca, Colombia, a town that would later serve as the blueprint for his fictional town of Macondo. He grew up in the home of his grandmother, and she would while away the hours telling him stories of ghosts and the fantastic, but with such a straight face that she presented it to him as cold reality. If a line can be traced directly from *100 Years of Solitude* back to García Márquez' youth, it would start here.

As a young adult, García Márquez was a middling student with more interest in novels and journalism than studying law, which was his intended path in life. He devoured works from authors including William Faulkner and Franz Kafka as he toiled at newspapers in Barranquilla and Bogotá. He then tried his hand at novel writing. In 1955, he published his first book, *Leaf Storm*, a novella that didn't sell and is now notable merely for being the first work featuring the town of Macondo. By all superficial accounts he had failed as a novelist, and he took to film critiquing and screenwriting in Mexico City. He was 38 years old.

INSPIRATION AND WILD SUCCESS

One day, whilst en route to a family vacation in Acapulco, García Márquez was struck with inspiration when a way to make a story idea he'd been toying with work on the page came to him. The book would follow multiple generations of the Buendia family as both they and their small town of Macondo changed and

grew. He turned the car around and drove right back to Mexico City, where he sequestered himself at home for 18 months in order to write. His sold his car; the family went into debt. But when it was finally published in 1967, *One Hundred Years of Solitude*, was an immediate runaway success. 30 million copies and one Nobel Prize in Literature later and García Márquez had been well and truly vindicated. When García Márquez was awarded that Scandinavian prize in 1982, many Colombians too felt vindicated – a brief respite from the violence and civil strife tearing their country apart. That's probably why Colombia's favorite son was never known as Señor Márquez or

Gabriel García Márquez in Cartagena, 1991.

Don Gabriel. No, then, now and forever they affectionately refer to him as Gabo.

A CONTINENTAL PROCLIVITY

García Márquez's masterpiece may have sparked a movement that gave identity to a genre without a name, but he wasn't the only author to toil with one foot in the fantastical and the other in reality. During the same time period a bespectacled librarian in Argentina named Jorge Luis Borges had already made noise with his labyrinthine, reality-bending shorts stories. So the spirit was there, but what García Márquez did was find a way to show that spirit to people beyond the borders of his own country, proving that you can come from nothing and change the world, so long as you can tell a good story.

Preparing food at a restaurant in Bogotá.

intarrosano
Morcilla antioqueña
Alcachofas con mozarella
Ensalada de cangrejo
Patatas bravas

FOOD AND DRINK

Colombia's cuisine is delightfully diverse, changing from region to region yet maintaining cohesive flavors through shared cultures and history.

For a long time Colombian cuisine was overlooked by the global foodie scene. Colombia didn't have sexy standouts like Peru's ceviche, world-class beef like Argentina, or the soulful cauldrons of *feijoada* found in Brazil. Or so people thought. But as the years go on and the country opens up more and more to tourism, people are discovering its myriad culinary delights. The food here is unlike anywhere else on the continent. Although the techniques may change from department to department, the majority of dishes are linked by a common theme: a commitment to quality ingredients and a humble approach to putting them together. The below is a regional breakdown of Colombia's best food and drinks.

BOGOTÁ

Ajiaco is the star of the show here. Every Bogotá and Cudinamarca resident eats it, and everyone's mother or grandmother prob-

Ajiaco.

There's a certain gastronomic ritual that many Bogtanos adhere to. This is known as 'onces' and it is an afternoon snack eaten around 5pm (despite its name meaning 11) that includes coffee, aromática, or chocolate, plus delectable pastries like almojabanas (Colombian cheese bread).

ably has their own special recipe. Essentially it's a chicken stew, made from yucca, maize, various types of potato (including the delicious, golf-ball sized *papas criollas*), and wild *campesino* herbs like *guascas*. It is served with capers, avocados, and crème fraiche. In the most traditional restaurants, it is served in an earthen bowl.

You can also find blood sausage (*morcilla*) and tripe (*chunchullo*) in and around Bogotá. *Caldo de Raíz* (soup of the root), is another staple, and only the most adventurous culinary aficionados need apply. Essentially it's a broth made with chopped up bits of bull penis and testicles, served with avocado. According to lore the dish is an aphrodisiac, although hard evidence is yet to transpire. To erase that image, consider one of Bogotá's great desserts: *cuajada con melao*, which is fresh cheese drizzled with dark cane syrup.

SANTANDER

Head to the colonial town of Barichara and almost right away you'll notice a curious ant (*hormiga*) theme about the town. Not only do the Barichara locals – and those throughout Santander – like to name things after ants, they also like to eat them. *Hormigas culonas* (large-bottomed black ants), are a famous culinary delight in the area. When in season (around Easter), you can find them in many stores and restaurants. They're surprising delightful, with a crispy, salty taste, similar to peanuts. In keeping with Colom-

sugarcane. *Bocadillo veleño* is a common sweet made from guava jelly and panela that is also found in other parts of Colombia.

THE CARIBBEAN

The order of the day in the Caribbean lowlands is fish. The most common type you'll find here is mojarra, a flaky white fish often fried and served with salad and fried plantains. Another typical side dish is coconut rice (*arroz de coco*), which is perfectly aromatic and best eaten by the sea. *Arroz de mariscos* (seafood rice) or *arroz de*

Fried fish is a popular dish in Barranquilla.

bia's obsession with food and sex, locals will tell you these produce aphrodisiac qualities as well, surprise, surprise!

Mute is a corn soup with different types of cereals, and it's sort of the Santandereano answer to *ajiaco*. Often it is made with beef ribs and pork. You can also find goat served with tripe and intestines throughout Santander, as well as pigeon. In the north exists a delicious dish called *rampuchada*, which is a spicy stew made with fish from the Zulia River. *Hallacas* are meat-filled pockets made from cornmeal that are reminiscent of a Mexican *tamale*, except bigger. *Carne orneada* is dried, salted meat that is not quite as tough as beef jerky, but of a similar texture, marinated in pineapple and unrefined

camarones (shrimp rice) are both popular dishes and are typically served as main courses. For street food, one option found in most coastal cities is *ceviche de camarones* (shrimp cocktail). This can throw many visitors, because Colombians don't have the same definition of ceviche as the Peruvians. If you get a *ceviche de camarones*, it is prepared shrimp and or *mariscos* or *pulpo* (shellfish and octopus) made in the typical cocktail style, meaning it is prepared fish mixed with lime juice, ketchup and mayonnaise and served with crackers.

One of the most famous dishes in all of Caribbean Colombia is the *cazuela de mariscos*, a boiling black cauldron of shellfish stew, rich and yellow, with all the flavors of fish, mussels, shrimp, langoustines, and more. *Sancocho de pescado* (fish stew) is an equally delicious soup but much lighter and typically made with just fish. *Chipichipi* (a frontrunner for best name for food ever) is a type of clam found along the coast and served with rice. Of course, *arepas* (cheese and flour patties served on its own or topped with meat) and *empanadas* are popular here as well, as they are in most other parts of the country.

NORTHWEST COLOMBIA

In Antioquia, you are treated to rich, humble food served in ample proportions. This is *campesino* fare – dishes intended to provide sustenance throughout a long workday. Case in point: the heavyweight-sized *bandeja paisa*, a tray loaded with a kaleidoscopic array of meats, including crispy pork skin (*chicharrón*) and sausage, finished off with a fried egg. As if this wasn't enough of an assault, they then load up the side with rice, beans (those from Antioquia are the

> The best way to take coffee in Colombia (aside from staying at a coffee finca) is from a street vendor. A tinto is a black coffee with sugar, café con leche includes milk, and if you want milk on the side you can ask for the leche aparte. If you like it strong, ask for café cargado.

best), *manioc*, fried plantains, and salad (just to keep it light). This dish has its origins around Medellín, but you can find it in most other parts of the country. Another similar dish is the *calentado paisa*, a kind of hash made from beans, rice, and *carne mechada* (stewed, tender beef), topped with an egg and served with *arepas*. *Natilla* is a circular sponge cake (kind of like a doughnut), that you can see being fried up in the bakeries and street vendors around Medellin. *Salpicón*, a fruit salad topped with crème and syrups, is also ubiquitous here.

SOUTHERN COLOMBIA

The most noteworthy aspect of southern Colombian cooking is that, unlike most other parts of the country, it doesn't often use

potatoes in its cuisine. Here corn, plantains, rice, and avocado are the staples. You can find many of these ingredients in famed Caleño dishes like *tamales*. Caleño *tamales* are slightly different than those found in other areas, such as Bogotá, as they are often bigger and feature larger portions of meat, although still wrapped in banana leaves. *Manjar blanco* is a popular dessert here, which, like caramel, is made from milk and sugar. *Cuy* (guinea pig), which is also popular in Peru and Ecuador, can be found close to the southern border.

Drinking fairtrade coffee in Medellín.

DRINK

COFFEE

This is of course a staple of Colombia and one of its principal exports. It will come as a surprise to many that most Colombians drink instant coffee at home, as they often don't have the budget to stock up on gourmet beans. Even more of an eye-opener is that the fact that the famous Juan Valdez was never an actual coffee company, but a character created to help sell coffee to other countries. You'll now see Juan Valdez gourmet coffee chains across the country, but even these were a direct response to the popularity of Starbucks (note the suspiciously similar design schemes of Juan Valdez when compared to Starbucks).

AGUAPANELA

Aguapanela is basically what the name implies: *agua* (water) combined with *panela* (unrefined sugarcane). You can drink it hot or cold and the outside temperature will determine which way is best.

AROMÁTICA

This is an herbal tea infused with various herbs and fruits. Flavors include *yerba buena*, *manzania*, limonaria, and *canela* (cinnamon). It's a great cold-weather drink and many of the street

Fresh watermelon.

vendors mix in rum or whiskey, which makes for a great Christmastime tipple.

CHOCOLATE

Hot chocolate is often drunk at breakfast in Colombia (and this could be a contributing reason the people in Colombia are so happy).

BEER

For a long time Colombia's beer selection was somewhat limited. The main brands, including Aguila, Costeña, and Club Colombia, were almost all produced by the Bavaria Group. Poker is probably the most palatable of the budget beers in Colombia. These days, where it concerns local beers, most people opt for those brewed by the Bogotá Beer Company, a national brewery and restaurant chain that does a solid lager and some interesting microbrews. You can find this dark-bottled beer in certain restaurants, most large-chain supermarkets, and many hostels.

CHICHA

Chicha is a fermented corn liquor that has its roots in the country. It's a *campesino* drink, not terribly strong but incredibly potent. Its thick texture is reminiscent more of chowder than of alcohol, and if you sit down at a *chicheria*, try not to smell it before downing it. There is also a non-alcoholic, sugary, fruit-infused version of *chicha* that has a smoother consistency and makes a great soft drink. You can find it in certain restaurants.

LIQUORS

Colombia is a drinking country, so teetotalers should know that they may be offered alcohol in local homes. Don't worry though – no one will be offended if you pass. Rum is popular in most areas of the country, as is whiskey. However, those on the coast tend to drink Old Parr. As for rum, Ron Medellín is probably the best brand. And, of course, it's the Paisas from Medellín that made *aguardiente* (an anise-flavored sugarcane liquor sometimes called *guaro*) famous. Spend more than a day or two in the city and the stuff will flow like water.

Wine is quite expensive in Colombia and you'll find the selection rather limited in many markets.

South American squirrel monkey (saimiri sciureus) at Amacayacu National Park.

WILDLIFE

Colombia is a country rich in biodiversity, and it's the influence of the nation's environment that creates the conditions necessary for these myriad species to thrive.

Conservation International have classifed Colombia as one of the 17 megadiverse countries in the world, which means it is home to high bio-diversity regions. Amazonas alone boasts 427 mammals, 378 reptiles, over 400 amphibians, and 3,000 types of freshwater fish. All in all, the Amazon Rainforest accounts for more than one-third of all animal species on earth. With such an abundance of life, it's no wonder conservation is such an important topic in Colombia. Sustainable tourism is the solution to ensure people can come and enjoy the region and its animal species for generations to come (for more information, see the Amazonas chapter).

Then there are the birds. Colombia is a birdwatcher's dream. It has the highest avian biodiversity of any country on earth, and is home to 1,889 species. This represents 20 percent of all the total species on earth. There are also 197 species of migratory birds that make their home in Colombia sporadically throughout the year. Unlike many species in the Amazon, these birds aren't just relegated to a single region. Prime birdwatching destinations include the Cauca Valley, the Sierra Nevada de Santa Marta, the Zona Cafetera, the Amazon, and the llanos Eastern Plains.

An often-overlooked destination for serious birdwatchers is the Pacific Coast region of the country. Here, in the Chocó Department, wet forests define the western Andes that slope into the sea and run into Panama's Darién Gap north into Panama. Perpetual clouds hang over these tropical forests, providing moisture and condensation that feeds the epiphytes growing on the dense clusters of trees and shrubs, which include orchids.

Golden poison dart frog.

Tanagers are rife in this area; Chocó has even earned an unofficial nickname – the Tanager coast – due to the abundance of these species. But they aren't the only ones; there are many other species endemic to the area. If you travel south, for example, to La Planeda, between Pasto and Tumaco, you will find a nature preserve covering 3,200 acres that is home to some 240 species of birds.

So what makes this possible? Why is Colombia such a hotbed of biodiversity? The answer lies in the variations of topography and the conditions of the Amazon. The Amazon River has the largest volume of water of any river in the world, and this, with help from the Orinoco River, has led to the creation of the most extensive tropical rainforest on the planet. This is fertile and expansive ground for a number of animal species.

The Andes must also be taken into account. The three cordilleras running through the country are part of the longest uninterrupted mountain chain in the world. These mountains create a wide range of habitats. Rivers drain these areas and create ideal living conditions. Add to that the various expanses of tree-covered open terrain, such as the llanos, and the arid desert regions, and you have the

Yellow-eared parrots (ognorhynchus icterotis) nesting.

conditions necessary to sustain a huge array of wildlife.

Geology and time have also played a key role in creating these conditions. Look at any map and what stands out about South America is that the continent is essentially an island. It's connected to the north via a narrow isthmus. At various points since the beginning of time, this land-link has been broken, cutting off migratory patterns from the north and isolating wildlife already existing on the continent, which means competitive conditions were mitigated, allowing more species to thrive. The present connection has been stable for a mere few million years – a relative blip on the timeline of planet earth. During that time, invasions of new migratory animals entered Colombia.

BIRDS

Out of the 1,889 species of bird mentioned earlier, some 71 are native to Colombia. Parakeets, finches, hummingbirds, woodpeckers, tanagers, and wrens are particularly abundant here. Some other species of interest include the *Cauca guan*, chestnut-winged *chachalaca*, blue-billed *curassow*, chestnut wood-quail, Bogotá rail, Tolima dove, yellow-eared parrot, black-backed thornbill, silvery-throated spinetail, Antioquia bristle-tyrant, and the Santa Marta *tapaculo*.

MAMMALS AND VEGETATION

As with the birds, Colombia's varied species of mammals thrive in certain parts of the country, depending on factors as landscape, temperature, and altitude. Many of these creatures are recognizable as woodland animals, like squirrels, mice, rats, tapirs, bats, sloths rabbits, and deer. The opossum is a primitive mammal that has thrived here in part because of the stable nature of the ecosystems. Other rodents in Colombia that are specific to South America include the capybara and chinchilla. Populating the list of Colombian mammals are alpacas, llamas, vicunas, cougars, bears, armadillos, porcupines, monkeys, wolves, and jaguars.

Where you find each of these animals depends on where you happen to be in the country. Some rare and unique mammals exist only at high altitudes here. For example, high in the Andes, between around 3,600 meters (12,000ft) and 4,400 meters (14,500ft), you'll encounter *páramo*

⊘ COLOMBIA'S NATIONAL BIRD

The national animal of Colombia is the Andean condor. With a wingspan of up to 3 meters (10ft), these carrion birds have been revered since before colonial times, when the indigenous regarded them as messengers of the gods. In recent times they have become a threatened species. Because of this, in 1989 an initiative was undertaken to reintroduce condors raised in captivity into the wild. Dozens have been released into Colombia's high-altitude páramos, in the Andes, which is their natural habitat. However, lack of efficient tracking methods makes it difficult for scientists to properly monitor these majestic animals, so only time will tell if the Andean condor will make a full comeback.

topography defined by straw grass (*pajonal*) and other moorland vegetation. Here, deep gorges offer some protection from the harsh weather conditions and icy winds. It's possible to find thriving shrubs and even the occasional orchid here. Look hard enough and you may just find the footprint of a white-tailed deer, also known as South Andean Deer or *huemul*, an endangered species.

Also found at high altitudes in the Andes (over 4,500 meters/15,000ft), are Polylepis forests, defined by gnarled evergreen trees that look like

difficult to spot mammals in the *páramo* during the day, as they tend to seek refuge amid the cover of that fringes these areas. At night is when they tend to come out to the moorlands, as the mists that swirl about the dark forests offer protection from the predators of the night. It's their tracks you have to look for, and often these will include those of pumas on the hunt. Birds in these high-altitude regions tend to be raptors like the mountain caracara and the red-backed hawk.

Speaking of cloud forest, this natural phe-

The spectacled bear is a relatively small species of bear native to South America.

something out of a dark fairy tale. Despite the high altitude, these forests are bright, and they drip water from the moist air on thriving tree ferns. Bromeliads live in abundance here, which is good as they are a principal food source for the spectacled bears in these areas. This is the only bear found in South America, and although it isn't endangered, it is classified as a vulnerable species due to losses of its habitat. It's typically a black-furred bear with distinctive beige or red markings around its face, lending it the spectacle look. Its closest relative, the Florida spectacled bear, is already extinct.

At the riverbanks it's not uncommon to see mountain tapirs and small Andean deer called *Pudu*. It's worth mentioning that it is quite

nomenon occurs only in the narrow strip of the Andean spine that runs from Colombia down to Ecuador and into Peru. In Colombia, these forests are often characterized by tall wax palms, which grow at between 2,000 meters (6,500ft) and 3,000 meters (10,000ft) above sea level on the western side of the central cordillera, and often peak above the cloud blanket. On the eastern side of the Cordillera Oriental Mountain Range, you'll find dense forests, which blanket the steep slopes and protect the streams running down that feed the Amazon River. These forests are overflowing with lichens, orchids, ferns and epiphytic mosses. This area typically get two meters of rain a year, which maintains the lush forests and help form the many clear-water streams running through them.

As the topography dips below 1,500 meters (5,000ft) the cloud forest disappears and transitions into the lowlands of the Amazon Basin. Here you'll find an abundance of animal species, including river mammals. For more info, see the Amazonian wildlife photo feature.

NORTH TO THE COLOMBIAN COAST

The Caribbean Lowlands are home to an array of animals that reinforce Colombia's reputation as a haven for diverse wildlife. The Caribbean Coast, for example, boasts species that are as unique as the culture itself. One of the most iconic of these animals is the iguana, and they are found all over, although you'll have to wander away from metropolitan areas to see them in their natural habitat. Usually they are milling about in trees and searching for fruits to eat, but it's also possible to catch them waddling across roads. More than a few iguanas can be found on the grounds at Quinta de San Pedro in Santa Marta. Also, if you visit Johnny Cay (just

Green iguana at Tayrona National Park.

⊘ CONSERVATION IN COLOMBIA

Colombia's various ecosystems and topographies have resulted in a mega diversity of wildlife. Some estimates state that around 10 percent of all the earth's species reside in this country. Such varied wildlife is a gift to locals and visitors alike, and the hope is that everyone should be able to enjoy Colombia's rich nature for many generations to come.

To this end there are currently a number of active conservation projects throughout the country aimed at addressing various concerns. Some such projects involve ensuring that Bogotá has clean drinking water for its residents by making sure that the cloud forests of the surrounding páramo continue to thrive. Others involve protecting the Magdalena River Basin, or ensuring sustainable tourism practices are being adhered to in the Amazon.

Climate change is also a threat to various areas of Colombia, including the northern Andean region and Amazonas. The direct danger is to the myriad species that live in these areas. Changing temperatures also have a negative impact on rural areas and the wild regions that surround them. Without action, whole ecosystems will be thrown in flux.

For more information, or to volunteer, visit www. nature.org or the Wildlife Conservation Society (www.colombia.wcs.org).

off San Andrés island), the central grasslands of the island are overflowing with these animals. Because they seem to enjoy a steady diet of food from enthralled tourists, most of them are on the chubby side.

If you're lucky you might spot a cotton-top-tamarin in northwest Colombia, between the Magdalena and Cauca Rivers. It's a small monkey notable for a white-patch of fur on its head that gives it a kind of mad-scientist look. Unfortunately these little guys are in danger of extinction. If you'd like to learn more about

> *Ever dreamed of visiting an island teeming with colourful squirrel monkeys? In Colombia there's just such a place: Isla de Los Micos (see page 265). Here you can walk among hordes of the most playful of critters, and if you've got food they won't be shy about approaching you...*

conservation of this unique species, feel free to contact Proyecto Titi (Calle 77 #65–37; tel: 5-353 1278) in Barranquilla.

The giant anteater also makes its home in northwest Colombia. If you travel between Cartagena and Barranquilla be on the lookout for road crossing signs featuring the image of an anteater. This animal can be found in other parts of South America, all the way down to northern Argentina, as well as in Central America. Fossil remains have been found as far north as Mexico. The animal is characterized by a pronounced snout, and is a close relative of the sloth. It used to exist in the mountainous Andes regions but has sadly since wiped out. Those who wish to see these elegant animals in their natural surrounding will need to visit the Caribbean Coast.

The red-footed tortoise is an animal commonly found on the Colombian coast as well as in southeast Panama. These tortoises are diminutive in stature, and earn their name from the red markings on their legs. Sadly this makes them quite the trophy for exotic pet owners. Still, go to the hottest parts of the coast, like Guajira, Magdalena, and the departments of Bolívar and Atlántico, and you may well see one moseying about in the wild.

COLOMBIAN FLOWERS

It's hard to address the diversity of wildlife in Colombia without also acknowledging the diversity of plantlife. Over 130,000 plant species exist here, and the richness of climate that allows for this vegetation is also responsible for the wide variety of flowers found in the country. Flower cultivation is so popular In Colombia that it has become an export crop that generates some US$1.5 billion annually. This has even resulted in the creation of one of Colombia's most famous festivals – Medellín's annual Feria

Cyrtochilum orchid.

de las Flores. Some common varietals include carnations, bromeliads, roses, *helliconias* and even the bird-of-paradise.

The most popular of all the species is by far the orchid. Colombia is home to over 3,000 species of this elegant flower, including the Flor de Mayo. You can see these gems on display at Colombia's largest botanical garden, the Jardín Botánico José Celestino Mutis (Calle 63 #68–95, Bogotá; tel: 1-437 7060; www.jbb.gov.co; Mon–Fri 8am–5pm, Sat–Sun 9am–5pm), or visit the Orchideorama at the Joaquin Antonio Uribe Botanical Garden in Medellín (see page 135). If you book a stay at Hacienda Venicia in the Zona Cafetera, be sure to check out the lady of the house's expansive orchid garden that she cultivates personally.

📷 AMAZONIAN WILDLIFE

The Amazon is a fragile ecosystem, home to a breathtaking array of wildlife.

The Amazonia region of southern Colombia is a formidable area. It encompasses six departments and covers some 403,000 sq km (155,600 sq miles) of land, mostly blanketed in tropical rainforest and jungle. The area is sandwiched between the Andes to the east and the borders of Venezuela and Brazil to the west. What feeds the incredibly diverse ecosystems here are a number of rivers, all of which drain into that most majestic of waterways, the Amazon River.

Within the main region of Amazonia are five sub-regions occupying various areas. These include the Amazon foothills, which are at the border of the Andes, as well as a number of river plains feeding water into the Amazon. The largest of these is the Caquetá River plains, followed by the Inírida River plains (where the southeastern Guiana Shield Mountains, the Cerros de Mavecure, are located), the Guaviare River plains in the east, and the Putomayo River plains. In the west you have the Serranía de Chiribiquete, which are also mountains of the Guiana Shield. Then there's the Amazon Trapezium (or Leticia Trapezium), which is a small strip of land that borders the Amazon River and includes the city of Leticia. This is where most visitors to Colombia's Amazon will arrive at, and it's a good base of operations for making excursions to visit the abundance of wildlife.

Pink river dolphin.

Harpy eagle (harpia harpyja) perched on branch.

A male wire-tailed manakin.

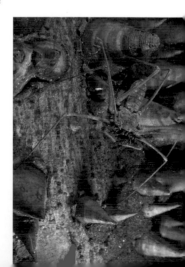

Jaguar in the Amazon Jungle.

Amazonian inhabitants

More than one-third of all animal species in the world live in the Colombian Amazon, making this area one of the most biologically diverse in the world. From Leticia you can make excursions to nearby Puerto Nariño to see some of these remarkable creatures, which include:

Pygmy marmoset
The adorable pygmy marmoset is the smallest monkey on earth. They live in family groups, in single trees and feed on tree sap (and bananas if they are around). You'll know a pygmy marmoset has been around when you see countless little teeth marks and holes in the tree bark.

Caiman
When you see a pair of glassy reptilian eyes on the surface of the water, you'll have found this iconic jungle predator.

Pink river dolphin
Born albino white but turning pink over time, these freshwater dolphins are one of the most iconic animals in the Amazon. They are even revered by the indigenous groups here.

Jaguar
The lion may be the king of the jungle in Africa, but here this spotted cat reigns supreme, no doubt due to the fact it possess the strongest bite of any feline on the planet.

Pygmy marmoset (cebuella pygmaea), Amacayacu National Park.

Spectacled caiman lurking in the water.

Tailless whip scorpion (heterophrynus sp.), waiting for prey on trunk of spiny tree.

Children playing soccer in the colorful streets of Cartagena's Getsemani district.

SPORT AND LEISURE

As with many South American nations, soccer dominates Colombia's sporting landscape. However, there's also a deeper sports legacy here, with some games dating back to pre-colonial times.

The Colombians are active people. After all, this is a country that grew from an agrarian society. Over the centuries, as communities emerged in the modern cities and towns that were founded, nature always played a crucial role. Even the largest of Colombian cities are located in and around mountain ranges, meaning that excursions and physical activities in the surrounding areas are commonplace.

Of course Colombia wouldn't be a Latin American country if soccer didn't play a role in the culture, and the pulse of "the beautiful game" can be felt throughout the country. When regular Colombians get too old (or too disinterested) to join a soccer game, they'll often settle back into other more esoteric sports that are unique to their country and that can often be enjoyed with a beer in hand. Below you'll find a list of those sports that define Colombia, from the national crowd pleasers to the regional favorites.

TEJO

It might come as a shock to visitors to Colombia, but, despite being played in almost every city and town, soccer isn't the national sport. No, that honor goes to tejo, an obscure (to foreigners anyway), game that has its roots in indigenous culture that heralded from the region known as Boyacá Department today. These days tejo is played everywhere, and it's become so ingrained in the Colombian consciousness that Congress passed a resolution in 2000, making it the official national sport.

On its surface the game isn't complicated. Players in teams of up to six people stand some 20 meters (66ft) from a small target made up of dirt or clay. (organized tejo is often played in enclosed areas featuring various narrow lanes where individual teams play) They throw a heavy,

The metal disc thrown in tejo.

palm-sized metal disc (the tejo) at folded paper triangles placed in a center ring within the target. The catch is that these paper triangles are filled with gunpowder, so if your tejo makes a direct hit, the triangle explodes and everyone in the general vicinity cheers. Needless to say, a direct hit results in more points than a standard. A standard point-scoring hit is any tejo that gets closest to the center medal ring; points don't count if the disc first hits the ground or backboard.

Legend has it that tejo has its roots in areas around Turmequé and Villa de Leyva, in Boyacá, and that indigenous tribes like the Muisca were the first to come up with the sport. Although historians generally agree that tejo dates back some 500 years, it's difficult to confirm this, due to the

> *Typically beers and often food are available during tejo games. Just remember never to walk across the lanes while a game is in full swing, or you could wind up getting hit by a tejo.*

Muisca's lack of recorded history. Whatever the origins, something about the game appeals to the Colombian culture greatly. No doubt this is at least partially due to the combination of beer

everyone plays it, from the rich kids in the north Bogotá suburbs to the poor Costeño youth kicking a ball around a trash-strewn dirt field between makeshift goalposts.

The Colombian national team had its golden era in the 1990s when they qualified for three world cups in the space of a single decade, a feat unmatched before or since. Although they never made it past the group stage, their performances solidified the country's reputation as a formidable soccer-playing country of Latin America. Colombia did not qualify for

Men playing tejo in Bogotá.

and explosives, which are ever-present during any *tejo* match.

You can find *tejo* games in most parts of Colombia. It's also becoming increasingly popular for hostels to arrange *tejo* outings during certain nights of the week. One such hostel that organises great *tejo* outings is El Macondo (www.macondohostel.com) in San Gil. They will organize the outing, arrange transportation, and explain the rules of the game.

SOCCER

It may not be the official national sport, but soccer is far and away the most popular sport in Colombia. Not only does everyone gather around the TV to watch televised games, but just about

a world cup during the 2000s, but they did win the Copa America in 2001 – their only win in the tournament's history. Colombia enjoyed a brief resurgence in the 2010s, led by a new golden generation of stars including James Rodríguez and Radamel Falcao. During the 2014 World Cup, they made it to the quarter finals, before being knocked out by the hosts Brazil (see box). If the national team are playing when you are in Colombia, head to a bar or better still, a house party, and when Colombia score a goal and the players celebrate with an impromptu salsa dance on the field, you'll feel like hitting the dance floor as well.

Despite Colombia's progress in the 2014 World Cup, they don't have a great international record, which helps explain why locals clubs are so popular in the country. The top league is Categoría Primera A, which is also known as Liga Aguila, after the league's beer sponsorship. It is regarded as one of the best leagues on the continent. Medellín's Atletico Nacional have won the Copa Libertadores (the most prestigious club competition in Latin America) on two occasions and are among the most successful domestic teams in the country. Other successful, popular teams in Colombia include Bogota's Millonarios and Santa Fe, together with Cali's América de Cali.

doing so in Colombia as well. Aiding the cause of the protestors is Bogotá's mayor, Enrique Peñalosa, a vocal advocate of animal rights, who succeeded in getting bullfighting outlawed in the capital city 2012.

However, in 2015 the courts overturned the ban citing the fact that bullfighting is a 'cultural form of expression' in Colombia. Refusing to take no for an answer, the protestors marched on Santamaria in early 2017. The demonstration soon turned violent, with police launching tear gas and pepper-spraying the protestors, who retaliated by

The Macarena Arena in Medellín during a bullfight.

BULLFIGHTING

The sport of bullfighting has a rich historical and controversial legacy in Colombia. For a long time Colombia was the South American capital of the sport; *plazas de toros* (bullrings) existed in many cities and towns. Colombia's most famous venue, the Colosseum-like Plaza de Toros Santamaria, in Bogotá, still operates today. The Feria Taurina, the annual bullfighting festival in Medellín, still takes place at the city's La Macarena bullring.

However, across the globe the sport of bullfighting has seen a pushback from the younger generation, who tend to view it as a barbaric relic from a less-enlightened era. These protestors have been making their voices heard in bullfighting strongholds like Spain, and now they are

⊘ 2014 WORLD CUP

After a 16-year absence, Colombia came roaring back in the 2014 World Cup. They thrashed Greece 3-0, and then edged out the Ivory Coast 2-1 before crushing Japan 4-1 to top their group for the first time in history. They beat Uruguay 2-0 in the round of 16, a result that cemented the 2014 Wold Cup as Colombia's most successful. They were eventually knocked out by hosts Brazil in the quarter-final, losing 2-1. After the final whistle, a clearly devastated and teary-eyed James Rodríguez was consoled by several Brazilian players, led by game winner David Luiz, in an iconic and touching moment. Despite their loss, Rodríguez was the tournament's highest goal-scorer, netting six times.

throwing bottles, stones, and bricks. This compelled the courts to take up the case yet again, but for now, the future of the sport remains in flux. Whether bullfighting is legal or illegal in the near future is wholly in the hands of the legal system, and is subject to change at a moment's notice.

RANA

This activity, colloquially referred to as the 'frog game', is similar to *tejo* in that it is a tossing game similar to horseshoes. In this one the object is to toss a brass ring into the mouth of a metal frog

Nairo Quintana.

(*rana*), which sits atop a metal or wooden box. The game is typically played in teams of two, and aside from scoring major points by landing the ring in the mouth, you can also score by landing the ring over one of the many the circular holes on the top of the box. It's a quintessential bar game in Colombia, but it's also great at backyard barbecues with a few beers and a few friends.

CHAZA

This handball/tennis-like game is actually the national sport of Ecuador, but it has made its way north, particularly to areas such as the Nariño Department, where it is played often. The game involves two teams of four people, each facing off in a rectangular area separated by a line, not unlike

Despite participating in the Olympics since 1932, Colombia didn't win gold until 2000, when María Isabel Urrutia triumphed in the weightlifting at Sydney. That was followed by another gold in the 2012 games, and then by three more in the 2016 games. Quite the improvement!

tennis. The object is to hit the *bombo* (ball) back and forth, and a player scores when they launch it into the opposing team's territory without them returning it. Typically *chaza* is played by hand, but sometimes paddles are used. Like *tejo*, *chaza* has its roots in pre-Columbian times, and many say the Incas were the first practitioners of the sport.

CYCLING

It's no surprise that cycling is such a huge sport and leisure activity in Colombia – the country's topography was made for the activity. The cordilleras challenge cyclists from all over to push themselves to the limit, as the terrain's steep grades and long climbs rival anything found in Europe. This is why Colombian cyclists have typically done well at the Olympics and the Tour de France. One such standout athlete is Nairo Alexander Quintana Rojas, a Boyacá-born professional who placed second in both the 2013 and 2015 Tour de France, and won the 2014 Giro d'Italia.

Colombia's mountains don't just breed athletes. Locals from Medellín, Antioquia, Cali, and Bogotá often like to unwind by cycling around the surrounding hills. It became such a popular pastime that the government got in on the act. In the 1970s, they created *ciclovia*, where every Sunday morning major thoroughfares are opened to pedestrians and cyclists. Today the *ciclovias* are the best times to get out and explore the cities of Colombia.

ROLLERSKATING

The inline skate craze of the early 1990s took many countries by storm – but Colombians really went wild for roller blades. It didn't take long for the trend to reach all corners of the country, and soon kids and adults in places like Cartagena, Bogotá, Cali, Medellín, and Valledupar were zipping along on streets and sidewalks. Many weren't content with skating as simply a leisure activity, and many Colombians went professional.

The national team annually competes at the World Roller Speed Skating Championships. As a testament to their prowess, they have taken home the title nine times in the space of just 12 years.

BASEBALL

Many sports fans know Latin American countries like Venezuela, Cuba, and the Dominican Republic as a breeding ground for baseball talent. However Colombia, a late bloomer as it may be, is slowly becoming known for baseball. Most of the fans and players are typically found on the coast of the country, from Cartagena all the way to the border with Venezuela. Games are particularly popular in Barranquilla, and this coastal city is even building a new baseball stadium that will play host to the 2018 Central American and Caribbean Games. The stadium will be named after one of Colombia's most famous baseball stars, Edgar Renteria, will seat 12,000 fans. Between this and the American scouts who keep coming to Colombia looking for fresh talent, expect baseball to become increasingly popular in Colombia for generations to come.

Radamel Falcao of Monaco scores against Manchester City in their Champions League tie, 2017.

⊘ FAMOUS COLOMBIAN SPORTS STARS

One of Colombia's most iconic soccer players is Carlos 'El Pibe' Valderrama, who played during the 1980s and 90s and whose distinctive blonde hair and flashy play made him a star. Of the current generation, there are three standouts: Radamel Falcao, who currently plays at Monaco, but has also played for Manchester United and Atletico Madrid, was one of the most prolific strikers in the world at his peak. Then there is James Rodríguez, who plays for Real Madrid, and goalkeeper David Ospina, who plays for Arsenal.

Ximena Restrepo, a 400-meter sprinter, won a bronze medal at the 1992 Olympic Games that was Colombia's first medal in the athletics category. Her time of 49.64 seconds is still a South American record. Another Colombian athletics star is Caterine Ibargüen, who has competed in the Olympics in the high jump, long jump, and triple jump categories, winning gold in the 2016 Olympics.

As for other sports, Colombian baseball player Orlando Cabrera claimed the 2004 World Series title with the Boston Red Sox. Edgar Renteria is another Colombian baseball star, earning World Series rings in 1997 with the Florida Marlins and then in 2010 with the San Francisco Giants. Juan Pablo Montoya is Colombia's most successful motorsports star, having competed in both Formula 1 and NASCAR.

Men singing and playing La Cumbia, a musical style typical of Colombia's Caribbean region.

MUSIC AND DANCE

As with all Latin American countries, music and dance are part of everyday life in Colombia, from socialising to celebrating.

Music feeds the soul of this country; it's the pulse that runs through the blood of every Colombian, from the cradle to the grave. In this chapter, learn more about how music in Colombia has evolved over time, together with the accompanying dance moves.

MUSIC

Some countries are musical by default. In Latin America, for example, most countries have developed musical genres that are an extension of their rich culture. However, only a few countries can claim that music is as much a part of their identity as any other aspect of their nation. Of course, Cuba and Brazil come to mind. Then there's Colombia. You can't talk about Colombia's cultural heritage without mentioning music – the two are that intertwined. As the culture varies from region to region, Colombian music also changes across the topography, making the country home to a

Folk dancers in Bahía Solano.

Colombians are crazy for salsa in general, and whether it's from Cuba, New York, Puerto Rico, or even their home country, they love it all equally. This is never more evident than it is in the south, where Cali has proclaimed itself the salsa capital of the country.

wide array of diverse musical genres. Go anywhere in Colombia, and you are guaranteed to hear great music.

This diversity is the result of disparate peoples, including the indigenous, Europeans, and Africans, all mixing over the course of several centuries. Their influences and culture have combined to create various styles of music that not only have roots in the cultural history of the nation, but have been adapted and have evolved over the years to find their place in the popular music scene. In Colombia, you'll hear local versions of rock and classical music, as well as types of salsa unique to Colombia that have been adapted to reflect the country's national identity.

The love Colombians have for salsa can be seen in the number of famous composers and musicians that have been born and bred in the country. Fruko y Sus Tesos is an iconic Colombian salsa group that is famous in the US, as well as Colombia and other South American countries. Jairo Vela, from Cali, is one of the most prolific composers in the genre and became famous as one of the founders of the influential salsa band, Grupo Niche. The other founder was Alexis Lozano. Some other noteworthy salsa artists from Colombia include Joy Arroyo, Cristian del Real; other famous bands include Alquimia, Los Nemus del Pacífico, Grupo Galé, Guayacán Orquesta (also founded by Alexis Lozano), and La Sonora Carruseles.

Shakira performing.

Move further toward the Caribbean Coast and you will hear eclectic styles that represent the aforementioned co-mingling of various influences. One such genre is vallenato, which was born in the city of Valledupar in the early 20th century and became popular in the 1980s. It's a good example of the merging of culture; within this genre you have instruments from Europe (the accordion), Africa (drums), and indigenous tribes (the *guacharaca*, a percussion instrument). The vallenato genre is a combination of four rhythms: *son*, *puye*, merengue, and *paseo*, and you'll know it the second you hear that accordion and *guacharaca* kick in. Today Valledupar hosts an annual vallenato festival, which is the largest in Colombia.

But aside from the most popular forms of music are a number of regional genres and sub-genres. These include *porro*, a kind of big-band style that originated in Sucre, on the coast. *Champeta* is a popular genre in Chocó, Cartagena, and Isla San Andres, and its West African rhythms have changed little over time. In the Andean region of Colombia you will hear *bambuco*, an indigenous musical expression with a slight European influence. It has melancholic, slow, folk-like rhythms and has been traced back to the Muisca Indians.

And of course one of the most famous musical expressions to be borne on the Caribbean Coast is cumbia (see box). Visitors lucky enough to spend time in Colombia's various regions will likely hear enough different types of music that they will begin to piece them all together and get a better picture of the country's musical scene. Even though the styles may be somewhat disparate, similar influences are found everywhere, and they all contribute to create something wholly unique yet undeniably Colombian.

DANCE

No single activity enjoys more popularity with members of the national population than this form of expression. In general, Colombians don't need much of a reason to go out and cut loose on the dance floor. It doesn't matter if it's the weekend, a weekday, a celebration, a birthday – pretty much any time is a good time to dance in Colombia.

Ø SHAKIRA SHAKIRA

International pop music icon Shakira has filled her cabinets with Grammy Awards and Billboard Latin Music Awards; she's toured the world and sold millions of albums. But her origins weren't exactly the stuff of legend. She was born Shakira Isabel Mebark Ripoll in Barranquilla, to a Colombian mother and a Lebanese father. She signed her first record deal at 13 and after a few setbacks achieved national success with the 1996 album *Pies Descalzos* (Bare Feet). From there it was a meteoric ascension to international success with hits such as *Whenever, Wherever* and *Hips Don't Lie*. Shakira went on to become the highest-selling Colombian artist of all time.

Most of the music that visitors encounter in Colombia was designed to go hand-in-hand with dance. Salsa, cumbia and vallenato are all popular music forms that were created specifically with movement in mind – and everyone takes part. The Colombian culture is such that both men and women are equally technically proficient when it comes to dancing. However, in truth most men learn from a young age because it's explained to them in no uncertain terms that if they want to impress a lady in the future, they need to learn how to dance.

The whole culture of dance is something Colombians take very seriously. To this end it isn't uncommon for male tourists to find themselves being dragged unwittingly to a bar dance floor by a single local desperate for a partner. Those who respond to a dance request with 'I don't know how' will most likely be met with bewilderment. To a Colombian, everyone can, and should, dance – the fact that one might not actually know how is purely incidental. Cali is the official salsa capital of the country (and it boasts the famous international festival), but visitors can rest assured that *salsotecas* abound throughout the country, in almost every city and town. At the very least you can be certain that even in the tiniest of watering holes, the proprietor will play some salsa over the loudspeakers at some point.

During Cali's salsa festival Colombia welcomes participants from all over the world to come and take part in a series of contests to crown the best dancer. Unsurprisingly Colombian locals often dominate the competitions, but their efforts have also been rewarded on the global stage. For many years salsa championships have been held in Las Vegas, Nevada, and Colombians have taken home first-place honors here as well. No matter where they compete, it seems that the Caleño style of salsa, unique to Colombia and technically different from Puerto Rican and Cuban styles, wows audiences and judges alike.

But Colombia isn't only salsa. Many of the country's most famous dances have their roots in the coastal regions of Colombia, in cities like Cartagena and Barranquilla. The African beats and frenetic rhythms of popular coastal music, such as cumbia, were born in the sultry nights of the area and live in the blood of the people. Coastal cultural heritage and history can be seen in the traditional folkloric dances of this region too. These are never more on display than during Barranquilla's Carnival (see page 202), when the parade's festivities showcase different types of dance. Many date back to the earliest colonial years of the Colombian Coast. This history is evident in the elaborate and colorful costumes of the dancers; costumes inspired by the African tribes that ended up on the shores of the Caribbean many centuries ago.

Cumbia dancer in Cartagena.

⊘ CUMBIA AND THE COAST

La Cumbia is the dance style most symbolic of Barranquilla's Carnival, and of the Colombian coast in general. It is based on the Colombian musical genre cumbia, which originates from three distinct ethnic groups: African, European, and the indigenous.

The European component to the dance is illustrated by the dress and interpretation of the music. The costumes worn by the dancers represent the European colonial period, while the instruments used and the rhythms of the dance are distinctly African. So what the Caribbean Coast offers in the form of dance is not only a fun activity, but a teaching tool used to express culture and history.

📷 SALSA DANCERS

Colombia has taken the salsa stylings of other nations and made it their own, resulting in one of the sexiest dances the world has ever seen.

It's true: Colombian salsa is different than other more traditional types found in Latin America. Much of this is to do with the history of the music in the country. Colombians fell in love with salsa in the 1940s and 50s, when the great big bands of New York, Cuba, and Puerto Rico were dominating the scene. They appropriated all forms of this music, creating a unique style that would eventually come to be defined as Colombian salsa. Compared to other styles of salsa, where there is more distance between the partners, Colombians get in close, which adds intimacy and passion, telling a story of romance and seduction not unlike the tango. Of course this music is faster, and Colombian salsa features four beats (with a break on the fourth), piston-like movements on the half step, always moving side to side or back to center, keeping the upper body still at all times: the way the Colombians dance salsa is all about the footwork. It's intended to be flashy, and it's intended to keep the focus and storytelling from the hips on down. To the typical Colombian, this dance is second nature and no great mystery; to the typical outsider, it's a maddening a conundrum and a cipher that few gringos ever master. But it sure is fun to try.

Cafe Havana, a salsa bar in Cartagena.

Salsa dancers perform during the Delirio Salsa show in Cali

Locals dance salsa in Cartagena.

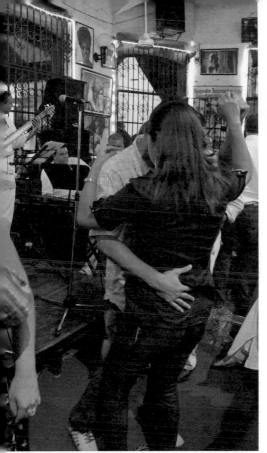

Salsa lessons in the colonial center of Santa Marta.

Colombian salsa

When Colombians began to create their own version of salsa music, it was inevitable that other musical genres would have influence on it. Cumbia played a large part in the evolution of Colombian salsa; salsa first arrived on the northern shores, where cumbia was already deeply ingrained. The syncopations, drums, guitars, and accordions of the Caribbean Coast informed the traditional stylings from New York and Cuba, and the next thing you knew you had something faster, unique to Colombia. The two genres are now so intertwined that, dancewise, they are often interchangeable. Whether it's cumbia or salsa, you're bound to see the similarities: partners dancing side by side, up close, moving from the hips down and mirroring each other's steps.

Salsa in Cali is a whole other animal compared to salsa from the north. Street-style salsa is what people think of when they think of modern Colombian salsa. This is flashier and faster than cumbia-based salsa, which is perfect for the nightclubs. Interestingly this style is rarely taught in schools; instead it's something Colombians learn from youth, or in the crucible of the glitziest *salsotecas* in Cali.

A dancer prepares to participate in the 7th World Salsa Festival in Cali.

Salsa dancers perform in Deliro.

Colombian dance group Salsa y Sabor at the 7th World Salsa Festival in Cali.

Wayúu indigenous woman weaving a chinchorro, a Colombian hammock.

TRADITIONAL CRAFTS

For indigenous Colombians, crafting is more than a hobby – it's a tradition handed down over generations.

Throughout Colombia you'll find no shortage of traditional crafts. These products are abundant in the cities, and the farther you venture into rural areas, the more you'll find entire communities whose economy revolves around the production and selling of crafts. Typically indigenous women will earn an income solely from making knit products, such as purses. These items represent more than money to the people who make them. They have a strong cultural significance deeply rooted in their native heritage. That's why authentic Colombian crafts are in such high demand, because they are much more than the sum of their parts.

SOMBRERO VUELTIAO

The sombrero *vueltiao* is perhaps the most potent symbol of Colombian culture. It's not hard to see why either: this wide-brimmed white hat, covered in black geometric patterns, is recognizable from a mile away. You may have seen them outside of Colombia too. Wherever there is a sizeable Colombian community in a foreign nation, the local politicians often pander to them by posing for photos in a sombrero *vueltiao*.

The hat itself has deep cultural roots, deeper than you might think. It actually dates back 1,000 years or more, to the indigenous Zenú people on the Caribbean Coast. They are typically made of *caña fleche* fibers, which are derived from a tropical grass. Also, the patterns imprinted on the hat are not merely decorative – they symbolize many different aspects of the cosmology on which this indigenous group formed their religious beliefs. Some are under the impression that the iconic Juan Valdez character is typically seen wearing a sombrero

Children making sombreros vueltiaos in Tuchin.

vueltiao, but this is a misnomer. His hat is a sombrero *aguadeño*, named after its town of origin, Aguadas, in Caldas.

MOCHILA WAYÚU

These bags are some of the most popular exports to fashion houses and stores across the globe. The craftsmanship is meticulous and the end result is an item of very high quality. Typically these bags are made from wild cotton and various other fibers. The process of making it involves twisting the fibers into z and s shapes, using a *ganchillo*, which is a crocheting technique. It's a painstakingly slow process: it can often take around 20 days to produce just one bag.

As with many crafts in Colombia, the methodology of producing these bags has been passed down from generation to generation. For the Wayúu people of the Guajira Peninsula, the act of making the bags is an expression of life. Legend has it that there was once a gigantic spider, named Wale'Kerü, in the area that was having trouble maintaining a steady supply of food. So he taught the Wayúu how to knit these bags in exchange for animals. There are various types of these bags, but one of the most common is the *susu*. These days it's seen on celebrities the world over.

Wayúu mochilas.

RUANA

The *ruana* is traditional piece of Colombian clothing from the Altiplano, which is made up of the highlands of Boyacá and Cudinamarca Departments. This is a type of poncho made from wool and designed to withstand the frigid temperatures typical of high altitude plateaus. These items are in demand as well, and in the town of Noba, in Boyacá, hundreds of families earn their living from the manufacture of *ruanas*. The proliferation of mass-produced *ruanas* means it can be easy to be duped into buying an inauthentic version. Therefore it's best to head to these little communities and show your support by purchasing one whose artisan values win out in the end. Many of the families who make them still sheer

> *If you are traveling toward the Ecuador/Peru border, then stop in at Putumayo Department. Here you'll find handmade beaded jewelry from the indigenous tribes of the region. They typically incorporate jungle seeds to make colorful pieces of jewelry, such as necklaces and bracelets.*

the sheep with scissors and thread the garment using spindles, a worthy commitment to craftsmanship that deserves recognition.

GUACAMAYAS

Guacamaya is the name of a town in Boyacá as well as a type of basket that hails from the area. These multi-color baskets are made by hand and are known for their distinctive weave, which involves rolling the fiber around a stem and then rolling again on a spiral. With this technique artisans are able to make a variety of items including bowls, trays, and baskets of varying sizes.

WÉRREGUE

This rare craft hails from the Chocó Department and is produced exclusively by women. The name derives from the Wérregue palm tree, whose leaves are woven so tight that they can even hold water, to form plates, bowls, pots and baskets. The original manufacturing process was brought to the area by missionary nuns hundreds of years ago, but the locals jazzed it up by adding flourishes of color and figures to the designs. Today *wérregue* crafts are distinct and famous products that are immediately known as being products of the Chocó.

FILIGREE JEWLERY

In Colombia, you'll notice the littler silver pieces of artisan jewelry, distinctive for their intricate and delicate designs that often resemble threads. In fact, the name derives from Latin, with *filum* meaning 'thread.' This technique of jewelry making is known as filigree, and despite existing throughout the world, from Europe to Asia and the Middle East, it was brought over to Colombia during colonial times by the Spanish.

This process of jewelry making first took hold in the Magdalena River towns on the Caribbean

Coast. Much of the gold the Spanish had pilfered passed through here, so local artisans had an abundance of material to work with. Over time locals adapted the delicate techniques to make them uniquely Colombian.

The Colombian technique of making filigree jewelry involves producing various parts of the item to be connected later to form a whole, not unlike a puzzle. The artisans make the framework out of silver, forming the individual shapes one by one. So every shape, be it a heart or a flower, has to be put together by hand. The artisans of today use modern tools, such as soldering irons and pliers, but overall it's a painstaking process that relies predominantly on the hands.

To create a piece of jewelry wholly from scratch is a good example of just how lengthy the process can be. The artisan starts with a chunk of silver, then melts it down to make the threads, before stretching them out until they reach the right size. This process can take a day to produce a single finished piece.

Purchasing filigree jewelry in Colombia represents the age-old question of commercialism: do you buy handmade or mass-produced items? On the international market, the type of filigree jewelry made in Colombia takes a backseat to cheaper, mass-produced imports. However, everyone likes quality, so visitors to Colombia often purchase the real deal because they know the authenticity and level of craftsmanship involved. They might pay more, but they're paying for a better product.

Still, authentic filigree pieces can be found at various prices. Some of the smallest pieces cost around US$5–10, while larger items like rings and bracelets can cost US$20–40. Larger and more intricate items can cost hundreds of dollars. Visitors to Bogotá should head to the markets at Usaquén to check out some authentic filigree jewelers.

One relevant organization well worth learning more about is Artesanias de Colombia (www.artesaniasdecolombia.com.co), which helps communities of artisan producers to monetize their items and turn their operations into sustainable businesses.

Men wearing ruanas in Tunja.

⊘ KUNA CRAFTS

There are so many beautiful crafts available from the various indigenous tribes in Colombia that seeing them all in one trip is an impossible task. However it's precisely this variety that makes Colombia a prime destination for travelers seeking to purchase quality, authentic goods made with heart and soul. To this end, it's best not to leave any indigenous stone unturned in the quest for great craftwork.

Enter the Kuna tribe. This indigenous group exists principally in areas of Panama, although there are some small communities in Colombia. Those who take the sailboat journey from Cartagena to Colon, in Panama (or vice versa), will be treated to a stop at the San Blas Archipelago of islands, where the Kuna have been living simply and off the land and sea, much as they've had for centuries.

They deal in trade, and one item travelers might come across is a *mola*, a traditional Kuna craft. *Molas* are multifunctional pieces of fabric with colorful designs that can be used as garments (they often form the front and back of dresses), or the coverings of bags.

Molas are perfect gifts for those who love crafting in their own right, as they can be sewn into pillows, furniture, cushions, and so on. You don't even have to visit the San Blas Islands in order to find these artisanal gems. They are on offer in the markets of Capurganá, near the Panamanian border.

THE GOLD MUSEUM AND INDIGENOUS CRAFTSMANSHIP

The Spanish yearned for it, and to this day it represents wealth and power. To Colombia's indigenous though, gold was just another element in the cycle of life.

goldsmiths held lofty positions in their communities due to the reverence people felt for their work. As a result, goldsmiths often held high political office or even became religious leaders. The precious metals were typically mined in alluvial fields, and from there they were smelted in the clay crucibles of makeshift furnaces heated over coal on tops of mountains,

A gold pectoral from the Calima people on display at Bogotá's Gold Museum.

It may be called the Museo del Oro, but there are a number of other items on display to compliment all that gold. For instance, the types of metals mined by these groups varied from tribe to tribe, depending on location. While *oro* was prized among certain Andean tribes like the Muisca, silverwork was also highly popular, especially in the Nariño Region. Platinum artifacts are also on display, most of which come primarily from the Chocó Region of northwest Colombia. In every case, the indigenous peoples who extracted these metals from the ground, and those who later formed them, were professionals of the highest calibre.

THE MINERS AND CRAFTSMEN

In pre-Columbian societies, both the miners and the

where the wind patterns could stoke the flames.

The earliest gold remains found in the museum date back to 500 BC, with the earliest metallurgical artifacts of any kind dating to 2100 BC. All pieces are very well persevered, which is testament to the extraordinary craftsmanship. The smiths hammered ingots against stone slabs, forming them into thin sheets. Talented craftsmen could then cut them with stone chisels and form them into various shapes, making jewelry, pins, statues, or ornamental attire, such as breastplates and headpieces, all of which can be seen at the museum. For more intricate work, indigenous craftsmen would sometimes cast various objects in beeswax, and then use it as a mould to transfer the shape to metal.

On the opposite side of the metallurgical exhibit is more goldwork, featuring funereal skull masks placed over the faces of the deceased before burial. There are also many ceramic artifacts representing daily indigenous life, often focusing on motherhood, as well some fertility statues. The ceramic artifacts on display are all the more impressive when you consider that the earliest ones are thought to have been made around 6000 BC. On the second floor there is also a screening room featuring a presentation on the history of the indigenous and metallurgy (in Spanish).

especially seen in the 'second-skin' artifacts, which are plate gold coverings that were worn by interpretive dancers who would move like animals.

The third floor also focuses on the chieftans of the tribes. It was customary to cover the recently deceased leaders in gold attire, mummify them, and inter them in caves or temples, so many of the artifacts remain as they were. However, no artifact in the entire museum is more interesting than *La Balsa de Eldorado* (the Raft of Eldorado), sculpted entirely of gold, and representing the offering ceremony performed by the Muisca people. The Muisca believed

At the Gold Museum in Bogotá.

WHERE GOLD MEETS SPIRITUALITY

A common symbolic thought among Colombia's many different indigenous tribes was that of transformation, and this is evidenced in many pieces throughout the museum, especially on the third floor. Interchangeable ornaments and diadems (crowns) are on display, many of them representing birds, frogs, pumas, deer, and jaguars. These early peoples held fast to the notion of different worlds, with the birds representing the upper realm, the humans, deer, and jaguars representing the immediate, and the snakes and bats representing the lower worlds. The artifacts on display here showcase a cosmology that expresses the idea that humans can transform into animals, and vice-versa. This is

that gold was the energy of the sun father, and therefore it was only ever borrowed. What gold they had they felt they needed to return to the lake, which represented the womb of the earth mother. Tribal leaders would cover themselves in gold dust, take a raft to the middle of the lake, then toss in gold ornaments, forming a pact with nature. *La Balsa de Eldorado* is a miniature representation of this ceremony: a raft featuring the leader and his various assistants, all rendered in gold of the most intricate detail. This exhibit is followed by the *sala de ofrenda* (offering room), which is a spectacular 360-degree showcase of hundreds of gold trinkets and items that the ancient Muisca would toss into the lake to appease their nature gods.

Rappelling on Juan Curi Waterfall.

ADVENTURE SPORTS AND ACTIVITIES

Unbeknown to many, Colombia's reputation as an adventure sports hotspot has been growing steadily for a number of years.

Colombia was made for adventure, and nowhere is this more evident than in Santander Department, where adrenaline junkies flock to engage in some of the most thrilling sports around. In this chapter, you'll find an outline of the different sports available throughout Colombia, and the best places to go to try them.

CANYONING

Colombia's striking scenery also allows for some truly unique and epic adventure sports such as canyoning, which is essentially abseiling down waterfalls. Canyoning is typically offered on a tour, which includes all the relevant safety equipment, such as helmets, harnesses, ropes, and, of course, guides. Heights vary from waterfall to waterfall, but the Cascadas Juan Curi, near San Gil, is 65 meters (213 ft) tall, which, together with the spectacular waterfall, makes it one of the most popular canyoning spots in the country.

The tours aren't only about the abseiling either. Typically these are multi-hour affairs that involve a good amount of trekking along a river to get to the site. Some of these tours also involve more than one descent, so it's best to find out exactly how many the tour company offers before making a reservation. Other good areas for canyoning include Medellín, Cudinamarca, Pereira (Zona Cafetera), and San Agustín, in Huila Department.

DIVING

Lest anyone forget, Colombia is the only country in South America to boast both a Pacific and a Caribbean coast, which means that there are plenty of great opportunities for diving here. Many tend to head straight to the Caribbean Coast, where there is an abundance of dive stores in the cities and towns. One popular place to reserve

Paragliding in the mountains near Medellín.

⊘ CUEVA DEL ESPLENDOR

Colombia's rivers have carved their way through various mountains across the country, creating beautiful underground caves that are well worth exploring. One such drop-dead gorgeous cave that every explorer (and abseiler) should visit is the Cueva del Esplendor, which is near Jardín, in the Antioquia Department. You'll find this fantastic cave just a few hours from Medellín, complete with a gushing waterfall crashing into the stone pools at its base. Get there via car or horseback on a day trip. You can reserve this excursion through Hostal Condor de los Andes in Jardín.

dive excursions is the fishing village of Taganga, near Santa Marta.

The islands of San Andrés and Providencia are also very popular. Conditions here are ideal due to the sheer amount of reefs, cays, and coral islands

> *Today, there's still only one reputable company for extreme rafting in San Gil: Colombia Rafting Expeditions (see page 159).*

Diver photographing pelican barracudas, Malpelo Island.

that are found throughout in this part of the Caribbean. There are plenty of good spots and dive operators in San Andrés. However, the nearby island of Providencia is less touristy and there are better reef conditions. On Colombia's southern Pacific Coast, Isla Gorgona has great conditions for diving.

RAFTING

San Gil, in Santander Department, really is ground zero for rafting. There are ideal conditions in the mountains at the Fonce and Suárez Rivers. However, this area wasn't always so well known as a rafting destination. It took an intrepid group of adventure-sport-loving locals and travelers in the early/mid-2000s to stake out and mark the best routes around San Gil. Through trial and error of

the most dangerous variety, these foolhardy rafters learned the safest routes as well as the various grades.

Depending on their level of comfort, visitors to San Gil should choose between rafting expeditions that are milder, such as grade I or II rapids, or more extreme, which go up to grade V. There's much adrenaline and excitement in rafting, especially with rapids of higher grades. It's fairly common to find that one or more members of your boat go overboard, so don't be alarmed if they do!

Colombia has an abundance of rivers, so San Gil isn't the only spot to enjoy some rafting. Other popular locales include San Agustín, in Huila Department, Río Negro in Tobia, Cudinamarca, the River Barragan in the Zona Cafetera, the Cauca Valley, San Juan in Antioquia, and Flandes in Tolima Department.

PARAGLIDING

Many travelers may come to San Gil and Bucaramanga for the paragliding, but this is not the only spot in which to enjoy this sport. From Santander to the Cauca Valley, conditions are great for paragliding; not only that, but the breathtaking scenery that defines much of Colombia means many regions are best seen from above. There really is nothing like looking down at Colombia's raw beauty – all those rolling green hills, cloud forests, and canopy jungles – from a few hundred meters up in the air.

As for the conditions, strong thermal winds are found throughout the country, which allows for ideal flights from elevated terrain. To this end, paragliders typically take off from hillsides or mountaintops, often over sheer drops. Beginners who purchase a tour will fly in tandem with an experienced paraglider. The team straps you into a front harness with the pilot in back. He then runs off the side of the mountain and takes flight, controlling the parachute by handbrakes. However, the act itself involves more than gliding around in a parachute. Professional paragliders have an innate understanding of wind patterns and thermal conditions, and know the differences between the various clouds – as some 'good' clouds are innocuous, while other 'bad' clouds will suck a parachute up into the air like a vacuum.

Anyone can reserve a tandem flight, and no previous experience or training is necessary. Many people come to Santander to fly over the

Chicamocha Canyon, which is the largest in Colombia. Soaring a few hundred meters over this gorge is an experience in itself, and these flights typically last 30–60 minutes. Paragliding tours also operate out of other locations as well, including Medellín and Cali. One of the best areas in the entire country is around the town of Roldanillo, in the Valle de Cauca.

KITESURFING

Come to the Guajira Peninsula, in particular Cabo de la Vela, and you'll find strong offshore winds that make this an ideal spot for kitesurfing. During the day, the skyline here is peppered with brightly colored canopies while on the surface of the sea happy folks zip along on flat boards. Cartagena is also an ideal spot for kitesurfing, and windsurfing.

MOUNTAIN BIKING

As mentioned before, cycling is one of Colombia's favorite sports, which means that there are plenty of opportunities to cycle throughout the country, with mountain biking being one of the more popular means of travel. This is due to Colombia's mountainous terrain, which not only gives mountain bikers quite a workout, but also provides beautiful scenery scarcely rivaled throughout the world.

Many head to Santander and cycle the mountains around San Gil and the Chicamocha Canyon. There are also great conditions outside of Bogotá in Boyacá, as well as in and around Medellín. In San Gil the best company for reserving a tour and renting bikes is Colombian Bike Junkies (see page 159).

ZIPLINING

Zipline activities are becoming increasingly popular throughout Latin America, particularly in areas with thick tree canopy. Colombia is rife with these ideal conditions, and not only are there canopy tours in lush hilly areas like those outside Medellín, but there are also tours over water in the Reserva Río Claro (see page 150). In San Gil, a zipline has been installed that runs a few hundred meters from one side of a canyon to another. The steep drops make for a wild ride.

Cyclists descending a mountain near Medellín.

⊘ COLOMBIA: DARLING OF THE PARAGLIDING WORLD

It's almost impossible to imagine Colombians of generations past – from those fighting in the War for Independence to those fighting through Colombia's subsequent civil wars – ever thought there would come a day when their beloved nation would become a base for people to launch themselves off mountains into the air for no other reason than the sheer fun of it. The beautiful mountainous terrain that served as the staging ground for many battles is equally perfect for fun and adventure.

The wheels were set in motion in the 1950s, when aviation buffs from the US and Europe discovered that it was indeed possible for a glider pilot to take flight simply by running off the side of a hill or mountain. The concept

evolved over time, and soon paragliding was an activity practiced on the world's most famous mountain ranges. It's not surprising, then, that aficionados eventually broadened their horizons and left the Alps for the Andes.

As soon as paragliders discovered Colombia, it was all over. In the adventure sports capital of Santander, the conditions are perfect for paragliding. There are always colorful bits of fabric dotting the beautiful skyline. In 2015, Colombia was officially recognized for its ideal conditions when the World Air Sports Federation (www.fai.org) held their 14th annual World Paragliding Championships in Roldanillo, in Cauca Department. Come here and experience the epic flight conditions yourself.

The ramparts of San Fernando de Bocachica Fort, Cartagena.

Driving between fields of coffee plants near the town of Trujillo.

On the banks of the Amazon River.

Playa Blanca, Rosario Island.

INTRODUCTION

A detailed guide to Colombia, with principle sites clearly cross-referenced by number to the maps.

Cable car to Monserrate.

For most of the 20th century, many of the so-called civilized countries of the world shunned Colombia, regarding it as nothing more than a rapidly failing state. For decades travelers avoided this destination out of fear that the numerous narco and guerrilla groups were going to do to them what they had done to so many others over the years. Then something amazing happened: seemingly overnight, there was a crack in the veneer of Colombia's infamous reputation, and the world saw through to a nation of unrivalled beauty, both in its landscapes and its people.

This is no longer Pablo Escobar's Colombia. It is a nation that is finally achieving its unparalleled potential; Colombia is welcoming visitors with open arms and every department is open for business. Come to Cudinamarca and soak up the culture and colonial heritage of the country's capital, Bogotá. Head southeast to Santander, and paraglide through the skies, or brave the raging rivers and class V rapids. Continue to Valledupar, home of Colombia's biggest music festival, the Fiesta de la Leylenda Vallenata, where the pace of life is markedly slower, and the area is teeming with running rivers.

Plaza Santo Domingo, Cartagena.

Then there's the coast. From the deserts of the Guajira Peninsula to the ramparts of Cartagena's walled city, Colombia has some of the most stunning beaches and national parks anywhere in the world. Fly to the Chocó, on the Pacific Coast, and go whale watching, or relax in Medellín, the City of the Eternal Spring. Continue to the Amazonas and discover your inner Indiana Jones with a nighttime wildlife tour, swimming with pink river dolphins, or fishing for piranha.

These are but some of the places in Colombia. You could spend your entire life traversing Colombia and you'd barely scratch the surface of this land of fantasy-meets-reality. It's true you'll probably never know all of Colombia, but what better way to spend your life than by trying?

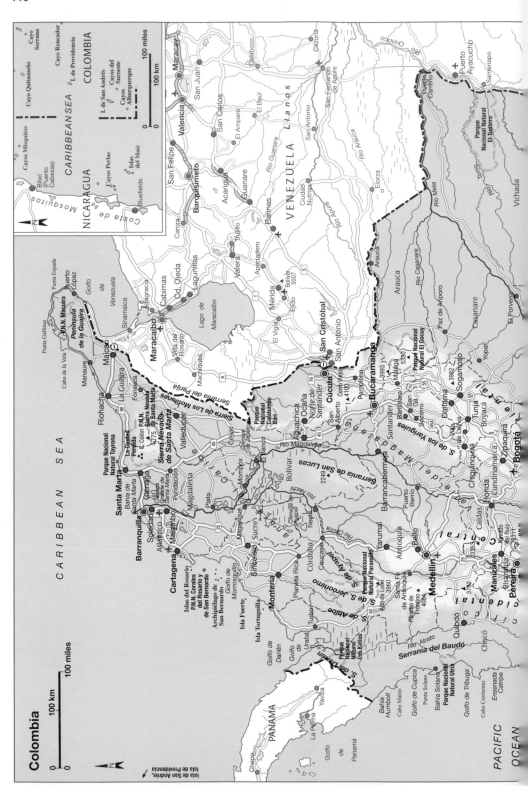

Colombia

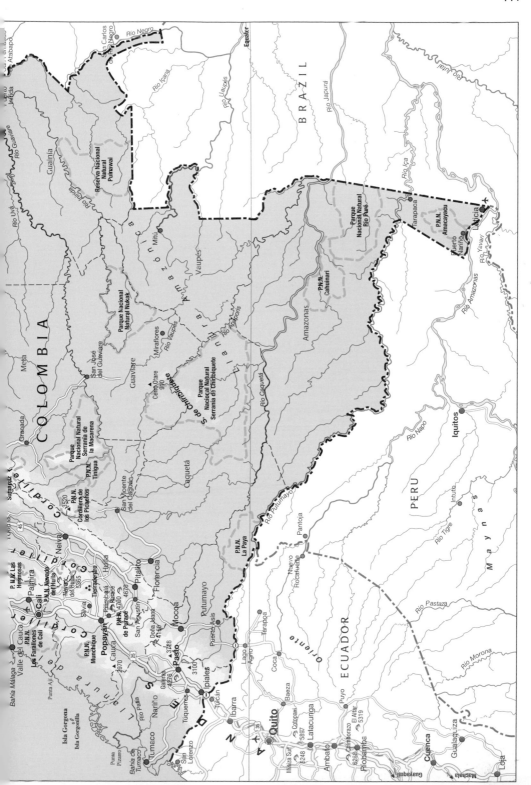

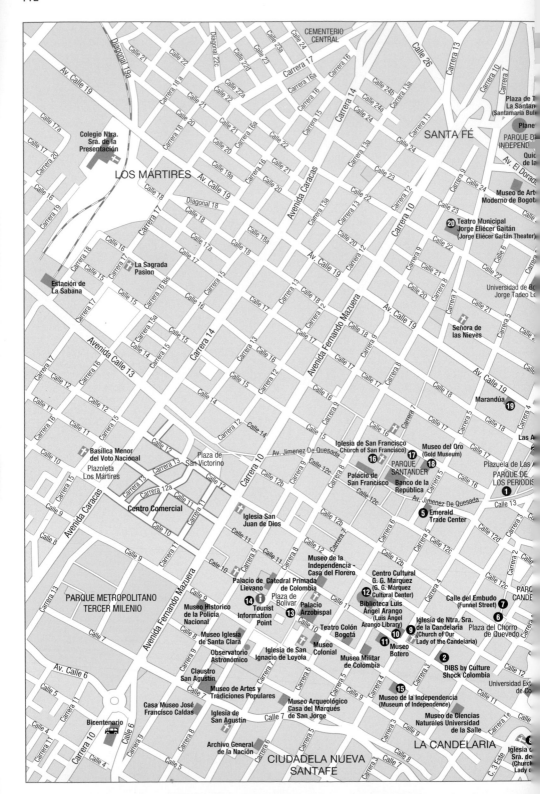

CEMENTERIO CENTRAL

SANTA FÉ

Plaza de T
La Santam
(Santamaria Bul

Plane

PARQUE D
INDEPEND

Quic
de la

Av. El Dorad

Museo de Art
Moderno de Bogot

Colegio Ntra. Sra. de la Presentación

LOS MÁRTIRES

20 Teatro Municipal Jorge Eliécer Gaitán (Jorge Eliécer Gaitán Theater)

Universidad de Bo
Jorge Tadeo Lo

La Sagrada Pasion

Señora de las Nieves

Estación de La Sabana

Marandúa 19

Basílica Menor del Voto Nacional

Iglesia de San Francisco Church of San Francisco

Museo del Oro (Gold Museum)

Las A

Plaza de San Victorino

Plazoleta Los Mártires

Av. Jimenez De Quesada

16

17

18

Plazuela de Las

PARQUE DE LOS PERIODIS

PARQUE SANTANDER

Centro Comercial

Palacio de San Francisco

Banco de la República

1

Av. Jimenez De Quesada

Iglesia San Juan de Dios

5 Emerald Trade Center

6

Museo de la Independencia - Casa del Florero

Centro Cultural G. G. Marquez (G. G. Márquez Cultural Center)

PARC
CANDE

PARQUE METROPOLITANO TERCER MILENIO

Palacio de Lievano

Catedral Primada de Colombia

12

Calle del Embudo (Funnel Street) 7

Museo Histórico de la Policía Nacional

14 Tourist Information Point

Plaza de Bolívar

Palacio Arzobispal

Biblioteca Luis Ángel Arango (Luis Ángel Arango Library)

6

13

Iglesia de Ntra. Sra. de la Candelaria (Church of Our Lady of the Candelaria)

Plaza del Chorro de Quevedo

Museo Iglesia de Santa Clara

Teatro Colón Bogotá

10 9

Observatorio Astronómico

Iglesia de San Ignacio de Loyola

Museo Colonial

11

Museo Botero

2

Claustro San Agustín

Museo Militar de Colombia

DIBS by Culture Shock Colombia

Casa Museo José Francisco Caldas

Museo de Artes y Tradiciones Populares

Universidad Ext
de Co

Iglesia de San Agustín

Museo Arqueológico Casa del Marqués de San Jorge

15

Museo de la Independencia (Museum of Independence)

Calle

Bicentenario

Museo de Ciencias Naturales Universidad de la Salle

Archivo General de la Nación

LA CANDELARIA

Iglesia d
Sra. de
(Church
Lady o

CIUDADELA NUEVA SANTAFE

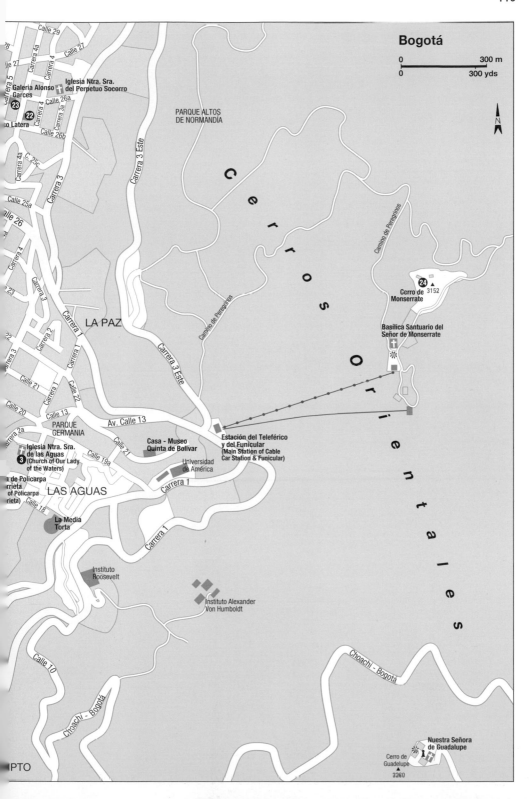

Bogotá

0   300 m
0   300 yds

N

Calle 29
Calle 27
Carrera 4a
Carrera 4
Calle 27
Galería Alonso Garces
Iglesia Ntra. Sra. del Perpetuo Socorro
Carrera 4
Calle 26a
23
22
co Latera
Carrera 3a
Calle 26b
PARQUE ALTOS DE NORMANDÍA

Carrera 4a
C. 25c
Calle 25a
Carrera 3
Carrera 3 Este

Calle 26

Cerros Orientales

Camino de Peregrinos

Carrera 4
23
Carrera 3

Camino de Peregrinos

24 3152
Cerro de Monserrate

LA PAZ
Carrera 1
Carrera 2
Carrera 3 Este

Camino de Peregrinos

Basílica Santuario del Señor de Monserrate

Calle 21
Carrera 1
Calle 22
Carrera 1

Calle 20
Parque 2a
Av. Calle 13
PARQUE GERMANIA
Calle 13

Casa - Museo Quinta de Bolívar
Estación del Teleférico y del Funicular (Main Station of Cable Car Station & Funicular)

Calle 21
Calle 19a
Iglesia Ntra. Sra. de las Aguas (Church of Our Lady of the Waters)
3
Universidad de América

a de Policarpa rrieta of Policarpa rieta)
LAS AGUAS
Carrera 1
Calle 18

La Media Torta
Carrera 1

Instituto Roosevelt

Instituto Alexander Von Humboldt

Choachi - Bogotá

Calle 10

Choachi - Bogotá

PTO

Nuestra Señora de Guadalupe
Cerro de Guadalupe
3260

Narrow street in La Candelaria.

BOGOTÁ

Nestled high in the Andes sits a modern Latin American capital and the seat of Colombia's political and economic power – where old neighborhoods and grand plazas provide a link to the country's colonial past.

When arriving in Bogotá by air, you'll be struck by the collision of the city's urban growth with the surrounding pristine nature. Bogotá's sprawling metropolis is ever expanding, slowly encroaching on the tranquil green valleys and misty Andean peaks of the Cordillera Oriental that surround it. Once you touch down at the airport, you're deposited right in the middle of the city's 1,590 sq km (613 sq miles) and amid its nearly 7 million inhabitants. You then have a choice: you can either push back against the kinetic energy or get swept up in the culture and pace of life in Bogotá.

Despite Bogotá's status as a modern capital, it has also retained some of the best-preserved colonial neighborhoods on the continent. These combined aspects – the old and the new – make the city an architectural melting pot; it's filled with shimmering office towers and swanky new restaurants that sit side-by-side with centuries-old churches, plazas, and homes that could have hosted Simón Bolívar for dinner in times gone by.

Everything in the timeline of the city – from the early Muisca period to the arrival of the Spanish conquistadors, to the founding of the capital, to its present day form – informs a unique culture unlike anywhere else in the country: a highland people with mixed European/indigenous roots, moving through the streets at a breakneck pace and each with a singular purpose – to hustle rent money, provide for the family, graduate from school, make it through the day, or revel in the night. Or just simply maintain the status quo. Ask a Bogotano what makes a Bogotano, and they might just tell you it's cold-weather adaptability peppered with high stress levels. But they're still Colombians, which means their welcoming spirit and warm-heatedness hasn't dissipated in the thinner air.

Torre Colpatria.

Main Attractions

La Candelaria
Plaza Bolívar
Museo del Oro (Gold Museum)
Cerro Monserrate
Alto Chapinero
Mercado Paloquemao
Villa de Leyva

Maps on pages 112, 126, 132

BOGOTA: THEN AND NOW

Like most colonized areas in Colombia, the first explorers arrived in search of gold. This was never truer than with Spanish Conquistador Gonzalo Jiménez de Quesada, who, in 1536, sailed south on the Magdalena River from coastal Santa Marta with a force of 900 men. They were in search of El Dorado, the famed lost city of gold. The journey was so perilous that by the time the expedition arrived in the Andes around present-day Bogotá, only 166 men remained. While no one ever did find the golden city of El Dorado, Muisca gold work can be observed today in the city's most impressive museum, the Museo del Oro.

Upon failing to find El Dorado, Jiménez de Quesada turned his attention to conquering the local indigenous population: the Muisca. It was these natives who called the area *Bocatá*, and when the colonists claimed the land in 1538 it would first be changed to New City of Grenada. Later, it was officially changed to Santa Fe de Bogotá. Jiménez de Quesada stayed in the region as more expeditions arrived and the settlement grew. This area became the base of operations for subduing other parts of the country, and Jiménez de Quesada was eventually offered a commission to conquer the llanos.

After the revolution, and Spain's final defeat at the battle of Boyacá, Bogotá became the official capital city of the new Gran Colombia, and remained so through the 19th and 20th centuries as other countries broke off from the coalition. Eventually the Republic of Colombia was founded. It has stayed true through civil wars, dictatorships, and every subsequent modification of Colombia's Constitution, the last one being in 1991. Bogotá, it seems, will always be Bogotá.

Not that the city always carried a stately reputation. For too many years Bogotá was known mostly for the corruption of its politicians and the violence in its streets, with the most ruthless act being the Palace of Justice siege in 1985 by M19 rebels. That's because Bogotá has been the convergence point in the ongoing struggle for

Tourists and locals in La Candelaria.

⊘ ALTITUDE SICKNESS

If you are visiting Bogotá for the first time, you will find that acclimatising to the altitude is just as important as getting your logistical bearings. The reason for this is that Bogotá sits at an altitude of 2,644 meters (8,675ft) above sea level. Many travelers may not notice the effects of *mal de altura* (altitude sickness) immediately, but they can sneak up on you at a moment's notice, especially when walking up the steeper streets of La Candelaria. Symptoms include dizziness, tiredness, loss of appetite, nausea, and shortness of breath. To avoid such unpleasantness, be sure to stay hydrated and steer clear of any strenuous activity for the first 24 hours, whilst your body acclimatizes to its new surroundings.

cessation of hostilities between government forces and guerrilla groups over the years.

However, as with Medellín, Bogotá has reinvented itself, shedding its dark and infamous past in favor of a present filled with rich culture, high fashion, world-class dining, raging nightlife, and a looming dream of peace. This capital city is where politicians craft complex peace agreements in concert with waning guerrilla forces in the hopes that a jaded populace will capitulate and up-vote their schemes for a better future.

GETTING YOUR BEARINGS

As with other South American metropolises, such as Sao Paolo or Buenos Aires, Bogotá viewed from above can be intimidating. It almost seems impossible that a new arrival with limited time in the city can adequately get his or her bearings in such a massive municipality. The good news is that, although Bogotá is enormous, travelers will be spend much of their time along the foot of the Cordillera Oriental, which runs from north to south. Using this mountain range as your anchor point, will make navigating Bogotá a lot easier.

Visitors will probably want to explore La Candelaria and Plaza Bolívar first, as these are the easiest areas to traverse on foot. Even so, traffic and congestion here can be just as fierce as anywhere else, with cars and taxis seemingly happy to bump into each other if they get too close. One of the main east–west thoroughfares in this area is Avenida Jiménez de Quesada, between Carrera 3 and Carrera 7. This marks the edge of La Candelaria, with the neighborhood stretching south to Calle 7.

Downtown follows Carrera 7 northeast past Avenida Jiménez all the way up to Calle 26, which, to the east, includes part of the thriving bohemian neighborhood La Macarena. While the rest of downtown includes many good shopping options, quick eats, and decent restaurants, parts of it, notably between Carrera 7 and Carrera 10, are best avoided after dark, as this is the city's red light district. Bordering La Macarena, from Calle 50 to 68, is one

Taking in the view from Monserrate.

⊘ Tip

One of the best local palliatives for altitude-related discomfort is *aromática*, a delicious infusion prepared with aromatic herbs and/or fruits, like a tea.

of the more affluent neighborhoods in Bogotá, El Chapinero. Beyond Calle 60 lies North Bogotá, which is home to some of the most popular tourist destinations such as the Zona Rosa and Zona G.

LA CANDELARIA

Parque Periodista ❶ lies at the northeast end of La Candelaria. It may be small, but you can't miss the center statue of Simón Bolívar housed in a domed stone gazebo. This park is also the embarking point for many of the neighborhood's bicycle and walking tours. Those who take the increasingly popular (and very worthwhile) graffiti tour will have the option to stop in at an intriguing little art gallery: **Dibs by Culture Shock Colombia ❷** (Carrera 3, no.11–24; tel: 300-312 2215; daily 10am–6pm), which features thought-provoking works by talented local and international street artists.

To the northeast of the park, where Avenida Jiménez runs alongside Carrera 2a, you'll find the charming **Iglesia Nuestra Señora de las Aguas ❸**

(Church of Our Lady of the Waters; Carrera 2, no. 18a–62; tel: 1-341 0674; mass times: Mon 7am, Tue–Fri 7am and 6pm, Sun 8am, 10am, noon, and 6.30pm), a quaint colonial church founded in 1633. Outside is a statue of Peruvian writer Don Ricardo Palma, who was a central voice in the struggle for independence. One block south from the church, also on Carrera 2a, is the **Estatua de Policarpa Salavarrieta ❹** (Statue of Policarpa Salavarrieta), a sculpture that honors a heroine of Colombian independence: Policarpa Salavarrieta or 'La Pola'. She was a pro-independence spy who was martyred at just 21 years old when the Spanish executed her in 1817. Just up the street you can see the small yellow house where the viceroy authorities arrested her (Carrera 2 between Calles 12 and 13).

Just south of Parque Periodista and across the Calle 13 lies the beginning of the colonial section of La Candelaria. A number of historic homes have been converted to bars, cafés, restaurants, hotels, and hostels. Boutique hotels used to be the order of this neighborhood, but the tourism boom of the last few years means it has become ground zero for hostels catering to the backpacker crowd. New options seem to be popping up monthly and the competition has had a positive effect – most of the hostels in the area are, at the very least, decent and often very good. **Casa Platypus** (www.casaplatypusbogota.com) is one such place, located in a converted colonial home complete with central courtyard. It enjoys the distinction of being the first real hostel in Colombia, and is one of many examples of local entrepreneurs earning a buck while still preserving the colonial spirit of the neighborhood.

Down from Parque Periodista, and along Avenida Jiménez, are a number of restaurants and banks, as this area borders downtown. Also here is the **Emerald Trade Center ❺** (Avenida

⊘ BECERRA, BIEBER, AND BOGOTÁ

Bogotá has a love-hate relationship with its street artists. On August 19, 2011, Diego Felipe Becerra, a 16-year-old boy, was shot in the back and killed, allegedly for the attempted robbery of a bus driver. However, evidence suggests that he was hiding from police officers after they caught him graffiting an underpass.

The tension between the city's graffiti artists and law enforcement was palpable, and it was only exacerbated when a certain Justin Bieber came to town. After a concert, Bieber decided to go and graffiti an underpass, under the protection of a police escort. To many Bogotanos, the fact that Bieber could spray paint a Canadian flag (with a cannabis leaf replacing the iconic maple leaf), with police permission and protection, was an affront to the memory of Becerra. The following week, some 300 street artists descended on the underpass, painting anywhere and everywhere (even over Bieber's original work), in a show of solidarity with their fallen brother.

Since then, Bogotá authorities have tried to work with local artists, sanctioning some street art. Despite this, authorities and street artists are unlikely to ever see eye to eye. As famous Colombian street artist, D.J. Lu, put it: "being told where you can paint goes against the spirit of graffiti." Becerra would likely agree.

Jiménez, no. 5–43; Mon–Fri 7.30am–7pm, Sat 8am–5pm). Emeralds are just as sought-after as gold in Colombia, and there's no greater selection in the country than at this shopping complex.

Travel south and up into the higher streets of La Candelaria, along Carreras 2, 3, and 4, and you'll start to see the graffiti wall art showcased in the tour mentioned earlier. At the corner of Carrera 2 and Calle 12b you'll the **Plaza del Chorro de Quevado** ❻, a popular colonial plaza where Bogotá is believed to have been founded in 1538. There's a small white chapel here, the **Hermitage de San Miguel de Principe**, which was constructed in 1969 in the same location as the first ever chapel in Bogotá. Most interesting nearby is the **Calle del Embudo** ❼ (Funnel Street) a narrow cobblestone street lined with old houses and *chicha* bars, which leads from the plaza down to Calle 12c. One such *chicha* bar, with a lovely terrace, is **Café del Chorro** (Carrera 12b, no.83), which also serves hot wine and juices. Be warned: *chicha* is fermented corn liquor popular with *campesinos*. The drink may not be too strong, but it is potent, and those who try it should avoid smelling it first (see page 67).

Continue into the hills of La Candelaria, where the roads are cobblestone or paved with bricks. The narrow *calles*, flanked by colonial homes with bougainvillea-draped wooden balconies, look down to all of Bogotá sprawling westward. At the very top of La Candelaria is the **Iglesia de Nuestra Señora de Egipto** ❽ (Church of Our Lady of Egypt; Carrera 4e, no. 10a–02; tel: 1-342 1230), a colonial church that borders the neighborhood of El Egipto, one of the poorer barrios in the city. It is considered a conflict zone in Bogotá, one plagued with gang violence. **Hostel Sue** (http://hostalsuecandelaria.com/) runs tours with local guides up to El Egipto, where visitors can have breakfast amid stunning hillside views and talk to local children and former gang members about life in the area. As for the church, it was built on the site of a hermitage constructed in 1556 and has undergone many renovations throughout the years. Recently it's gotten quite the facelift,

The intersection of Carrera 5 with Calle 11 in La Candelaria.

⊘ Tip

Look out for petty crime in Bogotá. In La Candelaria at night, drug-pushers can be particularly prevalent.

with its neo-Gothic white facade with new gold trim complementing the jutting central bell tower. It was even declared a national monument in 1975.

Down Calle 11 you'll find the **Iglesia de Nuestra Señora de la Candelaria** ❾ (Church of Our Lady of the Candelaria; Carrera 4, no.11–62; tel: 1-384 5787; Mass times: Mon–Sat 7am and 6pm, Sun 9am, 11am, 6pm). This church was built in 1686, but, like many other *iglesias* in the area, it has undergone several reconstructions to keep it sturdy and its yellow front facade and twin bell towers looking their best. Inside there are three naves lined with adornments and ceiling artwork, and at the back there are a number of impressive gold altarpieces.

Next to the church of La Candelaria, also on Calle 11 you'll find the **Biblioteca Luis Ángel Arango** ❿ (Luis Ángel Arango Library; Calle 11, no. 4–14; http://www.banrepcultural.org/blaa; Mon–Sat 8am–8pm, Sun 8am–4pm), a multistory library with a small English section on the fourth floor (mostly English-as-a-Second-Language textbooks). There

At the Botero Museum.

are free Wi-fi and internet stations here, though. At the exit is a small Sala de Musica, an exhibit featuring Colombian musical instruments over the centuries. This includes everything from violins and harps to indigenous Muisca xylophones.

Diagonal to this is another important cultural house: the **Museo Botero** ⓫ (Calle 11, no. 41; www.banrepcultural.org/museo-botero; Wed–Sat and Mon 9am–7pm, Sun 10am–5pm, closed Tue), a must-visit museum dedicated to one of Colombia's most famous artists, Fernando Botero. You won't just find Botero sculptures here; there are also his paintings and drawings. Many of them feature that signature Botero style: human subjects of exaggerated proportions just begging you to reach out and touch them.

A block downhill is the **Centro Cultural García Márquez** ⓬ (Gabriel García Márquez Cultural Center; Calle 11, no. 5–60; www.fcecol.info; Mon–Sat 8am–6pm). The center is home to a bookstore with a small literature section in English where you can find

works by Garcia Marquez, among others. On the bottom floor of the center is a free art gallery featuring exhibitions that change monthly – one month it could be showcasing the works of Frida Kahlo, and the next displaying indigenous art and sculpture. The center is also home of the *feria de libros* (book fair), which takes place once a year during different months, although the most famous often occurs in April.

Farther down Calle 11, just before Plaza Bolívar, you'll see a row of traditional Colombian eateries, the oldest of which, **La Puerta Falsa** (tel: 1-286-5091), has existed for over 200 years. Most of these restaurants focus on Bogotá staples like *ajiaco* and *tamales*, and they are all of comparable good quality.

PLAZA BOLÍVAR

When you arrive in **Plaza Bolívar**  you'll be in the colonial and historic heart of Bogotá. This sprawling square has seen quite a bit since it was first founded as the Plaza Mayor all the way back in 1539. Today many humans swarm the area, but most visitors are of the avian variety, with countless *palomas* (pigeons) milling about the square. If you'd like to feed them, you can purchase bags of corn from local vendors for US$0.30. Watching over it all is a statue of a stately Simón Bolívar, sword in hand and clad in robes and military dress. The statue was sculpted by an Italian, Pietro Tenerani, in 1839, and became the first public monument in the Bogotá. Today, many plazas in other towns and cities throughout Colombia and Venezuela are named after the Liberator.

Real history can be found on all four sides of the square. The looming **El Catedral** (Cathedral; Tue–Fri 9am–5pm, Sat–Sun 9am–6pm) sits on the plaza's northeast corner. This large cathedral was actually erected between 1807 and 1823 and took the place of a smaller chapel, which was built in 1553 and was the site of the first ever mass

said in Bogotá. The church itself is expansive and elegant, painted white with wide columns ringed with carved decor painted gold. Crystal chandeliers hang from the ceiling and frescoes adorn the walls just below the center dome. In the rear is the small chapel **El Topo**, featuring a choir loft of sculpted walnut. If you're lucky you'll enter El Catedral when the organ is playing, and the entire space comes alive.

Next to El Catedral is the **Capilla del Sagrario** (Carrera 7, no. 10–40; tel: 1-341 1954; mass times: Mon-Fri noon, Sat noon and 5pm, Sun 10am, noon, and 5pm), a 17th-century chapel not nearly as grand as El Cathedral, but nonetheless with an impressive red and gilt ceiling. Next to that is the **Palacio Arzobispal** (Archbishop's Palace; Carrera 7, no. 10–20), which features elegant brass doors and facades. Other structures include the original site of the Viceroy's Palace, the **Capitolio Nacional** (completed in 1927 after over 70 years of work), and the **Casa de los Comuneros** (corner of Carrera 8 and Calle 10), a 17th-century former commercial

Plaza Bolívar and the cathedral.

center. Today it houses the city's main **Tourist Information Point**  (Carrera 8, no. 9–83; http://bogotaturismo.gov.co; Mon–Sat 8am–6pm, Sun 8am–4pm). The English-speaking staffers are very friendly (and patient), and will provide useful maps of the city. This office also offers the only truly free walking tour in the city – the rest operate based on tips. English-speaking tours leave from the office Tuesday and Thursday at 10am and 2pm and cover various historic sites in the nearby areas.

On the west side of the plaza is Bogotá's City Hall, the **Alcaldia** (Carrera 8, no. 10–65), also known as the Palacio Lievano, constructed in French style, with a long arcade fronting the building. On the north side the **Palacio de Justicia** (Palace of Justice) dominates the plaza. The original building was badly damaged when M19 guerrillas laid siege to in 1985, and it was rebuilt in 1999, with a focus on creating symmetry within the prized public space. Today its muscular design projects an image of fortification and security above all else.

On the northeast corner of Calle 11 you'll find another stellar museum: the **Museo de la Independencia**  (Museum of Independence; Carrera 7, no. 11–28; tel: 1-334 4150; www.museoindependencia. gov.co/Paginas/english.aspx; Tue–Thu 9am–5pm, Sat–Sun 10am–4pm), also known as the Casa del Florero. This museum takes a unique approach to Colombia's history, inviting guests to not only see it, but also touch it via interactive video exhibits. These take up two floors in an old colonial house dating back to the late 16th century and feature a copy of the *Acta de la Revolución,* which was drafted in 1810. There are also video presentations of various periods in Colombia's history, including a harrowing retelling of the Palace of Justice Siege by M19 guerrillas. You'll also see the base of the vase that played such a crucial role in the 'flower vase incident' that occurred on July 20th, 1810, and was an attempt by *criollo* patriots to provoke the Spanish viceroy. They did this by requesting a vase from a local businessman named José Gonazáles Llorente to present to a visiting dignitary at a dinner. The *criollos*

Capitolio Nacional.

knew he would refuse, and when he did, it sparked protests that would eventually lead to Colombia's independence. There are some 2,000 artifacts of the independence era on display in the museum, and most of the exhibit text is in Spanish. Daily guided visits in Spanish only.

CARRERA 7

If you head north on Carrera 7 from Plaza Bolívar, you will find that it is solely a pedestrian-only throughway for many blocks. Retail outlets and fast food restaurants primarily line the street, but there are many vendors and street performers as well. This is a good area to try some Colombian street food, such as fresh mango cut into slices, sprinkled with salt, and drizzled with lime juice.

At the corner of Calle 15 and Carrera 7 is the **Iglesia San Francisco** ⓰ (Church of San Francisco; mass times, multiple daily Mon–Sat 7am–6pm; Sun 8am–7pm), which was built between 1557 and 1595. Inside it's dark and moody, with elaborate gold-painted altars lining the walls. The church is

directly across from **Parque Santander** ⓱, which has existed since the mid-16th century and features a statue of Francisco de Paola Santander.

THE GOLD MUSEUM

On the west side of the park is the entrance to the **Museo del Oro** ⓲ (Gold Museum; Carrera 6, no. 15–88; tel: 1-343 2222; www.banrepcultural.org/gold-museum/exhibition-in-bogota; Tue–Sat 9am–7pm, Sun 10am–4pm). If you go to one museum in Bogotá, go to this one. Colombia has a pronounced and well-preserved indigenous heritage, and there are few places where you'll get a more tangible sense of this culture than here. The museum, located in the modern Banco de la República building just off Parque Santander, is home to over 35,000 pieces of pre-Columbian gold work and ceramics.

The entrance is off Parque Santander, and the first floor contains a restaurant, gift shop, and information kiosk, which provides free maps in English. This is also a good place to inquire about guided tours, which the museum

Museo de la Independencia.

Iglesia San Francisco.

Exhibit at the Gold Museum.

offers in both English and Spanish. From February through October, there are typically two tours per day; one in the morning and one in the afternoon. In November and December there are six tours per day; three in the morning and three in the afternoon. Most of the displays here are found on the 2nd and 3rd floors, and they focus heavily on the pre-Colombian indigenous groups and their relationship to the land and precious metals. One half of the 2nd floor, for example, is devoted to the metallurgical history of Colombia's indigenous tribes and the processes they used to mine and shape gold, bronze, and copper. The third floor features, among other things, *la balsa de Eldorado*, a small gold raft sculpture representative of the Muisca people's ceremonial offering to their gods. (For more information, see page 96).

DOWNTOWN TO PARQUE INDEPENDENCIA

Carrera 7 continues as a pedestrian-only thoroughfare past Calle 19, which is an area known for its raucous local bars and quick eats. One place that's worth a stop is the delicatessen **Marandúa** ⑲ (Calle 19, no. 4–25; tel: 1-243-0070; Mon–Sat 9am–8pm, Sun 10am–6pm, closed Fri) Locals stand shoulder-to-shoulder at the counters in this Spanish-style deli, eating cheap, delicious pork-leg sandwiches and drinking imported beer from Spain.

After Calle 19, you'll find the **Teatro Municipal Jorge Eliécer Gaitán** ⑳ (Jorge Eliécer Gaitán Theater; Carrera 7, no. 22–47; tel: 1-379 5750; www.idartes.gov.co/teatrom-jeg) an art-house movie theater that features Colombian and short film festivals, as well as smaller international releases. Three blocks north is where the pedestrian-only walkway ends and the cars take to the street again. Also here is the lush green **Parque Independencia**, a terraced park that runs from Carrera 7 up to Carrera 5.

Here you'll also find the area's premier bullfighting ring, the **Plaza de Toros Santamaría** ㉑ (Santamaría Bullring; Carrera 6, no. 26b; tel: 1-327 4850). Built in 1931 and seating some 14,500 spectators, this impressive Colosseum-style arena stands out in an otherwise modern neighborhood. There's been some controversy regarding this structure, however. Enrique Peñalosa, Bogotá's pro-animal-rights mayor, banned the popular sport of bullfighting in 2012. But in 2015 a constitutional court overturned the ban, and now bullfighting is technically legal again. This will continue to be a thorn in the side of younger Colombians, who typically oppose the sport. Bordering both the park and the bullring to the northeast is the trendy bohemian neighborhood of La Macarena.

LA MACARENA

As fun as La Candelaria can be, it's nice to get away to a more peaceful area. **La Macarena** might just be the best option as it's located next to Parque Independencia, about a 20-minute

walk from La Candelaria. This tiny yet bustling enclave is nestled at the hilly foot of the cordillera, surrounded by a leafy residential neighborhood of upscale apartments and 100-year-old brick homes.

In a few blocks (between Carreras 5 and 4, and 29 and 26), you'll notice a collection of international restaurants: La Macarena is fast coming into its own as a mini Zona G, another trendy Bogotá neighborhood. Aside from fine dining, La Macarena is a great place to come for a coffee or hot chocolate, as independently owned cafés abound. For chocolate lovers, the star of the neighborhood is **Lachoco Latera** ㉒ (Carrera 4a, no. 26b–12; tel: 1-774 9621; Mon–Wed 12.30–8pm, Thu–Sat 12.30–9pm, Sun 1–7pm), a café that also serves creative chocolate refreshments. They offer run-of-the-mill teas and juices, but it's their various hot chocolates – imbued with flavors like ginger, mint, clove, and cinnamon – that are the real draw here. A great spot for coffee is **Librería Luvina** (Carrera 5, no. 26c–06; tel: 1-284 4157; http://luvina.com.

co), a corner bookstore/café that serves sandwiches and salads too. Most of the books here are in Spanish, but there are a couple of English offerings from wandering expat authors.

There are also several small art galleries in the area, featuring works by local up-and-coming artists. The pick of the bunch is the **Galeria Alonso Garces** ㉓, (Carrera 5, no. 26b–92; tel 1-337-5827; www.alonsogarcesgaleria. com/info.htm; Mon–Fri 8.30am–1pm, Sat 10am–2pm, closed Sun), which features some fantastic work, by both national and international artists.

UP TO MONSERRATE

There are some truly spectacular views in South America: the 360-degree panorama of Rio from Christ the Redeemer; the towering green peaks surrounding Machu Picchu; and last but not least, looking down at Bogotá's sprawling metropolis from the top of **Cerro Monserrate** ㉔ (www.cerromonserrate.com/en; funicular railroad operates Tue–Fri 6.30am–11.45am, Sat 6.30am–4pm, Sun 6.30am–6.30pm; cable car operates

The view from Monserrate.

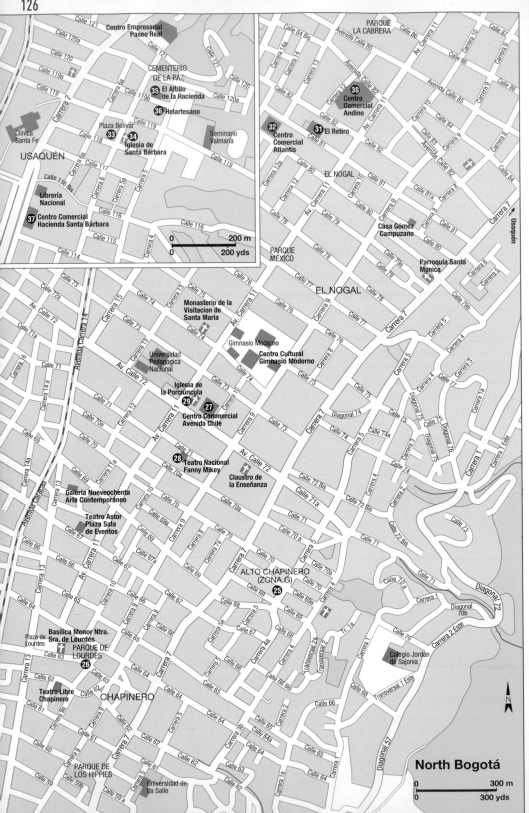

Calle 121
Calle 120a
Calle 120
Calle 119a
Calle 119
Centro Empresarial Paseo Real
Calle 121
Calle 121
Calle 120
CEMENTERIO DE LA PAZ
Carrera 6a
Calle 119b
35 El Altillo de la Hacienda
Calle 120a
Calle 120
Carrera 7
Calle 119
36 Helartesano
Plaza Bolívar
33 **34**
Iglesia de Santa Bárbara
Calle 119
Seminario Valmaría
Calle 119
USAQUÉN
Clínica Santa Fe
Carrera 7
Carrera 6
Carrera 5a
Carrera 5
Calle 117
Calle 116 Bis
Librería Nacional
Calle 116
37 Centro Comercial Hacienda Santa Bárbara
Calle 116
Calle 115
Carrera 4
Calle 114

PARQUE LA CABRERA
Avenida Calle 85
Carrera 14a
Carrera 14
Carrera 13
Calle 84 Bis
Calle 86
Carrera 11
Carrera 10
Carrera 9
Calle 87
Calle 86
Avenida Calle 82
Carrera 12
30 Centro Comercial Andino
Carrera 11
Calle 85
Calle 84
32 Centro Comercial Atlantis
31 El Retiro
Calle 81
Calle 82
Avenida Calle 82
Calle 83
Calle 84
EL NOGAL
Calle 80
Carrera 12
Carrera 11
Carrera 10
Calle 81
Calle 81a
Carrera 9
Carrera 8
Calle 78
Calle 79
Casa Gómez Campuzano
Calle 81
Calle 80
Usaquén →
PARQUE MÉXICO
Calle 78
Calle 79a
Carrera 6
Carrera 5
Parroquia Santa Mónica
Calle 79b

EL NOGAL
Calle 76
Calle 77
Calle 78
Carrera 9
Carrera 7
Monasterio de la Visitación de Santa María
Gimnasio Moderno
Centro Cultural Gimnasio Moderno
Universidad Pedagógica Nacional
Av. Calle 72
29
Iglesia de la Porciúncula
27
Centro Commercial Avenida Chile
28 Teatro Nacional Fanny Mikey
Claustro de la Enseñanza
Galería Nueveochenta Arte Contemporáneo
Teatro Astor Plaza Sala de Eventos
ALTO CHAPINERO (ZONA G)
25
Basílica Menor Ntra. Sra. de Lourdes
Plaza de Lourdes
PARQUE DE LOURDES
26
Teatro Libre Chapinero
CHAPINERO
Colegio Jordán de Sajonia
PARQUE DE LOS HIPPIES
Universidad de La Salle

North Bogotá

0 — 300 m
0 — 300 yds

0 — 200 m
0 — 200 yds

Mon–Fri 6.30am–midnight, Sat noon–midnight, Sun 10am–4.30pm).

Take the cable car to the top of this hill in the Cordillera Oriental and you'll pass over tall, bushy eucalyptus trees until you reach your destination, at a height of 3,152 meters (10,340ft) above sea level. Prevailing over the summit is the bright white **Santuario Monserrate** (tel: 1-284 5700; mass times: Mon noon, Tue–Fri 10am and noon; Sat 8am, 10am, noon, and 2pm) a church built in 1915 on the same spot were a 17th-century monastery once stood. From the steps of this church and its surrounding stone pathways, you will have a 180-degree view of the city stretched out before you. The view stretches from the south to the north, and all the way west to where the houses end and the green valley begins. Nothing beats this bird's-eye view of the sprawling metropolis that is Bogotá.

Adjacent to the church is a useful **tourist information kiosk** (Mon–Sat 8am–5pm, Sun 9am–4pm). Just north of here is a row of stands selling souvenirs, including some Indigenous purses, but they're often of dubious authenticity and quality, so be careful. Down toward the funicular elevator (a travel option with often shorter lines than the cable car), are two restaurants, the upscale and very French **San Isidro** (www.restaurantecasasanisidro.com), and **Casa Santa Clara** (tel; 1-243 8952; www.restaurantecasasantaclara.com; Mon–Fri noon–midnight, Sat–Sun noon–4pm). The stunning views from the patio tables at Santa Clara make for a great place to enjoy a hot chocolate and an *almojabana*. There are few better places in Bogotá from where to watch the sun set.

EL CHAPINERO

About 3km (2 miles) north along Carrera 7 is the upper-middle-class neighborhood of **El Chapinero**. This barrio is more diverse than it appears on its surface for a couple reasons:

younger generations of Colombians are moving into its stately old houses, and it is home to one of the most thriving gay communities in the city. In fact, the area has an official **LGBT community center** (Calle 66, no. 9a–28; tel: 1-249 0049; www.ccdlgbt.blogspot.co.uk). Gentrification, for better or worse, means the neighborhood is getting a younger facelift and might someday even rival the Zona Rosa, 10 blocks to the north.

It's best to divide El Chapinero into two zones. The modern **Alto Chapinero** ⑳ (also known as Zona G), the gastronomic heart of the neighborhood, located between Carreras 7 and 5 and Calles 70 and 69a, and the **Quinta Camacho** located nearby on Carrera 11, between Calles 67 and 72. The latter makes for an especially pleasant stroll because of the architectural beauty of the area. In the late 19th and early 20th centuries wealthy Bogatanos started building homes here in the English Tudor style; today the streets are lined with lovely houses whose overtly British design is refreshingly out of place in Latin America.

The cable car to Monserrate.

Toward the south of Chapinero you'll find **Parque de Lourdes**  (Calle 63 at Carrera 13), a plaza notable for the imposing church standing on its eastern side. The **Iglesia de Lourdes** was built in 1875 and features a stunning facade of three pointed, arched doorways with ornamented cornices. The elegant white interior has three naves, with gold-painted decor throughout. The church was built in neo-Gothic style and is one of finest examples of such architecture in the city.

The English houses and tranquil neighborhoods disappear around Calle 72, a busy thoroughfare lined with chain restaurants and the **Centro Commercial Avenida Chile** (CC Av Chile; Calle 72, no. 10–34; www.avenidachile centrocomercial.com; daily 10am–8pm), the first of many modern shopping complexes in the area. Just before it, on Calle 71 between Carreras 11 and 7, there is a line of cheaper places to eat than those you'll find in the Zona G, although most are fast food outlets. Also here is the **Teatro Nacional Fanny Mikey** (Calle 71, no. 10–25; tel: 795

7457; www.teatronacional.co), a theater featuring local and international performances that plays an important role in helping local acting talent develop.

Standing out the sea of modernity that is Chapinero is an old twin-steeple church, the **Iglesia de la Porcíuncula** (Calle 72, no. 11–82; mass: Mon–Fri 7am, noon, 6pm, and 7pm, Sat 8am, noon, 5pm, and 7pm, Sun 8am, 1pm, 5pm, and 8pm). Built in 1930, this church, with its whitewashed facade and carved wood double doors, is another great example of Colombian neo-Gothic architecture. From here it's easy to continue north to the **Zona Rosa** (Zona T). There's no need for a taxi as the walk between the two neighborhoods, along Carrera 11, is brisk and pleasant.

ZONA ROSA NIGHTS

At Calle 82 and Carrera 11 you'll find the beginning of Bogotá's **Zona Rosa**. It's hard to miss because three giant shopping complexes convene right here. First there's the **Centro Andino** (www. centroandino.com.co; Mon–Fri 10am–8pm, Sat 10am–9pm, Sun noon–6pm) then

Tudor-style architecture in Alto Chapinero.

El Retiro ③ (www.elretirobogota.com; daily 8am–9.30pm), and finally **Centro Comercial Atlantis** ㉜ (http://atlantisplaza.com/en; daily 8am–11pm). Take your pick: each of these offers limitless retail and boutique options. One reason to venture over here, other than for conspicuous consumerism, is to try one of Bogota's much-beloved steak restaurants: **Andres de Carne de Res** (www.andrescarnederes.com). The heart of the Zona Rosa area is just to the north of the shopping centers, where there is a pedestrian-only throughway. This relatively small area features a wide array of dining and drinking options, including *cervecerias*, gastropubs, and Irish pubs. There are even a couple small casinos around, including **Crown Casino** (Carrera 13, no. 82–85; tel: 1-649 7288; www.crowncasinos.com.co), which offers little more than blackjack, roulette, and a few slots – but provides all the thrill and spills of losing money nonetheless. The younger crowd come here once the sun sets on a weekend night to take advantage of the glitzy discos and lively atmosphere.

USAQUÉN AND THE FAR NORTH

If you head farther north along Carrera 7, to the point where the *calles* hit triple digits, and you'll eventually arrive in **Usaquén**. This neighborhood is so far on the north side of Bogotá that it wasn't even absorbed into the city until 1954. Usaquén was originally founded as its own town, meaning it has its own **Plaza Bolívar** ㉝, a model of tranquility complete with center fountain and a bust of the Liberator himself watching over the area.

More impressive is the **Iglesia de Santa Bárbara** ㉞ (Church of Santa Bárbara; Carrera 6; tel: 1-213 3298; mass times: Mon–Fri 6.30am, 8.30am, noon, and 6pm, Sat 6.30am, 8.30am, and 5pm; Sun 7.30am, 9am, 10.30am, noon, 6pm, and 7.30pm), which was founded in the middle of the 17th century. The front facade is painted white, with a towering central bell tower. Inside the church, the nave is a little smaller than it appears from the outside. However, behind the pulpit is a gleaming altarpiece of carved, gilded wood that frames certain paintings featuring various Biblical

The Andino Mall.

scenes, such as the Annunciation and the Crucifixion of Christ.

There are some other attractive colonial buildings surrounding the plaza, some of which have been turned into upscale eateries and chain restaurants. However, Usaquén's reputation as an up-and-coming Zona Rosa means that there are a few fine places to eat and drink within just a couple city blocks. There are also some charming cafés, with one of the best being **El Altillo de la Hacienda** ❸ (Calle 119b, no. 5–48; tel: 1-523 1695; Tue–Fri open 24 hours, Sat until noon, Sun 9–10am, Mon 10am–noon). Come here for the ambience if nothing else – although the sandwiches have a good reputation – as the exposed brick wall, French bistro tables, and hanging plants turn this open-fronted space into a secret garden of sorts. At the back is a store selling artisanal goods, as well as an art space where adults can craft and paint while sipping a glass of Argentine wine on sale from the adjacent bodega.

Another great stop for a refreshment is the **Helartesano** ❸ (Calle 119b,

no. 580; tel: 310-812 8110; Mon–Sat 12-7.30pm, Sun 11am-7.30pm), an artisanal ice cream parlor that also does brownies. Located a block away from the plaza, they make each cup of ice cream to order and often have multiple mixers going at one time, releasing great plumes of white fog from all the liquid nitrogen being added. The finished product is delicious, and the store features flavors like mango, raspberry, and Nutella.

Just above Helartesano, on Carrera 5, you can see some fine street art along the blue wall of the city parking lot. Head down two blocks to Carrera 6A and walk south, you'll pass by a number of street vendors and stands selling everything from jewelry and clothing to books and antiques. This road leads to the entrance of **Centro Comercial Hacienda Santa Bárbara** ❸ (Carrera 7, no. 115–72; tel: 1-612 0388; daily 10am–8pm), another chic and modern shopping complex that would look at right alongside those in the Zona Rosa. For shopping, try to come on a Sunday, when Usaquén holds an

Usaquén's flea market.

outdoor *feria de pulgas* (flea market), around the plaza on Carrera 6a and around Calle 120. For more details, see www.pulgasusaquen.com.

MERCADO DE PALOQUEMAO

If you're looking for an excuse to head out west and spend some time with real *Bogtanos*, then there's no better option than the **Mercado de Paloquemao** (Calle 19, no. 25–04; tel: 321-253-4290; www.plazadepaloquemao.com; Mon–Sat 4.30am–4.30pm, Sun 5am–4.30pm). This is one of great municipal markets of Latin America, and this one is big, taking up around half a city block in total. Inside, the market is just as large and labyrinthine as it appears from the outside. Narrow walkways cut through entire neighborhoods of fruit and vegetable stands, each of them selling fresh produce from local farms as well as purveyors located throughout the country. This is the best place in the city to find some of Colombia's most exotic fruits in one location, and sampling these delicious items is a must. Some highlights include *feijoa*, which is shaped like a small cucumber and has a taste like guava; *guanabana*, a large egg-shaped spikey fruit that looks almost extraterrestrial, but has a delicious sweet-and-sour inner white flesh; *carambola* (star fruit), which comes in two varieties, green or gold. Then there's *pitaya* (dragonfruit), and various other types of passion fruit, like *granadilla*, an orange-colored fruit containing inner sweet jelly and edible black seeds.

Other areas in the market of note include rows of countless butcher stations (the smell will give its location away) and *pollerias*, selling recently plucked chickens and fresh eggs, as well as an entire wing dedicated to seafood, both fresh and frozen. Toward the rear of the market, in the northwest zone, you'll pass by some lovely greenhouses selling fresh flowers, and the pleasant aroma complements

a quick meal perfectly. Luckily there's a nearby row of tiny family-run restaurants. These eateries are open for breakfast and lunch, and serve dishes made from the produce and products in the market. These include humble Colombian fare like *gueso marrano* (stewed pork arms), *sancocho de pescado* (fish soup), *ajiaco de pollo* (chicken soup) and various fish dishes. One dish with a very potent flavor is *caldo de raíz*, a soup made with chopped up bits of bull penis and testicles. It's easy to guess the effect the locals say eating it will have on your libido.

This market is a must-visit for visitors to Colombia: it gives a great sense of the people and the tastes and flavors that make the country what it is today.

AROUND BOGOTA

ZIPAQUIRÁ AND THE SALT CATHEDRAL

Zipaquirá (colloquially known as Zipa) is a municipality about 45km (30 miles) north of Bogotá. This is cattle-ranching country, but the reason it's popular with

> **Tip**
>
> The Mercado de Paloquemao is located on the western edge of El Centro, a poor and run-down area with a high crime rate, so don't wander too far from the market and keep your wits about you at all times.

The Salt Cathedral of Zipaquirá.

tourists is because of its 15th-century **rock salt mine and spectacular Cathedral de Sal** (salt cathedral; www.catedraldesal.gov.co; daily 9am–5.40pm). Early miners originally dug a shrine in the tunnel, and then in 1950 they went all in and built the church. In 1954 they dedicated it to the Patron Saint of Miners, Nuestra Señora del Rosario. The original church was closed in 1990 and in 1995 a new cathedral was opened 500 meters from the original site.

The entrance to the salt cathedral is in the hills 20 minutes west of Zipaquirá. There is also a museum and information center and the cost of admission includes a 75-minute guided tour. Upon entering you'll see the 14 stations of the cross, each with its own 4-meter (13ft) high cross sculpted by a different artist. These give way to the choir, baptistery (with its own natural water supply), narthex, and sacristy sections of the church. The nave is located at the very bottom, 180 meters (590ft) below the surface.

Getting to Zipaquirá is a straightforward affair. Going by bus is one option,

and most hostels and hotels in Bogotá arrange tours to the cathedral that include transportation. Another way to get there is to take the tourist train from Bogotá (see page 279).

VILLA DE LEYVA

Drive for around 3 hours from Bogotá, along many twisty-turny roads through beautiful cordillera hills blanketed with evergreens, and you'll arrive in **Villa de Leyva**. The town is in the department of Boyacá and sits at an elevation of 2,149 meters (7,000ft), roughly 500 meters (1,640ft) below Bogotá. Due to its relative isolation from major trade routes, Villa de Leyva is almost as it was when it was founded in 1572, making it well worth the journey.

The starkest example of this preservation, and the geographical star of the town, is its expansive central plaza, the **Plaza Mayor**, which is spread over a staggering 14,000 sq meters (150,700 sq ft) and was outfitted with rough cobblestones in the 1960s. The grand size also means that it might just be the largest colonial plaza in South America. It's no surprise, then, that there's an equally antiquated colonial church fronting the plaza: the **Iglesia de Nuestra Señora del Rosario** (northwest side of Plaza Mayor; mass times: Mon–Fri 6pm, Sat noon and 7pm, Sun 7am, 10am, noon, and 7pm, festivals noon and 6pm). The church is long but humble in its appearance. Inside, stone floors lead through a dark nave to a pulpit backed with gold-painted altarpieces depicting various saints. When you combine the plaza, this church and all the whitewashed colonial homes with terra-cotta roofs that make up the town, then you'll see why this is a popular destination, for local and international tourists alike.

There's a tourist information desk at the plaza (daily 8am–noon, 2pm–7pm), which is run by the police. However, the English spoken here is limited at best. Around the plaza you'll find plenty of interesting and upscale restaurant

Villa de Leyva

0   100 m
0   100 yds

N

Teatro Municipal
Calle 13
Calle 15
Convento Padres Carmelitas
Iglesia del Carmen
Placa del Carmen
Carrera 11
Museo Prehistorico
Carrera 10
Casa Museo Luis Alberto Acuña
Calle 13
Calle 14
Carrera 9
Cacao Heladería Artesanal Ⓐ
Plaza Mayor de Villa de Leyva
Iglesia de Nuestra Señora del Rosario
Carrera 11
Calle 12
Carrera 10
Ⓑ Museo del Chocolate
Carrera 8
Calle 13
Calle 11
Carrera 9
PARQUE ANTONIO NARIÑO
Transversal 10
Ⓔ Casa Antonio Nariño
Ⓘ Ⓓ Antonio Nariño
Ⓒ Astral
Calle 10
Carrera 10
Ⓚ Capilla San Jose
Carrera 8
Calle 11
Carrera 7
Calle 12
Carrera 9
Terminal de Transporte
Hospital San Francisco
Calle 10
Calle 11
Carrera 6
Calle 8
Carrera 8
Claustro San Francisco
Carrera 7
Calle 10

options, most of them operating out of converted colonial homes. One place just off the plaza to stop in for ice cream is **Cacao Heladeria Artesanal** Ⓐ (Carrera 10, no. 11–85; tel: 310-259 4562; daily 11am–8pm), which serves all things frozen, from gelato sandwiches and frozen yogurt to unique ice cream flavors like lychee and aloe vera. They even have vegan and sugar-free options. More delectable sweets can be found at the northern corner of the park at the **Museo del Chocolate** Ⓑ (Carrera 9, no. 11–02; tel: 300-265 4498; daily 9am–7pm). Just up the street you'll find a bakery run by an expat Frenchman, **Astral** Ⓒ (Calle 12, no. 7–56; tel: 8-732 0811; Mon–Thu 8.30am–7pm, Fri–Sat 8.30am–8.30pm, Sun 8.30am–5pm), which does the best baguettes and croissants in town, perhaps even the whole of Colombia.

There are a couple parks in town that celebrates Villa de Leyva's most famous residents: **Parque Nariño** Ⓓ, which boasts a monument to Antonio Nariño, one of the early supporters of Colombian independence. The **Museo**

Casa Nariño Ⓔ (Carrera 9, no. 10–25; tel: 8-732 0342; Thu–Tue, 9am–5pm; free), is located near Plaza Mayor and is where Nariño died. It's filled with colonial items such as independence-era military attire, 19th century revolvers, knives, and even cattle brands. On the exterior courtyard wall is a ceramic bust of Nariño and a wall sized copy of el *Declaracion de los Derechos del Hombre y del Ciudadano Colombia* (The Declaration of the Rights of Man), which Nariño translated from French to Spanish in the late 1700s.

There are several excursions that can be done in Villa de Leyva and the surrounding area, including a 3-hour horseback riding tour around town and visit to the Fossil Museum, full or half-day hiking tours to Angela's Step, which affords spectacular, panoramic views of the Moniquira Canyon, and hiking tours to the Iguaque Flora and Fauna Sanctuary. Reserve these excursions through the local tour company **Colombian Highlands** (www.colombianhighlands.com), located at Hostel Renancer in Villa de Leyva.

Ⓞ Tip

Getting oriented in Villa de Leyva isn't difficult so long as you keep centered around the Plaza Mayor. You'll probably arrive at the terminal, which is only three blocks southwest of Plaza Mayor

Plaza Mayor, Villa de Leyva.

The Palace of Culture.

MEDELLÍN

Nestled in the rolling green hills of Antioquia lies Medellín, the capital of the department and a thriving contemporary city rich with unique Paisa culture.

Colombians call Medellín the 'City of the Eternal Spring.' Spend a little time here and it isn't hard to see how the nickname came to be. At 1,496 meters (4,900ft) above sea level, it's located high enough in the Cordillera Central to enjoy a perpetual springlike climate; temperatures average around 72°F (22°C) year round. The effects of the altitude are negligible to the average visitor, with few experiencing any form of discomfort. This makes strolling the streets of Medellín a must for anyone.

The city began as a humble village, known as a *poblado*, founded by the Spanish colonialist Francisco Herrera Campuzano. This area is located in the present-day neighborhood of Poblado. In 1675 the Queen Consort of Spain, Mariana of Austria, founded the Señora de la Candelaria in the present-day city center. In 1826 the city became the capital of the department of Antioquia, and the Colombian Constitution of 1886 recognized it as the capital of the Federal State of Antioquia in 1888. It quickly became a thriving commercial center of the country, enjoying success first with gold, and then with coffee exports.

Northwestern Colombia, including Medellín, was settled mostly by the Basques, rather than the Spaniards, with the first wave of immigrants arriving during the 17th century. This has given the regional culture a slightly

Heading to El Poblado.

idiosyncratic quality when compared to other parts of Colombia. The Medellinense move to their own beat, so to speak, and you'll find little differences here: the tango genre, for example, is more popular in Medellín than it is anywhere else in Colombia. Medellín is also an industrial center, and by many metrics it is a prosperous city. This is evidenced in the ever-pulsing current of commercialism, and the city has no shortage of upscale shopping malls.

So that's what Medellín is today: a modern, thriving metropolis of about

◉ **Main Attractions**

Plaza Botero
Museo de Antioquia
Joaquin Antonio Uribe
  Botanical Gardens
Avenida 33

Map on page 136

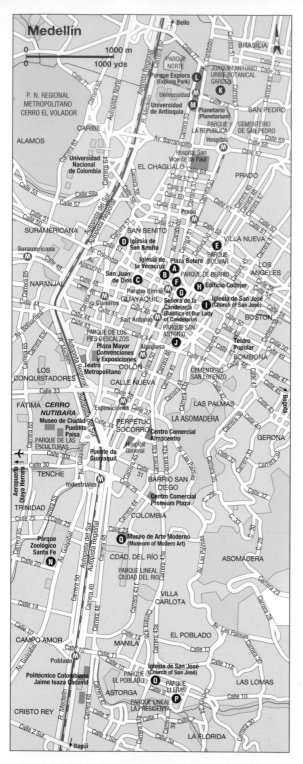

Medellín

3.8 million people that's the second-largest city in the country. It's a hotbed of art, music, commerce progressive politics, and progressive thought processes. True, in a city that's constantly looking to the future, you won't find much evidence of Medellín's colonial past – although there are some nice churches and plazas – but what you will find in abundance is progress.

A VIOLENT PAST BUT A BRIGHT FUTURE

Most who travel here will be at least partially aware of Medellín's chequered past. For a long time the city's image was one of violence caused by drug trafficking, with some of the most heinous crimes committed by the infamous cartel leader and son of Medellín, Pablo Escobar. It was during Escobar's heyday, in the late 1980s and early 90s that Medellín had the unwanted reputation as the most dangerous city in the world, with a murder rate that peaked at 380 people killed for every 100,000. At the time, the city's population was around 2 million. Talk to any Medellín resident who was alive during that period, and the chances are they won't speak fondly of it at all.

In 1993, when the police finally killed Escobar, the drugs or cartels didn't disappear – in fact it created a vacuum that guerrilla groups were all too eager to fill – but it did give the city a fresh start, like demolishing a faulty old building in order to build something modern in its place. With nowhere to go but up, civil servants began to think long and hard about how to turn their smouldering wreckage of a city around. In the mid-1990s at the department of social civic planning, a core group of planners eschewed long-held doctrines of top-down policy in favor of focusing on connecting the poorest neighborhoods of the city, areas that had been all but lost to gangland violence and abject poverty, with new metro transportation. It was a revolutionary idea for the time, and one that would succeed beyond anyone's wildest dreams.

This visionary group of planners foresaw more than just connecting the hillside neighborhoods to the city center through a sophisticated metro system involving buses, trains, and *telefericos* (cable cars). To truly succeed they felt that they had to include new literacy projects, libraries, schools, and arts centers – all to be located in the midst of former bullet-riddled narco warzones. To do this, they went into Medellín's outer neighborhoods and approached public enemy number one: the narcos themselves. Ultimately they persuaded the neighborhood kingpins to allow this experiment of civic engineering married to community outreach. They accomplished this in no small part because they were naive enough to try in the first place, unencumbered by the circumspect non-action of politicians to which many were accustomed.

The metro was built, and as the cartel's influence in Colombian cities waned, the government stepped in and offered the poorer neighborhoods a deal: peace and job creation in exchange for leaving the drug trade behind. Today the metro now connects those in the poorest areas to the city center, where they can now earn an honest living. Since the deal, community projects in the poorest areas have thrived, with schools and libraries being built on former narco battlegrounds. Children, who 30 years ago would have been dragged into a life of gang violence with the cartels, are today using their library cards to check out books on the life of Simón Bolívar.

True, there is still some crime in Medellín's poorest neighborhoods, but the progress is stark and undeniable. By 2011, the murder rate had dropped to 70 people per 100,000; by 2015, it had dropped to just 20. Today it's negligible, and if this tenuous trend continues, then Medellín can truly be considered a global success story.

FINDING YOUR WAY AROUND MEDELLÍN

As Colombia's second-largest city, and with a population of around 3.8 million, getting your bearings in Medellín can

Medellín's metrocable system.

be daunting. There are tourist information points in various locations in the city, including the international **Jose Maria Cordova International Airport** (tel: 4-287 4028) both **north** and **south bus terminals**, and **Plaza Botero**. They will give out maps of the city.

Medellín's streets have names as well as numbers. The north–south Carrera 46 is one of the most prominent thoroughfares in the city, and also goes by the name Avenida Oriental. Carrera 81 is a road running to the west of the city, also known as Avenida Ochenta. Calle 51 runs east from downtown and is called Avenida La Playa, and Calle 33, which crosses the river and is a hotbed of nighttime disco fun, is also known as called La Treinta y Tres.

By far and away the best way to get around Medellín is on the city's fine metro system. This includes a network of trains, buses, and *telefericos*, all serving the center, west, and south of the city. A one-way ride costs about US$1.25. Regular buses are another plentiful transportation option and cost about US$0.60 per ride.

PLAZA BOTERO

Plaza Botero (also called Plaza de los Esculturas after the many sculptures in the area) is the central plaza and one of the most famous in Medellín. It is located at Calle 52 and Carrera 52 and contains some 23 works donated by Colombia's most famous sculptor, Fernando Botero. Although each is different, the sculptures all possess that unmistakable Botero style – round, sensual, and voluptuous figures whose smooth texture is as important a part of the aesthetic as any other aspect.

The imposing Gothic building on the north side of the plaza is the **Palacio de la Cultura Rafael Uribe** (Mon–Sat 8am–noon, 2–5pm; free), which was designed by Belgian architect Agustín Goovaerts and finished in 1937. Today it's a cultural center and art gallery. Opposite is the **Museo de Antioquia** (Carrera 52, no. 52–43; tel: 4-251 3636; www.museodeantioquia.co; Mon–Sat 10am–5.30pm; contact the museum in advance to organize guided visits in English), featuring many works by Botero as well as contemporary

Plaza Botero.

Ⓞ PARTY ON A CHIVA BUS

If you've ever thought about converting a windowless bus into a mobile disco – and even if you haven't – then this uniquely Colombian excursion might just be for you. Chiva bus tours are popular throughout Colombia, but they are especially popular in Medellín. The concept is simple: fill up a bus with people, give them a few drinks, play some lively music and drive them around Medellín for a while. The chiva bus is essentially a club on wheels; be warned though, space is at a premium and the quarters may be a little too cramped for some. Most hotels and hostels in Medellín can easily arrange these tours, and they often last 3–4 hours, taking place on Friday and Saturday nights. The cost is typically around US$15–20.

paintings and sculptures. There's also a room exhibiting paintings by Colombia's Francisco Antonio Cano Cardona

A block south of Plaza Botero is the **Iglesia de la Veracruz** (Church of the Veracruz; Carrera 51, no. 52–58). Construction of this church began in 1682 by the Spanish who settled the area and it was finally finished at the end of the 18th century. The church includes an altar brought over from Spain and triple bells on the steeple. It's believed to be the oldest church in the center of the city. Other churches in the area include the **Capilla San Juan de Dios** (San Juan de Dios Chapel; Carrera 54, no. 59–85) and the **Iglesia de San Benito** (Church of San Benito; Calle 51, no. 56a–76).

PARKS OF MEDELLÍN

Located northeast of Plaza Botero is the **Parque Bolívar** a long, stately park featuring fountains and an equestrian statue of The Liberator himself. The first Saturday of every month a craft market, the **Mercado de San Alejo** is held here. Overlooking the park from the north is the **Catedral Metropolitano**, one of the largest all-brick buildings in the world. Optimistic locals may claim that it is the largest church in Colombia; it is certainly the largest in Medellín. The church features an impressive, all-brick interior, Spanish stained glass, and a marble altar.

Located three blocks south from Plaza Botero is **Parque de Berrio**, a major metro stop in the bustling heart of Medellín. It also has some interesting landmarks, such as the **Señora de la Candelaria** (Basilica of Our Lady of Candelaria; tel: 4-231 4907), a whitewashed church with twin steeples dating from the mid-17th century. You can also see an iconic Botero sculpture here: *El Torso de Mujer*, a female torso without arms and head.

A couple of blocks east is the **Edificio Coltejer** (Calle 52, no 47–42), a commercial building notable as the tallest in Medellín. Built as the headquarters of a Colombian textiles organization, today the building is mostly offices. Near to this, on Avenida Oriental, is the **Iglesia de San José**, (Church of

⊙ **Tip**

The best people-watching spots in Parque San Antonio are from the tables of the outdoor bars selling *micheladas*.

Catedral Metropolitano.

San José; Carrera 43, no. 9–30), which dates back to the 17th century, but was modified repeatedly until 1903. It was the last building designed by Nicaraguan architect Félix Pereira and houses the oldest painting in the city – one of San Lorenzo, the patron saint of Medellín. The old and dignified church almost looks out of place in the hectic commercial zone where it sits.

Parque San Antonio ❶ (Calles 44/46 and Carrera 46) is one of the best people-watching spots in all of Medellín. The park is located a few blocks south and was inaugurated in 1994. It features an expansive plaza complete with an amphitheater. In its short existence the park has endured tragedy: in 1995, a bomb planted by FARC went off at a concert here, killing 23 people and injuring dozens more. The blast also partially destroyed a Botero sculpture, *El Pájaro de Paz* (the Bird of Peace). Botero requested the original sculpture be left as is, as a symbol of the futility of violence. There are many Botero sculptures in the park tiday, including the *Torso Masculino*, which

is the male version of the female torso found in Parque Berrio.

THE BOTANICAL GARDEN AND AROUND

The **Joaquin Antonio Uribe Botanical Garden** ⓚ (Calle 73, no. 51d–14; tel: 4-444 5500; www.botanicomedellin.org; daily 9am–4pm; free) is a 14-hectare (34,595-acre) park featuring 1,000 living species of animals and some 5,500 species of plants and trees. The park itself almost never came to be. In 1972 it was rescued from developers by botanist Joaquin Antonio Uribe and turned into the lush grounds you see today. It features a lily-filled pond as well as various pathways leading to, among other things, the famous 'Orchideorama,' which protects a vital collection of orchids. This structure is the result of a competition held for local architects to design the new space. The winners created this 20 meter (65-ft) -tall 'Orchidarium', a wood-meshwork canopy with flower-tree structures that collects rainwater and protects the orchids and also contains a butterfly reserve.

The Orchideorama at the Joaquin Antonio Uribe Botanical Garden.

Near to the Botanical Garden is the **Parque Explora**  (Explore Park; Carrera 52, no. 73–75; tel: 4-516 8300; www.parqueexplora.org; Tue–Fri 8.30am–5.30pm, last entry at 4pm, Sat–Sun 10am–6.30pm, last entry at 5pm), a science and tech museum with more than 300 interactive exhibits plus a 3D theater and aquarium. It's a fun outing for both adults and kids, and the exhibits touch on, among other things, technological advances, and how they relate to the natural world, geology and climate. Also nearby is the **Planetario** (Planetarium; Carrera 52, no. 71-117; tel: 4-516 8300; www.planetariomedellin.org; Tue, Wed, and Fri 8.30am–5pm, Thu 8.30am–6pm, Sat–Sun 10am–6.30pm), which has a projection room with capacity for 300 plus a 200-seat auditorium.

SOUTH AND EL POBLADO

South of the city center and just west of the river is the **Zoológico Santa Fe** (Zoo; Carrera 52, no. 20–63; tel: 4-444 7787; www.zoologicosantafe.com; daily 9am–5pm), where you can see many South American animals and birds. The zoo is particularly interested in threatened species, like the Andean condor, cotton-top tamarind, and spectacled bear. There are also plenty of mammals here that are found throughout Colombia, such as the jaguar, anteater, and tapir.

Across the river and to the east is El Poblado, where Medellín first began as a humble village. Today, it is one of the trendiest, most affluent areas of the city. While you're certain to find plenty of bars and upscale restaurants in this neighborhood, remnants of its colonial past are more difficult to come by, with the exception of the **Iglesia de San José** (Church of San José; Carrera 43a, no.9–50; mass times: Mon–Sat 8am, noon, and 6.30pm; Sun 7am, 8am, 10.30am, noon, 6pm, and 7pm). The church was founded in 1616 and features an expansive pulpit and fine stained-glass mosaics.

Three blocks east of here is **Parque Lleras**, an area commonly known as Medellín's Zona Rosa. Here you'll find a high concentration of bars, clubs, and chain restaurants. During the day the park is filled with street artists and their paintings, and there's a nice tranquil vibe. During the evening, especially on weekends, the area gets quite touristy.

Farther to the north is the **Museo de Arte Moderno** (Museum of Modern Art; Carrera 44, no. 19a-100; tel: 4-444 2622; http://elmamm.org; Tue–Fri 9am–6pm, Sat 10am–6pm, Sun 10am–5pm). Housed in a former steel factory, the museum's permanent collection features works by Colombian artists including Enrique Grau, Óscar Muñoz, Manuel Hernández, and Jorge Julián Aristizábal. North of here, just west of the river, you'll find a stretch of Avenida 33 that is the true Zona Rosa of the city, and a nice alternative to tourist-centric Poblado. Here you'll find an array of discos, rock bars, pubs, lounges, and dives, many of which offer drink specials, happy hours, and creative cocktails. It's a good place to come to rub shoulders with the Medellinense and lose yourself in the warm and welcoming spirit of Medellín.

> **⊙ Tip**
>
> The center of Medellín is becoming increasingly seedy in the evening, with petty crime and prostitution being common at night. It is best to visit this area during the day.

Condominiums in El Poblado, known as the Milla de Oro (Golden Mile).

View over the Guatapé Reservoir.

ANTIOQUIA

In central-northwestern Colombia lies a region defined by green mountain landscapes of spectacular beauty, a perfectly temperate climate, and regional culture distinct from any other place in Colombia.

The land is known as Antioquia, and the people that inhabit it, Antioqueños. There's a dominant cultural group here, and they identify as Paisas. This may seem like a superficial designator on the surface, but to experience Paisa culture first hand is to catch a glimpse into a Colombia at once familiar yet slightly askew. It was Paisa industriousness that turned Antioquia Department into the industrial capital of the country. The department's capital, Medellín, is an example of what Paisas are capable of: here sleek and shiny office parks and apartment towers are connected to even the poorest neighborhoods via one of the most advanced metro systems in the world – something that, the more you spend time here, seems like it could only have ever happened in Antioquia.

Yet outside of the capital city, the pace of life slows to a crawl in the idyllic colonial villages dotting the countryside. Spend time here, eating hearty plates of *comida Antioqueña*, strolling cobblestone streets amid whitewashed homes and surrounded by rolling green hills, and you can't help but wonder how something as ugly as violence could ever affect one of the most beautiful regions of the world. Again, Antioquia is as complex as its people, and you could spend years here without ever finding a truly satisfactory answer.

Relaxing in front of a coffee house in Jardín

A BRIEF HISTORY

The Muisca indigenous people didn't only exist in the Bogotá region – in pre-colonial times they could also be found in Antioquia. However, they weren't the only indigenous group in this area. The southern Antioquia region was inhabited by the Quimbaya people, who were known to produce some of the most detailed gold work of any pre-colonial native group. Other areas of Antioquia were inhabited by native groups, including Carib 'families' such as the Nutabes, Catías, and Tahamíes. It was

Main Attractions
Santa Fe de Antioquia
Jardín
Reserva Natural Cañon del Río Claro
Hacienda Napoles

Maps on pages 144, 147

these principal indigenous groups – the Caribs, Muisca, and Quimbaya – that the first conquistadors encountered when they made their way south from the coast and into Antioquia.

Relations between the natives and the conquistadors started off badly and quickly got worse. The populations of the Quimbaya and Muisca were smaller in Antioquia, and those that weren't subdued by the Spanish quickly dispersed. The Caribs had the numbers and the will to fight, but were outgunned by the Spanish, and those who refused to live under Spanish rule were soon killed. These encounters were defined by their gruesomeness – so much so that many Caribs killed themselves rather than submit to being conquered. Those who

didn't take their own lives scattered to neighboring departments, like Chocó, which is why today you'll rarely see Paisas with native blood – the population of Antioquia as a whole is less than 0.5 percent indigenous.

Of the Spaniards who did settle in Antioquia, a great majority of them hailed from Spain's north coast, particularly the Basque region. For years it was unclear just how many Basque wound up in this area in the early days of the 16th and 17th centuries, as there is almost no record of the Basque language, Euskara, being spoken. Scholars attribute this to the fact that any Basque who wished to resettle in Colombia at the time likely were forced to speak Castilian. This changed

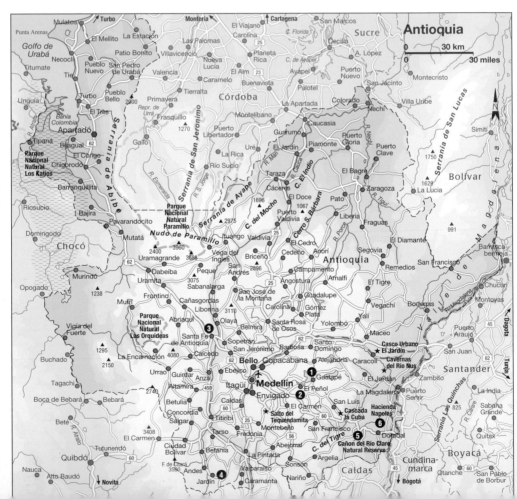

slightly after the Spanish Civil War when a new wave of Basque immigrants came to settle in Antioquia, and this time they brought their language with them. However, they flew so far under the radar for so long, that it took an American historian, Everett Hagan, flipping through a Medellín phone book at random in 1957 to realize that a significant portion of the surnames in it were of Basque origin.

Some say that the Paisa reputation for industriousness is a direct result of their Basque roots. A more likely explanation is that the Paisa facility for trade and industry was born out of necessity rather than DNA. Antioquia as a region is geographically isolated and mountainous, meaning it couldn't sustain very many crops. As a result, Paisa residents were forced to become dependent on trade, first with gold and then, over the centuries, with things like textiles and, unfortunately, cocaine.

Yes, the drug trade in the 1980s and 90s tore through the whole of Colombia, but it was particularly cruel to Antioquia. Pablo Escobar was a natural-born Paisa, and his Medellín Cartel operated out of the capital city. The ripple effect of his operation extended to all corners of this region, but it is only in the last few years that Antioquia is finally beginning to shake off the legacy of one Pablo Emilio Escobar Gaviria.

ANTIOQUIA AND ITS PEOPLE TODAY

Today Antioquia has a population of around 6 million people, with over half of them living in the capital city of Medellín (see page 135). It seems the Paisas could only have ever existed in this particular part of Colombia. This is especially true when you consider the departments bordering Antioquia. To the west and north is the Chocó, where the culture is dominated by indigenous blood and tribal rhythms passed down through generations from Africa. To the south is the Zona Cafetera, which even the Paisas refer to as 'frio' (cold). No, Paisas wouldn't want to live anywhere else, or be anyone else. After spending even just a little time here, you'll start to understand why.

A street full of colorful houses in Guatapé.

○ Tip

Pack light when traveling to Antioquia. Many cities and towns, such as Medellín, enjoy a spring-like climate all year round.

GUATAPÉ AND EL PEÑOL

When Paisas want to get away for a day trip or weekend excursion, they oftentimes come to **Guatapé** ❶, located about 93km (58 miles) east of Medellín. Once you arrive you'll see why: Guatapé is adjacent to El Peñol, a town and sleek granite rock, which juts 200 meters (650ft) out of the ground like a bullet, and is one of the major tourist attractions in Antioquia. That said most people prefer to stay in Guatapé as opposed to El Peñol because this lakeside town is an explosion of color and activity, which is most pronounced on the *zócalos* (lower exterior portion) of the colonial houses that are found here. Even some of the mototaxis are decked out in all the colors of the visible spectrum.

Guatapé is a small lakeside town with hardly more than 6,000 residents, making it even more of an attractive location for those escaping the hustle and bustle of nearby Medellín. On weekends it is positively packed, with families and couples strolling along the *malecón* (waterfront promenade) beside the lake and enjoying ice cream

and other snacks. Here you'll see plenty of pleasure boats cruising the waters, blaring salsa and vallenato like there's no tomorrow. One water-based activity that stands out here is the zipline that runs over the lake. Those who come during the week will find the town to be quieter and the lodging options to be much more reasonably priced.

The **main plaza** ❹ is surrounded by colorful houses and a red-and-white Greco-Roman church, the **Parroquia Nuestra Señora del Carmen** ❸ (mass times: Sun 8am, 10am, noon, 4pm, and 7pm). The church dates back to 1812 and the interior has many impressive wood carvings and columns. Head over to **Calle de los Recuerdos** ❹ and see some houses whose *zócalos* have been embellished with intricate sculptures depicting local families and political events. It's a unique form of public art. Another religious institution here is a Benedictine Monastery, the **Monasterio Santa Maria de la Epifania** ❹, which holds Sunday services at 11am, accompanied by Gregorian chanting. To visit, simply take a mototaxi from the plaza.

The Stone of El Peñol, also known as the Rock of Guatapé.

Just 3km (2 miles) away from Guatapé is the town of **El Peñol ②**, which was founded in 1714. Although it doesn't hold a candle to the former as far as lodging options go, people flock here for the rock of the same name, whose summit looks out over a network of interconnected aquamarine lakes like something out of a fantasy-adventure video game. To reach the summit involves climbing 649 steps, which takes about 30 minutes. It's a must visit for the views alone.

SANTA FE DE ANTIOQUIA

Some 80km (50 miles) northwest of Bogotá is **Santa Fe de Antioquia ③**, a medium sized town of about 23,000 residents with a whole lot of colonial history. Jorge Robledo founded this town in the Cauca River valley in 1541. Located at a lower altitude, the town enjoys a more tropical climate, and is hotter than Medellín. The town was initially founded as a gold-mining town, and it was the location of the first such mine in the area. Santa Fe came into its own in 1584, when it officially became the capital of Antioquia. It remained the capital until 1826, when it was replaced by Medellín.

Santa Fe de Antioquia retains so much grandeur from its time as the capital that the town was even named a National Monument of Colombia in 1960. The colonial spirit is thick here, as you'll see from the narrow cobblestone streets and architecture of the great balconied mansions that line them. This makes for a great weekend getaway for those who want to escape the modernity and tourist hordes of Medellín's Poblado neighborhood. Having said that, Santa Fe de Antioquia has seen something of a boom in tourism in recent years, with new hotels and hostels popping up all the time. Visitors will be particularly impressed with the annual Christmas and New Year festivities.

Immediately striking is the **Plaza Mayor**. You won't find a more beautiful colonial-style plaza anywhere else in Colombia: there's an elegant center *fuente* (fountain), which has been supplying Santa Fe with water for the better part of 450 years, with a central bronze statue of Juan del Corral, who was president of Antioquia during a brief period of independence from 1813 to 1826.

The most dominant building around the plaza is a neoclassical cathedral, the **Catedral Basilica de la Inmaculada Concepción de Santa Fe** (Cathedral Basilica of the Immaculate Conception; mass times: Mon–Fri 6.45am, Sat 6.30pm, Sun 11am and 6.45pm), which was constructed between 1797 and 1837 and looks over the plaza from the west. Inside is an 18th-century sculpture depicting the Last Supper. Local artisans built the shrine in the church, with its embossed silver ornamentation, which was then decorated with local gold pieces. Unfortunately,

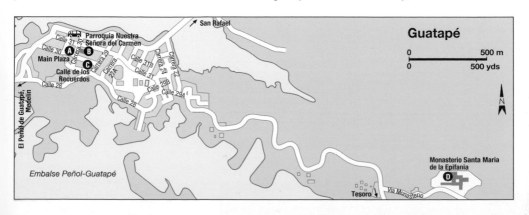

however, the gold was stolen in 1986. In the plaza around the church you'll also find many artisan kiosks selling souvenirs and handicrafts, as well as local products like honey and dried fruits.

Another standout church is the **Iglesia de Santa Bárbara** (Calle 11, no. 8–53; mass times: Mon–Sat 8am and 6pm, Sun 8am, 10am, and 8pm), which is located two blocks from the Plaza Mayor. This gem was finished in 1728, at which point it was given to the Jesuits. The front is in Rococo-style (late Baroque) and the interior walls are in Calicanto-style. Adjacent to the church is the **Museo Juan del Corral** (Calle 11, no. 9–77; tel: 4-853 4605; Mon–Tue and Thu–Fri 9am–noon, 2–5.30pm, Sat–Sun 10am–5pm, closed Wed; free), housing collections of historical items and local gold work. West of the Plaza Mayor is another interesting public area, the **Plaza José Maria Martinez Pardo**, which contains a statue of Jorge Robledo.

JARDÍN

Iglesia de Santa Bárbara.

Jardín ❹ is a small town 133km (83 miles) southwest of Medellín that is home to around 14,000 people. It is located in a valley between the western Cordillera Oriental and the San Juan River, and there are actually a number of rivers and *arroyos* in the area, making Jardín one of the major trout-fishing destinations in Antioquia. There are also a number of trout farms in the surrounding hills. The town itself stands out as one of the most idyllic colonial villages in an area already teeming with idyllic colonial villages.

The history of Jardín is an interesting one in that its original site belonged to the Emberá-Katío, an early indigenous group. In 1863 Indalecio Peláez, a settler, claimed the land here between the two *arroyos*. The story goes that these first outsiders to arrive in the area were so taken back by the jungle valley, surrounded by bright green hills, that they started referring to it as a garden. Even today visitors will note just how apt this name is.

Then, later in the 1860s, a group of priests arrived, and they officially founded Jardín as a parish in 1871. Their main goal was to create a village with more independence than others in the region; one where locals and farmers wielded control of the municipality. However, in 1882 the president of Antioquia State, Luciano Restrepo, declared it a town. For a while the people of Jardín were predominantly growers of such crops as plantains, sugarcane, and beans.

Tourism eventually overtook other industries as the driving force of Jardín's economy. Perhaps the main reason for this is because the village is another one of those places that has changed little in the intervening years since colonization. Colonial whitewashed homes with colorful doors and bougainvillea-draped balconies still line the streets, and the plazas and churches pay homage to earlier centuries. As Jardín is such a picture-perfect representation of another time, there has been a huge influx of hotels

opening in town. Some estimates place the number at around 40, which is about four times as many as there are in the bigger town of Santa Fe de Antioquia. Visitors can rest assured they'll be able to find a bed for the night.

As for the village, the central plaza, **Principle Park** (sometimes called Plaza El Libertador), is where all the action occurs. There's a large fountain here, surrounded by colorful patio chairs and well-manicured bushes. The stones that make up the plaza come from the nearby Tapartó River. There's an abundance of shopping, dining, and lodging options around the plaza, and locals sit outside the bars surrounding the plaza whiling away the afternoon hours, while vendors sell fresh fruit juices from carts. There's a bright white statue here featuring the loving representation of the Madre de Jardín. During the weekend evenings, local horseback-riding enthusiasts ride into the plaza and show off various gaits for the amusement of the locals and tourists.

Jardín's neo-Gothic church, the **Templo Parroquial de la Inmaculada Concepción**, is well worth looking around. Built between 1918 and 1942, the church is a National Monument of Colombia. The striking facade was made with hand-carved stones that parishioners brought from a nearby quarry as a way to atone for their sins. Inside, there's an impressive altar, made of Italian marble, and an eight-point star in the apse. Impressive sculptures of Christ and the apostles sit behind the pulpit, and there are beautiful stained-glass mosaics throughout.

Visitors to Jardín will also want to take a ride on the cable cars. There are two cable car lines here, which were originally meant to help connect residents from the nearby villages so they could sell their goods in Jardín. These lines are also a gambit to boost tourism, with one traveling from the north to the top of a mountain peak locals call the Alto de las Flores (Flower Hilltop). It affords great views of the town and there's also a restaurant there. The other line, the *garrucha*, is an older cable car that runs from the south up over a river to a hill lined with plantain

Local man wearing traditional straw hat called a sombrero vueltiao, Jardín.

Principle Park, Jardín.

Where

The Reserva Natural Cañon Rio Claro and Hacienda Napoles are about 20km (12 miles) apart. Since these locations are at roughly the midpoint between Medellín and Bogotá, it makes sense to visit them on the same excursion.

trees. There's a terrace bar offering good snacks like *empanadas*, beer, and *aguardiente*. The views of the town from here are stunning.

Lastly, you can't come to Jardín without visiting **Dulces de Jardín** (Calle 13, no. 5–47; tel: 4-845 6584; www.dulcesde jardin.com; daily 8am–6pm), a famous local confectioner that supplies candy, chocolate, and jelly to the rest of the country. Even if you don't have a sweet tooth, be sure to try the *curuba* (banana passion fruit) and rose petal marmalades. They also serve a tasty breakfast of yogurt with fresh fruit.

RESERVA NATURAL CAÑON DEL RÍO CLARO

In a country filled with immense natural beauty, there's no shortage of dreamlike locales teeming with otherworldly charm. One such place is the **Reserva Natural Cañon del Río Claro** ⑤. The canyon was formed by water carving its way through the countryside on a marble riverbed, leaving sheer cliffs and hidden caves in its wake. The running waters here twist and turn their way

Men relaxing at the end of the day in Jardín.

through Antioquia, creating large pools and gulleys that act as natural bathtubs of the most vivid shades of jade.

THE HISTORY OF CAÑON RÍO CLARO

The preserve (www.rioclaroreservanatural. com) is located 165km (103 miles) southeast of Medellín on the way to Bogotá, about a three-hour journey. Interestingly, had the Medellín–Bogotá road never been completed it's likely this area would have remained little discovered other than by local *campesinos* and only the most intrepid of backpackers. But the road was built, and a certain Pablo Escobar built his home some 20km (12 miles) away, making it all but inevitable that Río Claro would one day open up to the masses.

It was just such a *campesino*, Eduardo Betancourt, who discovered the gorge that has now become one of Colombia's prized tourism destinations. In 1964 Betancourt was losing his livestock to a savvy jaguar, and the humble farmer decided to end matters once and for all. It took him six weeks,

but he finally succeeded in tracking the animal to the canyon. Just as Betancourt was bearing down on the animal, preparing for the final assault, the jaguar slipped away forever. However, it did lead Betancourt to the area that would later become the park. There were locals in the area, but they never entered that part of the canyon because they believed it to be cursed.

Betancourt returned to his landowner, Juan Guillermo Garcés, emptyhanded but with a tale of a canyon paradise. This intrigued Garcés so much that he never got the tale out of his head. Then, in 1970, a government engineer on a survey mission to build a bridge for the new highway, spotted the canyon from a helicopter. With news that officials had now come across the canyon as well, Garcés enlisted the help of Betancourt to lead him to the fabled area. Over two days they hacked through dense jungle and pulled themselves upriver on a raft, but finally they arrived.

It was intended to be a short trip but Betancourt and Garcés stayed in the canyon for a few months, exploring caves under the canyon walls and building shelters there. It was a good vantage point from which to observe a wide array of animal species that were previously unknown, such as the cave-dwelling *guacharo* bird. Upon experiencing this bio-diverse ecosystem, Garcés was inspired to protect it, and thus he developed it into a private nature preserve.

Of course the reserve gained more notoriety when Escobar's profile rose to the point that he was the most famous Colombian in the country. Journalists staking out the famous Hacienda Napoles often wandered over to the preserve, and the area got its fair share of free press. The buzz around the canyon was so strong that on the weekend the new Medellín–Bogotá road opened, some 1,500 visitors descended on Reserva Río Claro. At that point the cat was out of the bag, and rather than fight the momentum, Garcés decided to promote sustainable tourism in the area while maintaining a protected preserve.

Reserva Natural Cañon del Río Claro.

⊙ Tip

Hotel Río Claro is the biggest and most developed of any of the lodging options in Rio Clara, featuring 32 bungalows, a swimming pool, a waterslide, and a restaurant.

WHAT TO DO AND WHERE TO STAY

The Reserva Río Claro is best visited over two or three days; there are plenty of activities and sights here that are going to keep you occupied for some time, so 24 hours just won't cut it. Among the activities available is rafting, not only down the river but under great limestone cliffs with water dripping from huge stalactites. The river has sculpted many caves and caverns along the canyon, so caving is also popular in this area. One such cavern cut by the El Bornego creek spans 400 meters (1,312ft) and is made up of tunnels with smooth marble walls. Of course swimming is also popular here, and there's also a zipline network that covers 500 meters (1,640ft), allowing you to glide over the river and through the tropical rainforest on its banks.

There are also a number of lodging options at the site, including a rustic refuge made up of four different lodges, where rooms have balconies offering views of the canyon. There's also the Blue Morpho eco-lodge, with two floors of rooms offering forest views. La Mulata consists of two family-sized homes perfect for large groups, and their elevated position makes them ideal for birders.

HACIENDA NAPOLES

In a place called Puerto Triunfo, Antioquia, some 150km (93 miles) east of Medellín, is the former home of the most notorious drug lord to have ever lived, **Hacienda Napoles** ❻ (road from Medellín–Bogotá at km 165; tel: 4-444 2975; www.haciendanapoles.com; Tue–Sun 9am–5pm). Really, calling it a home is a misnomer – this was an expansive estate covering a massive 20 sq km (7.7 sq miles) of land. Pablo Escobar built Hacienda Napoles to be his prime country estate, and indeed he made it one of his principal residences. Today the home itself has fallen into disrepair, and the whole property is now a theme park complete with hotels.

Back in its heyday the hacienda symbolized everything large and ostentatious about Escobar. Not only was it home to a sprawling residence, but it possessed a 1,280-meter (4,200-ft)

Entrance to Hacienda Napoles.

-long private airplane runway. To put that in perspective, this personal airstrip was large enough to land a Boeing 747. Needless to say, Escobar didn't build it to accommodate passenger jets.

Certainly vast quantities of drugs were shipped to and from this airfield, but that wasn't all. A smuggler by trade, Escobar used the landing area to secretly bring in exotic animals. He did this for the singular purpose of building his most prized area of the property: his own private zoo. However, the zoo wasn't so totally private, as Escobar – in keeping with his carefully cultivated image as a Robin Hood type figure – opened it up to the locals. Here Antiqueños would come and see animals never before seen on the continent, such as elephants, giraffes, and hippos, among others.

In the late 1980s, as Escobar was beginning to feel the pinch of government intrusion into his narco operation, he fled Hacienda Napoles, leaving it to its own slow, inevitable march to the state of decay it is in today. In the immediate aftermath scavengers came to pilfer hidden stashes of cash and drugs, and many of the zoo animals died or escaped. This was the case with Escobar's hippos, who ran off into the Magdalena River (see box).

The property was eventually taken over by the Colombian government. A private company built a safari theme park, and you even enter the grounds through great tall gates not unlike those seen in the film *Jurassic Park*. Part of this theme park is the old zoo, which is now a nature preserve featuring a number of animals, including elephants, buffalo, wild cats, ostriches, llamas, and monkeys, as well as an entire herd of hippos. There are even life-size dinosaur models here, which were originally created for Escobar.

As for the main house, it was left abandoned and fell into disrepair. You can still visit it today, and you'll notice holes in the swimming pool that treasure hunters dug looking for stores of hidden cash. It will likely strike some that the house is on the small side, odd for a man who, at the height of his powers, pulled in $22 billion dollars a year.

Exhibit at Hacienda Napoles.

⊘ PABLO'S HIPPOS

After the Colombian police began to get the better of Escobar and he went on the run, his private zoo at Hacienda Napoles soon became neglected. As a result, some of the hippos escaped, and made their way down to the Magdalena River. Over the years the hippos thrived, even more so then back in their native habitat in Africa. The region agreed with them too, and they soon began breeding in large numbers. Today there are too many hippos in the Magdalena River region in Antioquia to count, but they are all descended from Pablo's hippos. Rumour has it that the original hippos that escaped from Escobar's property, the mothers and fathers of this unusual colony, are alive and well today.

SANTANDER

Head north of Bogotá, just east of the Magdalena; when the cold and misty Andes give way to tropical cloud forest, you've arrived in Santander Department.

Colombia's central northern Santander Department exists as a municipality due to the early Spaniards' insatiable desire for gold. In the pre-Columbian era, a confederation of native tribes, such as the Muisca, Laches, Yariguí, and others, coexisted here in peace and harmony, cultivating the land of the surrounding mountainous areas. That all changed when the first expedition to the area, led by conquistador Antonio de Lebríja, passed through here in 1529. Eventually the natives were conquered and those who persisted in the fight soon found themselves extinct. Martín Galeano, a conquistador who was part of Gonzalo Jiménez de Quesada's Bogotá expedition, founded Santander's first town, Vélez, in 1539.

Local governments were established and they oversaw the enslavement of the remaining native population, who were forced to work in the fields and mines. As the centuries passed, and independence came to Colombia, Santander Department was officially established in 1857. Today the area is thankfully known more for adrenaline-pumping adventure sports than its checkered past. In fact, Santander is the unofficial adventure sports capital of Colombia: here you can indulge in some hair-raising feats including whitewater rafting, paragliding, caving, and ziplining.

SAN GIL

On its surface, **San Gil** ❶ may seem like a small colonial town populated by a mere 50,000 people. However, its strategic location in the valley of the Río Fonce makes it an ideal destination for any thrill seeker. The river systems of the Fonce, Chicamora, and Suárez cut through the gorges of the surrounding Andes, facilitating some of the best rafting and kayaking in the country. Local and international travelers flock to San Gil to conquer these rivers, but they also come to trek in the lush green hills of

Main Attractions
Exploring the Cañon de Chichamocha
Abseiling in San Gil
Paragliding in San Gil and Bucaramanga
River rafting in San Gil
Barichara

Maps on pages 156, 160

Paragliding in San Gil.

the surrounding countryside, bathe in the natural pools and falls of the Pozo Azul, cycle through the mountains and paraglide over the Chicamocha Canyon.

ARRIVING IN SAN GIL

If traveling by bus, you'll most likely be arriving at the transportation terminal, which is about 2km (1 mile) from downtown. At the bus depot, you'll also find buses to Bucaramanga (3 hours) and Tunja (4 hours) in the north, or Bogotá (6 hours) in the south. There are also quick minibuses to surrounding colonial towns like Barichara and Socorro, which take roughly 30 minutes. Currently there is no tourist information at the bus depot, but there are plenty of stores and snack sellers around. A

taxi from the terminal to downtown shouldn't cost more than US$2. Alternatively, it is only a short walk.

AROUND TOWN

The town's north and south sides are bisected by the Río Fonce, which runs along Carrera 11. Just south of the river and up a hill is the imposing **Central Comercial El Puente** (Calle 10, no. 12–184; tel: 7-724 4644), a huge shopping complex with a movie theater and a plethora of dining and retail options. Across the river is the **Parque Gallineral** (8am–5pm). This 4-hectare (10-acre) park is named after the *chiminango* trees that flourish throughout, hanging low and providing welcome shade for roosting hens (*gallinas*).

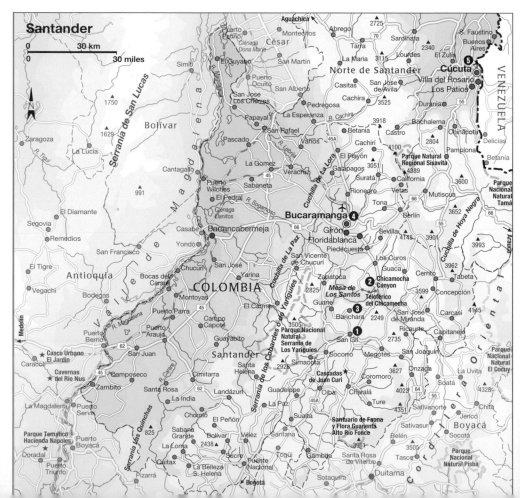

The park is a lush green oasis in the middle of a lush green town, and the mini rivers running through it turn the area into a botanical garden complete with various species of birds and butterflies. Heliconia, shine vermillion, and bright bromeliads cover the trees. There's a lovely natural pool here too, where weary locals come to cool off. Guides are happy to show you around the park and answer questions about the flora and fauna, for a generous tip, of course.

The historic heart of the town is centered around the lively and beautiful **Parque Principal**. At the center of the park is a large fountain; the outer realms are dotted with ceiba and heliconia trees. At the north end of the park is the **Catedral de la Santa Cruz** (Calle 12, no. 8–44; mass times: Mon–Sat 6am and 6.30pm, Sun 5am, 7am, 9am, 10.30am, noon, and 6.30pm), an old colonial church founded in 1791. Its charming brick exterior may look like it is being lost to the slow march of time, but the church was remodeled in 1965, so it should be around for some time

to come. All of the park, including the church, looks fantastic at night when it's lit up in soft colors. Here you'll also find the best nightlife in town – no bar or disco offers a better experience than having a drink with the locals who congregate on the square nightly.

CAÑÓN DE CHICAMOCHA

The **Chicamocha Canyon** ❷ flows from Boyacá Department to Santander, where it cuts the deepest gorge on earth, near Bucaramanga. The result is a stunning natural phenomenon that is one of the biggest canyons in the world, and the biggest in Colombia. One of the best ways to see it on land is on the route from San Gil to Bucaramanga. About 25km (16 miles) north of San Gil is the small colonial town of Aratoca (www.aratoca-santander.gov.co), which is known mostly for its impressive colonial stone church. Here the road descends along the cliffs to the valley below, making for one of the most dramatic views in the country. Of course, the best and most awe-inspiring way to experience the canyon is by air.

Monument to Santander culture in the Chicamocha Canyon.

⏲ Tip

First-timers on the adventure sport scene in San Gil may want to start small with paragliding. You can opt to take a shorter, 15-minute your first time out that might be easier than the longer 45-minute options.

ACTIVITIES IN AND AROUND SAN GIL

Every extreme sport that Santander is famous for can be found in San Gil. Even though most high-end hotels will be happy to arrange for these activities, it is highly recommended to go through the town hostels, like Macondo, as they have been working with local providers day-in, day-out for years and are definitely the place to go for advice on adventure tourism.

ABSEILING

What better way to get the blood flowing than with a 60-meter (197ft) descent alongside a gushing cascade of the Juan Curi waterfall? Advance reservations are essential, and it is best done in the morning; you can hike to the falls or cycle from San Gil. Alternatively, take a bus from the main terminal in San Gil toward Charalá and ask the driver to let you out at Juan Curi and walk from there.

CAVING

This is a pretty straightforward activity that offers plenty of thrills in the form of spider- and bat-filled caves. Cuava Vaca, located near Curití is the most beautiful and most extreme cave in town. You'll be given a helmet with headlamp and sent on your way to crawl through mud and swim between caverns. This cave is ideal for spotting stalactites and stalagmites. Take the bus to Curití for around US$2 or a taxi for around US$10.

HIKING

There's no need to take buses between all the charming colonial towns around San Gil when you can simply hike the network of trails – called the Lenguake or Camino Real – that connects them all. The full circuit takes three days to complete, but there is a popular and scenic hike that takes just 1.5 hours, and goes from Barichara to Guane.

PARAGLIDING

For paragliding enthusiasts, the area around Bucaramanga and San Gil is something of a mecca. Once you take to the skies you'll see the appeal: face-to-face with carrion birds, with all of Santander's beautiful countryside

Zip lining through the Chicamocha Canyon.

sprawled out 200 meters (650ft) below, is an experience that will stay with you for a lifetime. A 20-minute ride near the town of Curití costs around US$25, while a more comprehensive flight above the great Chicamocha Canyon (the largest in Colombia) lasts 30–60 minutes and costs US$60.

KAYAKING

Three-day kayak training courses for beginners are available in San Gil. These typically start in a swimming pool teaching fundamental manoeuvres (like the eskimo roll), before moving to the Río Fonce.

RAFTING

Another main reason people flock to this little town is to brave its wild rivers. There's still only one truly reputable operator in San Gil for extreme rapids: Colombia Rafting Expeditions (Carrera 10, no. 7–83; tel: 7-724 5800; www.colombiarafting.com), and they welcome all levels of experience. The Río Fonce is ideal for beginners and families as it boasts tamer grade II–III rapids. There are daily trips in the morning and afternoon that cost US$12, with 1.5 hours spent on the river. Beginners are also welcome at the Río Suarez, but be warned: this river quickly hits class IV–V rapids, so you better plan on at least some of the people in your boat going overboard during the 20km (12-mile) -trip. It lasts 1–2 hours and costs around US$45, leaving once a day at 10am.

SWIMMING

Most swimming enthusiasts head out to the natural pools formed by rock formations in San Gil's many rivers. Pozo Azul is one such option, and it's located just outside of town. Pescaderito is another, perhaps more stunning option, located slightly farther away, near Curití. If you don't want to venture out of town, try the swimming pool at Parque Gallineral.

MOUNTAIN BIKING

Colombian Bike Junkies (tel: 316-327 6101; www.colombianbikejunkies.com) is the only company offering comprehensive mountain biking trips around San Gil, including passing through the Suarez or Chicamocha Canyons. They offer two different all day tours (8am–6pm), each covering a different 50-km (30-mile) route, costing US$80. Breakfast, lunch, drinks, and snacks are included.

ZIPLINING

One of the newest adventure sports attractions in San Gil is the 500-meter zip line, running from one side of Canyon Quebrada Seca to the other, and offering stunning views of San Gil below, particularly at sunset. It's located at the Peñón Guane Activity Center, which is 3km (2 miles) outside San Gil and also features a giant slingshot and activities for children.

BARICHARA

In the competition among Colombia's many idyllic colonial towns as to which one reigns supreme, **Barichara ❸** can

Rappelling down Juan Curi waterfall.

> **⊘ Fact**
>
> Officially the game of *tejo* is Colombia's national sport. Unofficially it's a great excuse for friends and family to toss a disc, cause some minor explosions, and enjoy a few beers in the process. The game is typically relaxed, with folks laughing and drinking while listening to ranchero or cumbia music. As a communal activity it is undeniably fun and addictive.

Dancers at a festival in Barichara.

be found near the top. More than a few visitors have described this colonial outpost in the mountains as the most beautiful in the country – and for good reason. Here the streets are paved with hefty stones, and many of the town's oldest buildings are made of an adobe-like substance called *tapia pisada*, which is a type of clay. The stores and residences are almost all whitewashed, with terra-cotta roofs, with green trim on the doors and *zócalos* (base of the building). The church and chapels you'll see here are uniquely beautiful, standing out from other majestic cathedrals throughout the country.

Due to the town's heritage and well-preserved colonial appearance, it was named a National Monument of Colombia in 1975. However, titles and awards matter little when you're strolling along the town's cobblestone streets, relaxing on the steps of a nearly 200-year-old church, or sampling some exotic cuisine – fried ants are the order of the day for many restaurants here. In fact, you probably won't be thinking about much at all: a trip to Barichara

offers the perfect chance to escape the fast-paced, adrenaline-pumping active life of San Gil and take it easy for a day or two. It's a great place to recuperate your body and rejuvenate your soul. After all, it was the native Guane people who first inhabited this area, and the indigenous name of 'Barichara' loosely translates to "the place of rest and flowering trees."

However, this isn't to say Barichara is a land lost in time. As with most beautiful municipalities in Colombia, the tourism boom has affected this tucked-away town too. New resorts, hotels, and hostels are popping up and wealthy opportunistic outsiders are buying up land. It's a more contentious issue here than it is in the big cities because many locals feel like they're being pushed out of their own town by rising rents. Add to that a protracted water shortage in 2015 due to a mass population increase and you have a town trying to find equilibrium between sustainable tourism and ensuring the locals don't lose their land and livelihood.

ARRIVING IN BARICHARA

Barichara is located 22km (14 miles) from San Gil, and buses make the trip frequently from San Gil (daily every 30 minutes from 6am to 8pm), dropping you off in the Parque Principal. As with many bus journeys in the Santander Department, this one is filled with twists and turns through rural mountain areas. The town sits on a *mesita* (little plateau) that tends to get hot. However, it also slopes upward, and when you're in the north, you can look down and survey all of Barichara below you. There's a useful tourist information point at the east entrance of town.

EXPLORING BARICHARA

This town is small enough (population around 10,000) that you can get around entirely on foot, as long as you are prepared to hike up some hills. It's best to use the main park – the **Parque**

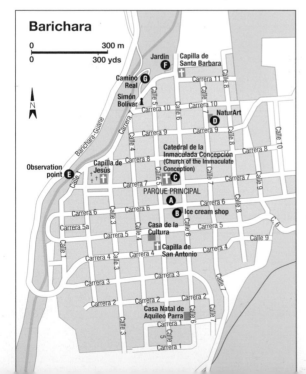

Barichara

0   300 m
0   300 yds

Jardin | Capilla de Santa Barbara

Camino Real G

Simón Bolívar

Carrera 11

Carrera 10

Carrera 10

NaturArt D

Carrera 9 | Carrera 9

Catedral de la Inmaculada Concepción (Church of the Immaculate Conception) C

Observation point E

Capilla de Jesús

Carrera 8

Carrera 8

Carrera 7 | Carrera 7

PARQUE PRINCIPAL A

Carrera 6 | Carrera 6

B Ice cream shop

Carrera 6

Carrera 5a

Carrera 5 | Casa de la Cultura

Carrera 5

Capilla de San Antonio

Carrera 4 | Carrera 4

Carrera 3 | Carrera 3

Carrera 2 | Carrera 2 | Carrera 2

Casa Natal de Aquileo Parra

Carrera 1

Carrera 1

Principal **Ⓐ** – as your main point of reference. Most of the best hostels and hotels are located just a block or two from here, as are the best restaurants and cafés. A popular place where everyone congregates is the **ice cream shop Ⓑ** on the southeast corner. The park itself is small but ideal, with lines of palms providing much-needed shade and a central stone water fountain where local children come to beat the heat.

On the northwest side of the park is the **Catedral de la Inmaculada Concepción Ⓒ** (Church of the Immaculate Conception; mass times: Tue–Sat 6am and 6pm, Sun 5am, 10am, noon, and 6pm), a great sandstone church with twin bell towers that is representative of the pristine colonial aesthetic of Barichara. Other churches of interest include **Iglesias San Antonio** (Carrera 4/ Calle 5; mass: Sun 8.30am), with twin bells atop a white steeple, and the all-brick **Jesus Resucitado** (Calle 3/ Carrera 7). One of the most charming is the **Capilla Santa Barbara** (Calle 6/ Carrera 11; open for weddings, baptisms, and communions), which sits at the top of town and looks down on them all.

Go off exploring on your own, wandering quaint streets lined with boutiques and *artesania* stores, such as the **NaturArt Ⓓ** (Carrera 6, no. 9–50; tel: 318-207 0996; Mon–Fri 9am–9pm), a charming store featuring international art, clothing, and various *artesanias* made by locals. Another great spot is the **Fundación Escuela Taller Barichara** (Carrera 5, no. 4–26; tel: 7-726 7425; http://tallerdeoficiosbarichara.com) a local school and workshop where locals who want to acquire a new skill learn the art of ceramics, jewelry making, artesania, and more. Here you'll find plenty of things for sale, including Guane purses. There's an attached gallery that exhibits local art, and the foundation also runs two very good restaurants, the on-site Las Cruces (Carrera 5, no. 4–26; tel: 726 7577) and the adjacent La Veranera (Calle 4, no. 5–17; tel: 7-726 7425).

For the best views, head to the north end of town and to the **observation point Ⓔ**. Here you'll be treated to panoramic views of the valley of the Río

Church of the Immaculate Conception, Barichara.

⏱ Where

Lots of people who want to learn how to paraglide head to Colombia Paragliding outside of Bucaramanga. They have a hostel there, right next to the launch site.

The Camino Real.

Suarez and the majestic Andes standing guard: you'll be hard-pressed to find a more humbling and awe-inspiring view in all of Colombia. It's only surpassed by the view of the Chichamocha Canyon on the mountain road as you travel from San Gil to Bucaramanga. There are also great views of the surrounding mountains when you walk up the road from the observation point to the **Jardin** , which is just behind the Capilla Santa Barbara. This pleasant little park features walkways lined with crotons of bright vermillion, stone aqueducts, and a small stone amphitheater, which hosts free live music concerts and events once every couple of months or so.

If you fancy a walk, take a hike around town on the **Camino Real** Ⓖ, an old path used by the Guane indigenous people that still contains some of the original paving stones. It leads out of town, along the countryside and through several orchards, until you reach the village of Guane, 9km (6 miles) from Barichara. The walk should take around 2 hours. This tiny community was once the Guane's capital, and there's a charming plaza and church with an imposing facade. In the plaza is a monument to Guaneta, a Guane chief, flanked by acacia trees. If you are planning on walking this route, bring your own water, although refreshments are on offer at various *fincas* on the route.

BUCARAMANGA

Roughly 420km (260 miles) from Bogotá is the city of **Bucaramanga** Ⓘ. If you're traveling north from San Gil, passing through the Cañón de Chicamocha, the sight of a giant modern metropolis appearing seemingly out of nowhere may well throw you. Industry is responsible for all this growth; this city of around 600,000 has boomed due in no small part to the success of Colombia coffee and tobacco on the international market. It's also a major transportation hub connecting Bogotá with Cúcuta, and on to the coast. Some of Colombia's best paragliding spots are just outside town. It's also a good base for other adventure-sports excursions.

BACKGROUND AND LAYOUT

Bucaramanga was founded in 1622, but expansion and evolution over the years means it has left much of its colonial past out of sight. However, there are a few areas in the city worth looking around, and one of them is the historic center. The palm-lined **Parque García Rovira**, with its center statue of the namesake – a local-born hero of the War for Independence – is the epicenter of this part of town. Here you will find many cultural centers and museums, including the **Casa de Bolívar** (Calle 37, no. 12–15; tel: 7-630 4258; Mon–Sat 8am–noon, 2–6pm), a colonial home where Simon Bolívar once lived when he made this then-village his base of operations in 1813. The museum houses some interesting artifacts from the period, and has a charming central courtyard. On the east side of the park is the **Iglesia San Laureano** (Carrera 12, no. 36–08), which was rebuilt in 1872 on the site of a 1778 church. The building that stands today has twin bell towers and a bright yellow exterior with white trim.

Parque Santander is the heart of the modern center of the city, and it is where many budget hotels can be found. This is where street vendors and artists peddle their wares, while nearby food carts offer iced orange, mandarin, and coconut juices, as well as cups of chopped fruit like mango and pineapple to help beat the mid-afternoon heat. This is the location of one of the most famous churches in Bucaramanga, the **Catedral de la Sagrada Familia** (Calle 36, no. 19–56; Mon 8am–noon, 1–3pm, Sun 8am–1pm). This stately white Romanesque church was finished in 1887 and has two sharp steeples flanking a statue of the Virgin and San Jose.

Other parks of interest include **Parque de Mejoras Públicas** (Calle 36, Carreras 29–32), a much larger and greener park than Parque Santander, and home to an impressive amphitheater. There's also the Parque de Los Ninos (Calle 30, Carrera 26), which features a famous ceramic sculpture called *Monumento Clavijero del Tiple*, by a Santandereano named Guillermo

Paragliding near Bucaramanga.

Espinosa. The large sculpture is the representation of the head of a tiple, a Colombian 12-stringed acoustic guitar. There is also the **Parque San Pio** (Carrera 5, no. 33), which is surrounded by nice restaurants as well as the **Iglesia San Pio**, a Modernist church featuring works by Oscar Rodríguez Naranjo, another Santandereano. Finally there's **Parque Las Palmas** (Calle 41, no. 30), which is named for its myriad palm trees. A couple of blocks away from Las Palmas is the **Museo de Arte Moderno** (Calle 37, no. 26–16; tel: 7- 645 0483; Mon–Fri 8am–noon and 2–6pm).

EXPLORING BUCARAMANGA FURTHER

South of the center you'll find the city's **country club** (Club Campestre de Bucaramanga; Carrera 21, no. 30–02), which is a sprawling operation on a stunning property. It features all the usual sports and activities (golf, tennis, etc.) and it has a fantastic swimming pool. There's also a hotel on the premises.

If you want to make the hike south to the neighbourhood of Floridablanco,

you can visit another worthwhile museum, the **Museo Aqrqueológico Regional Guane** (Carrera 7, no. 4–35; tel: 7-619 8181; www.casadeculturapiedradelsol.gov.co; Mon–Fri 8am–noon and 4pm–6pm; free), which showcases around 800 artifacts of the Guane indigenous people, from textiles and woodwork to necklaces and ceramics.

South of Floridablanco are the botanical gardens, the **Jardín Botaníco Eloy Valenzuela** (Avenida Bucarica; tel: 7-634 6100; Tue–Sun 8am–4pm). Here visitors can stroll through the gardens and see some of the park's 3,500 or so species of native plants, including orchids and heliconias.

CÚCUTA

Cúcuta ⑤ is the capital of Norte de Santander Department and, located a mere 16km (10 miles) from the border, is the closest major hub to Venezuela in the region. The city is notable for its tree-lined streets, which provide a nice respite from the average heat of around 84°F (29°C). The city was founded in 1733 and its population has since grown to around 600,000 – a far cry from its dusty border town beginnings. One point of interest for urban-planning enthusiasts is that Cúcuta is one of the few cities in the world – and certainly the only in Colombia – where the street grid system starts at zero.

SIGHTS AROUND CÚCUTA

The **Catedral de San José** (Avenida 5 Norte, no. 10–73) sits at the east end of Parque Santander, a green, pigeon-filled park whose avian residents like to make their home on the noble statue of General Santander. The church was originally founded in the mid-19th century, but an earthquake in 1875 destroyed the building and the version that stands today was finally completed in 1956 after 50 years of work. Despite its grand size and muscular bell towers, the most impressive thing about

---

⊘ SCORING GOALS FOR PEACE

In the north of Bucaramanga is a neighborhood called Dos Olas. Unfortunately, like too many communities in Colombia, this neighborhood suffers from high unemployment, poor nutrition, deprivation, mass school dropout rates, and the prevalence of *pandillas* (gangs). As the whole region of Bucaramanga – and indeed Colombia – tries to recover from decades of armed internal conflict, too often neighborhoods like Dos Olas, and the young people who inhabit them, are left behind.

Enter Goals for Peace is a charitable organization which started in 2012 through the combined efforts of Kasa Guane in Bucaramanga, the United Nations and FIFA International Global Peace Games Day. The objectives were simple but ambitious: promote ethically responsible tourism through social enterprise projects comprised of a network of enthusiastic volunteers and supporters. Goals for Peace focuses on Dos Olas in particular, using sports training as well as educational, artistic, and recreational projects to support and facilitate the at-risk youth population, teaching these young community members values like teamwork, respect, tolerance, and self-discipline.

Anyone can help the cause, and you can do so through donations as well as volunteer work in Colombia and remotely. For more info on volunteer opportunities contact Goals for Peace (info@goalsforpeace.com).

the church is its minimalist aesthetic. There's no flashy paint job, just a simple stone facade.

The **Casa de la Cultura** (Calle 13, no. 3–67; tel: 7-571 6689; Mon–Fri 8.30am–noon, 3–6pm) houses a museum dedicated to Cúcuta's rich history. Much of this has to do with the War of Independence, as Cúcuta was a strategic point due to its proximity to Venezuela. Southeast of the city you'll find the **Puente Internacional Simón Bolívar**, a bridge that crosses the Río Tachira and links Colombia to Venezuela. The small town of **Villa del Rosario**, where congress met in 1821 to decide on their new country's constitution, is located near the border. The area where the documents were signed is now a park, which is located near to the **Casa Natal del General Santander** (Km 6, San Antonio Villa del Rosario; tel: 7-570 0265; Tue–Sun 8am–11.30am, 2–5.30pm; free), a hacienda-style home where the independence hero and future president was born on April 2, 1792. In 1959, the home became a National Monument of Colombia.

BORDER CONSIDERATIONS

Exit and entry formalities between Colombia and Venezuela are handled at the office of **Migracion Colombia** (Avenida 1, no. 28–57; tel: 7-573 5210; www.migracioncolombia.gov.co; daily 8am–noon, 2–5pm). Despite Venezuela's ongoing economic difficulties, the border remains open, with foreigners free to move as they please. However, US residents need to apply for and receive a visa in their home country before entering Venezuela. To enter Colombia, foreigners must first obtain an exit stamp from Venezuelan immigration and then a Colombian entry stamp at the Migracion office.

To enter Venezuela, foreigners must get their exit stamp at the Migracion office. Buses leave for the border from Avenida 3 in Cúcuta. It is also possible to take a taxi for around US$2–3 (a taxi from Cúcuta airport costs around US$10). The first Venezuelan town on the other side of the bridge is San Antonio del Táchira. Taking a vehicle across the border requires a stamp from the SENIAT office in San Cristóbal, Venezuela (Tel: 0241-8563007).

Statue of General Francisco de Paula Santander in Santander Square, Cúcuta.

Hacienda de Guayabal coffee plantation, Manizales.

ZONA CAFETERA

East of Bogotá and south of Medellín, there lies rolling green hills and high altitude mountains that enjoy a tropical climate, making this area the premier coffee-growing region of Colombia.

Collectively the departments of Risaralda, Caldas, and Quindío make up what is known as the axis of the Zona Cafetera – the region where Colombia's world-renowned coffee is produced. The notion of this area being ground zero for bean production can be perplexing at first. There are towns and cities here, such as Manizales, located at an altitude of well over 2,000 meters (6,500ft). Yet the Zona Cafetera enjoys a tropical climate, making the sharp and steep mountains that cut through the region perfect for coffee cultivation. The landscapes here are lush and green, outshining even the rich green valleys and rolling hills of Antioquia, giving the area a Middle Earth look.

The methods used in the coffee production are from the region's agrarian past. The great coffee plantations in Zona Cafetera are typically passed down through the generations, keeping the business in the family. Most importantly, the beans are still picked by hand. During the harvesting season you'll see plenty of workers – many poor migrants from Chocó – navigating the steep hillsides, rooting through the short, fat plants in search of the red berries, slowly filling bushels to be taken to the processing facilities. The personal, individual effort involved in harvesting Colombia's coffee beans not only results in a better product, but

imbues it with character, not unlike drinking a quality bottle of wine made from hand-picked grapes.

Sadly however, these two factors aren't enough to overcome the economic demands of mass production in the modern world. As Brazil and other countries increasingly rely on mechanized harvesters to reap their crops, the global price of coffee has dropped. This has hit the local Colombian plantation owners particularly hard, and they've had to come up with other revenue streams in order to make ends meet.

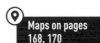

Main Attractions
Plaza Bolívar, Manizales
Parque Chipre, Manizales
Staying on a working coffee farm
Salento
Parque Nacional Los Nevados

Maps on pages 168, 170

Woker at a coffee plantation.

Catedral Basílica Metropolitana de Nuestra Señora del Rosario, Manizales.

One of these has been to open the doors of their haciendas to tourists. Those who choose to stay on a working coffee *finca* will bear witness to the process and tour the fields. Meals are often included and, most importantly, so is all the coffee you can drink during your stay.

MANIZALES

It's hard to believe that for all of the Zona Cafetera's breathtaking natural beauty, Colombians from other parts of the country can look down on certain parts of it so. Residents of Medellín often regard nearby **Manizales ①** as *frio* (cold), due to its high elevation and Bogatanos, who themselves reside in the thin air of the frigid and misty Andes, often remark that the only thing

colder than the Zona Cafetera, are its residents. Inter-departmental feuding aside, no trip to Colombia is complete without a visit to this part of the coffee-growing region, as one of its best coffee *fincas* is located just outside of town (see box).

HISTORY AND LOCATION

Despite being the capital of the Department of Caldas, Manizales is a smallish city of about 500,000 residents, that's relatively new in the grand scheme of things. It was founded in 1848 by a group of settlers who were trying to flee a situation of civil unrest in the capital. Manizales itself was settled at an altitude of 2,150 meters (7,000ft), on the narrow saddle of a

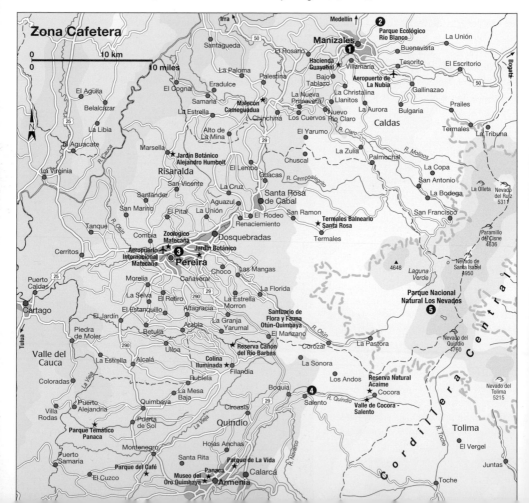

mountain with precious flatland to spare. The area was ideal as a settlement in the 19th century, but as the city has grown it has been forced to expand eastward into any habitable space, no matter how precipitous. This includes ridges between the town of Chinchiná and the Quebrada Olivares. Still, the fact that so much of the land slopes dramatically down to the valleys below Manizales means that the city offers stunning panoramic views on clear days – sometimes as far as to the Nevados Mountains to the east.

Even today Manizales is a city that is still in touch with its roots, celebrating its founders and heritage. Left to its own devices, it is likely that Manizales would have changed little in the intervening years since its founding, but fate had other plans. Parts of Manizales were destroyed during earthquakes in 1875 and 1879, and also by fires in 1927 and 1954. Much of the city has been rebuilt, but there are still some areas where you can see the republican architecture of old, such as the historic center.

NAVIGATING MANIZALES

The center is a good base for exploring the city. The area is good for walking, but the narrow streets are often congested with traffic. Also *telefericos* transport people up and down the streets of the sloping municipality. The main thoroughfare is Carrera 23 (sometimes called Avenida Santander), which runs from one end of the city to the other. The road then leads 8km (5 miles) southwest to La Nubia airport, and then all the way to Bogotá.

In the center of Manizales is the **Plaza de Bolívar Ⓐ**, which features ceramic murals detailing Colombia's history, by famed local sculptor Guillermo Botero. You certainly won't miss the towering bronze statue *Bolívar Condor*, which was created by Rodrigo Arenas Betancourt in 1991. It stands guard over the center of the plaza and depicts Simón Bolívar in mid-transition into a condor, his severed head protruding from the base of the statue.

At the north end of the plaza is **La Gobernación Ⓑ** (www.gobernaciondecal das.gov.co/web; Mon–Fri 7am–5pm), a

Downtown Manizales.

neocolonial government building with one of the most striking facades on the square. It's so impressive that in 1984 it was declared a National Monument of Colombia. Perhaps the only other building on the place that eclipses it is the **Cathedral Basílica Metropolitana de Nuestra Señora del Rosario** **C** (Basilica Cathedral of Our Lady of the Rosary of Manizales; Carrera 22; tel: 6-883 1880), which not only dominates the plaza, but the entire city. Rebuilding of the church began in 1927 after a fire had destroyed the original building the previous year. The plans were drawn up by Julien Aguste Polti, a French architect who designed it in the neo-Gothic style, and it was finally finished in 1939, after some delays owing to the Great Depression. It's an expansive cathedral that can accommodate 5,000 people, measuring 2,400 square meters (25,800sq ft). The building is constructed mainly of reinforced concrete with a spire that is over 100 meters (328ft) high. Each of its four towers is dedicated to a saint: Paul, Francis, Inés, and Mark. The interior stained-glass mosaics are very impressive, and there's a rose window at the west end. Over the altar hangs a suspended cross, and the wooden choir stalls are elegant.

The **Parroquia Sagrado Corazón de Jesús** **D** (also known as Iglesia de los Agustinos; Carrera 19, no. 18–53; mass times Mon–Sat 7am, noon, and 6.30pm, Sun 8am, 11am, noon, 6pm, and 7pm) also stands out due to its whitewashed facade with sharp towers. Overlooking the Parque Caldas is another white church in the neo-Gothic style, the **Iglesia de la Inmaculada Concepción** **E** (Church of the Immaculate Conception; mass times: Mon–Sat 7am, 8am, noon, and 6pm, Sun on every hour 7am–noon and 5–8pm). It was built between 1903 and 1921, and the interior boasts elegant cedarwood pillars. The **Teatro Los Fundadores** **F** (Fundadores Theatre; Carrera 22 at Calle 23; tel: 6-878 2530; free) is a great example of modern architecture, and the foundation itself hosts some fine exhibits, featuring works by Guillermo Botero, among others.

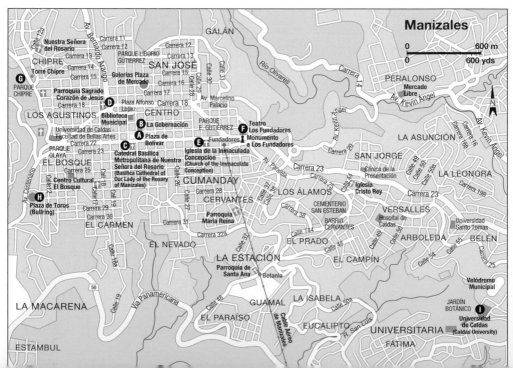

WEST OF THE CENTER

If you travel along Avenida 12 de Octubre you will reach the **Parque Chipre** , which affords great views of the city to the east, and of coffee country to the west. From here you can see all the way down toward the Río Cauca. The stunning views and the park amenities make this a popular spot with locals on weekends. On the promenade here vendors sell *obleas*, large wheat wafers that are fairly tasty. There's an iconic water tank here, known as El Tanque, which stands guard over all of Manizales. There's also the Mirador de Chipre, just north of Parque Chipre, which offers even better views. Also here is the Monumento a los Colonizadores, a monument to the colonists of the area made from melted-down keys. South of here and to the west is the **Plaza de Toros**  (Bullring; Carrera 27, no. 10a–07; tel: 6-883 8124; www. cormanizales.com). It was built during the 1950s in Moorish style and is a replica of the bullring in Cordobá, Spain. It holds 20,000 people and bullfights typically take place during the Feria de Manizales in January. For more details, see www.feriademanizales.gov.co.

EAST OF THE CENTER

East of the city center is the **Universidad de Caldas**  (Caldas University; Calle 65, no. 26–10; tel: 6-878 1500; www.ucaldas.edu.co), home to the **Centro de Museos** (tel: 6-878 1500 ext. 24132; Mon–Fri 8am–noon, 2–6pm), which has exhibitions on archeology and geology. East of here is the **Universidad de Manizales** (Manizales University; Carrera 23, no. 40; tel: 6-887 9680; www.umanizales. edu.co), which is located in an interesting building that used to be a train station.

EL CABLE

If you follow Carrera 23 east in the direction of Bogotá, you'll eventually reach Calle 65 and the **old cableway terminal**. This cable line once ran 75km (46 miles) from Manizales to Mariquita, and was used primarily to transport coffee. It was in operation from 1922 until the 1960s, and acted as an easy means for shipping products over the 3,700 meter (12,140ft) Alto de

Manizales city center.

Las Letras pass. The coffee was then transported from Mariquita to the Río Magdalena for shipment up river. Today this area is known as El Cable, and it is Manizales' Zona Rosa, filled with upscale bars and trendy restaurants.

PARQUE ECOLÓGICO RÍO BLANCO

Just a few kilometers northwest of Manizales is the **Parque Ecológico Río Blanco ❷** (tel: 6-887 9770; www.aguas demanizales.com.co), a protected cloud forest covering 4,932 hectares (12,187 acres). Many organisations, including the World Wildlife Fund, consider this to be the best spot for birdwatching in a country already famous for great birding sites. There are more than 350 known species here, including 33 species of hummingbird, four kinds of toucan, the royal woodpecker, and a rare type of rusty-faced parrot. There are also 40 different types of orchids and 350 species of butterfly here.

The park is owned and run by Aguas de Manizales because the area supplies the city with roughly 35 percent of its drinking water. Therefore if Río Blanco were to become corrupted or polluted, Manizales would suffer. The well-maintained preserve is the reason why Manizales' water is considered to be among the purest in the world. Before the area was protected it was home to many *campesino* families who still live on the land. They've been retrained as park rangers with the assistance of an organization called the Fundación Ecológica Gabriel Arrango Restrepo. Those coming here on birdwatching or photography excursions can stay overnight at a hut run by the Foundation. Contact the technical director, Sergio Ocampo, at tel: 6-887 9770 or sergiofundegar@gmail.com.

COFFEE IN AND AROUND MANIZALES

Manizales is the epicenter of coffee production in the region, and some of the best haciendas can be found just outside of town. With coffee prices declining in recent decades, many farms have been forced to get creative with how they supplement their income. To this end they've opened

Hummingbird feeding on nectar from a trumpet flower in the Río Blanco Reserve.

⊘ HACIENDA VENICIA

To experience a Colombian coffee operation from within is almost like being transported back in time: ride through coffee fields on horseback, passing among the plants with their waxy green leaves. In season their leaves hide bundles of little red berries, sweet on the outside and possessing the engine-revving coffee bean on the inside

Stay at Hacienda Venicia (www.haciendav-enecia.com), just outside Manizales for a few days and experience it for yourself. Here, you'll be given a primer on the history of the bean from the hacienda's excellent staff. You'll also stay at a hacienda that's been in the same family since the 1800s; the pictures of familial generations lining the walls offer a unique narrative that carries you from the days of Simón Bolívar all the way through to the digital age.

their doors to visitors, and coffee tours have become big business. Visitors shouldn't be shy about joining one of these excursions, and from Manizales most hotels and hostels will arrange them. Still, it's best to reserve an overnight stay, because doing so will give you a real feel for the operation. It will also allow you time to get to know the *finca* owners, gleaning insight into their family history and how they run their businesses.

PEREIRA

Located 56km (35 miles) southwest of Manizales, **Pereira** ❸ is the service capital of the coffee zone and the official capital of Risaralda Department. It sits on a plateau at an altitude of 1,411 meters (4,629ft) and makes a nice spot to visit: it's less touristy than Manizales and the surrounding countryside is just as beautiful. From the city you can see all the way to the peaks of the Cordillera Central. Two rivers bind the city: the Río Otún in the north and the Río Consota in the south. A viaduct links the town of Dosquebrados just beyond

the Otún to Pereira, making it more or less part of the city.

For centuries, the location of Pereira was rarely stable. It was founded as a settlement in 1541 by Mariscal Jorge Robledo but the site was moved to present-day Cartago on the Río la Vieja. This was due to the fact that the local indigenous tribe, the Quimbaya, weren't amenable to receiving uninvited guests. In the 19th century a man named Francisco Pereira left Cartago with the intention of founding an official town in the location of present-day Pereira, but he died before achieving this goal. His friend, Remigio Antonio Cañarte, who was also a priest, carried out his friend's final wish, and in 1863 he founded Pereira.

Today Pereira is a thriving city of around 475,000 people, with an industrial spirit evident in its many commercial institutions. The climate is agreeable and short rain showers are common here. These allow the area to cultivate more agriculture than just coffee, such as sugarcane, cacao, and livestock, and the food in Pereira is as good as it gets.

Bolívar Desnudo (Nude Bolívar), in Pereira.

⊙ **Fact**

Colombia's annual coffee production averages roughly 11.5 million bags per year. This makes it the third-highest coffee producer in the world after Brazil and Vietnam.

Unfortunately, like some other areas in the Zona Cafetera, Pereira is prone to seismic activity, and earthquakes have been known to occur here. The worst examples occurred in 1995 and 1999 when hundreds of people died and many houses were destroyed. The center of the city revolves around the **Plaza de Bolívar**, and visitors can walk to most points of interest from here. The areas between Carreras 10 and 12, as well as east-facing streets like Calle 14, are known for high crime rates, and are therefore best avoided.

By far and away the most striking thing you'll see in the plaza is the sculpture *Bolívar Desnudo*, by Rodrigo Arenas Betancourt. It was commissioned for Pereira's centenary in 1963 and features a nude Liberator astride his horse, carrying a torch. It's a fine sculpture with plenty of artistic merit; however, this was lost on the locals when it was first unveiled. Today Colombians have come round to the sculpture, but don't expect this laid-back attitude to nudity to spread too far afield; it's highly unlikely we'll see a nude George Washington statue in the US anytime soon. Other works by Betancourt in the city include the *Monumento a las Fundadores* (Avenida Circunvaler/Calle 13); *El Prometeo*, located in the **Universidad Tecnológico de Pereira** on Calle 14; and *Cristo sin Cruz*, a crucified Jesus minus cross located in the **Capilla de Fátima**.

Also on the plaza is the **Catedral Nuestra Señora de la Pobreza** (Cathedral of Our Lady of Poverty; mass times: Mon–Fri 7am and 6pm, Sat 7am, noon, and 6pm, Sun 8am, 10am, 11am, noon, 6pm, and 7pm), which has a rather unimpressive exterior. However, inside it is cavernous and elegant, with a bare wooden interior that has been left in its most basic state after the 1999 earthquake, with chandeliers hanging from the nave. There are also three other parks in the city (each with their own church) that are well worth exploring: **Parque del Lago Uribe Uribe**, which has a large, colorful man-made lake; **Parque Gaitán**; and the **Parque la Libertad**, which features a colorful mosaic by the artist Lucy Tejada.

Waterfall at the the hot springs of Santa Rosa de Cabal.

It's also worth stopping in at the **Jardín Botanico** (on the Universidad Tecnológica de Pereira campus; tel: 6-313 7500; Mon–Fri 8am–4pm, Sat–Sun 9am–2pm), which is a great spot for birdwatchers as it contains over 168 species. Those interested in an excursion should head out of town to **Termales de Santa Rosa de Cabal** (located midway between Pereira and Manizales; Santa Rosa de Cabal Thermal Baths; tel: 6-365 5237; www.termales.com.co; daily 9am–11.30pm). These thermal baths are located amid stunning surroundings complete with romantic waterfalls cascading down terraced hills. There's a hotel here, and a taxi from Periera costs around US$35. Alternatively, you can take a bus from Periera to Chinchina and then from Chinchina to Santa Rosa de Cabal. Be warned – these baths get very busy on weekends.

SALENTO

On the road toward Parque Los Nevados, in the foothills of the Cordillera Central, is the little town of **Salento** ❹. It sits at 1,985 meters (6,500ft) above sea level and is the oldest town in the Quindío Department, having been founded in 1842. Flowers and crops flourish here, which is a direct result of the regular rainfall the area receives. To the east you can see the snow-capped peaks of Los Nevados.

There was a time when Salento was a quiet, sleepy village. Those days are long gone: today, Salento is a popular weekend destination for locals and tourists alike. Despite this, it still makes for a worthwhile visit as the town somehow manages to retain much of its village charm. People love the brightly colored houses, and the surrounding hilly countryside and the Valley de Cocora makes for great treks among the wax palms. There's a stunning **central plaza** in town, with a center sculpture of a saber-wielding Bolívar, as well as a standout church, **Nuestra Señora del**

Carmen. A good trip from the plaza is to walk up Calle Real (Carrera 6) for some more great examples of colonial architecture. You can then climb 250 steps to the *mirador* (lookout point), which boasts stunning views of the Cardenas and Quindío rivers, which are part of the Valle de Cocora.

PARQUE NACIONAL LOS NEVADOS

In central Colombia there exists a small range of volcanic peaks that make up the **Parque Nacional Los Nevados** ❺. These peaks include the snow-covered Nevado del Ruiz, Nevado del Santa Isabel, and Nevado del Tolima. Other high peaks without snow cover include Paramillo del Cisne, Paramillo de Santa Rosa, and Paramillo del Quindio. This cluster of peak is a nine-hour excursion from Bogotá, or four hours if you are traveling from Manizales. Interestingly enough you can actually see the snow-capped peaks of Nevado del Ruiz, the highest of all the volcanos in the range at 5,321 meters (17,457ft), from Manizales.

Colorful houses in Salento.

This volcano is still listed as active, and it has a tragic history of eruptions. The most recent eruption was in 1985, and a lahar (a type of mudflow) created by the eruption all but destroyed the nearby town of Armero, killing some 25,000 people. Today there is still seismic activity in Nevado del Ruiz, but rather than large explosions, scientists are worried about small-scale eruptions. The risk here is to the glaciers at the peak; if they were to be destabilized by small eruptions they would create more lahars that could travel over 100km (62 miles) along the river valley below, causing significant death and destruction. Scientists estimate that if even 10 percent of this glacial ice were to melt, it would produce mudflows with a volume of 2 million cubic meters (2,615,900 cubic yds). Nevado del Tolima is also listed as active.

At the moment, however, this is all conjecture, and Los Nevados remains open to visitors – although certain areas are restricted. Here you'll not only find massive peaks, but there's also an abundance of volcanic lakes, hot springs, and stunning landscapes featuring high-altitude volcanic vegetation and *frailejones* shrubs, with some growing as high as 12 meters (39ft). You can arrange tours of the area in Manizales and there are good treks to be done the park. Perhaps the most famous and toughest is the six-day hike from Ibagué, in the south, north to Manizales.

For those coming from Manizales, the route follows the highway to Bogotá until La Esperanza, where you turn off to the right. From there it's a further 17km (10 miles) to the northern park entrance, located in Brisas. If you're trekking or on horseback, you can enter Los Nevados overland from the west and south of the park. This can be done from Pereira (which will take you through Parque Ucumari), Salento (via the Valle de Cocora), and Ibagué (along the Río Combeima).

Many choose to make this excursion from Manizales and arrive at the north entrance. It's the easiest way to access the park, therefore most tourists and trekkers end up here. There's a road that runs from the entrance at Brisas

Hikers in the Los Nevados National Park.

to a parking area located at the base of Nevado del Ruiz. A rough road (accessible by four-wheel drive only) continues to Laguna del Otún, which sits at an altitude of 3,900 meters (12,800ft). Many in the past have chosen to climb Nevado del Ruiz over all the others, as this is the tallest volcano in the park. There's an easy hike to a lookout point at 5,100 meters (16,700ft), but unfortunately this has been closed to visitors since 2011. The entire area of Brisas is currently restricted, and visitors are only allowed as far as the Valles de las Tumbas. This route is open daily from 8am–2pm and hiking the route takes around three hours. It is not necessary to obtain permits to visit the Brisas sector of the park, but you must be accompanied by an approved guide on a tour or excursion, which can be arranged in Manizales.

Farther south in the park there is a **visitor center** at El Cisne, which sits at an altitude of 4,200 meters (13,780ft). From here it's possible to trek to Laguna Verde, which is at 4,300 meters (14,100ft). As the name

implies, this lake is green and beautiful. It's located between El Cisne and Nevado de Santa Isabel.

Those who want to visit the Nevado de Santa Isabel sector and arrive at the glacier of the same name do require permission and the company of an official guide. Permission can be obtained at the **PNN Los Nevados Office** in Manizales (Calle 69a, no. 24–69; tel: 6-887 1611; nevados@parquesnacionales.gov.co; Mon–Fri 8am–6pm). The hours are daily 9am–5.30pm, but those who wish to hike to the top of the glacier should enter the area no later than 4am. Nevado de Santa Isabel is at an altitude of 4,965 meters (16,290ft) and is inactive. At the summit you'll be treated to a fine view of Nevado del Ruiz to the north and Nevado del Tolima to the south. Laguna del Otún is the biggest lake around here, and you can fish for trout from April to August. It's possible to camp at El Cisen, but be warned that you will need to bring all your own gear. Also, as the altitudes here surpass 3,800 meters (12,467ft), temperatures can dip below freezing at night.

◎ Tip

The national park office recommends all visitors check the seismic activity warnings at the Colombian Geological Survey (www2.sgc.gov.co) before planning their trip to Los Nevados.

Frailejón plants growing in the Los Nevados National Park.

Cartagena's 17th-century Convento Santa Clara.

CARTAGENA

When strolling the ancient ramparts of Cartagena, part of you will expect to see pirate ships and Spanish galleons appearing just offshore – such is the timeless quality of Colombia's most majestic colonial city.

Even during the 1980s and 90s, when Colombia was only known for internal strife, visitors came from all over to see Cartagena, which tells you all you need to know about the appeal this famous destination possesses. Even today, as Colombia's doors are firmly open to visitors, the well-peopled cobblestone streets and fortresses of bustling Cartagena still exude their 16th-century authenticity and charm.

Cartagena is located on Colombia's central Caribbean Coast, where all Costeño people and traditions converge, forming one unique culture that is both homogenous and eclectic. The cuisine – the shellfish, the *ceviches*, the fish, and the *sancochos* – represents this eclectic mix of flavors and styles, as does the music.

This well-preserved ancient hub is also one where the old and the new converge. Many visitors head straight to the walled city, where the cobblestone streets and palm-filled plazas are as romantic and indelible as anything from Márquez's *Love in the Time of Cholera*. Modernity does encroach at Bocagrande, where new condominiums, high-rise hotels, and apartments dominate the skyline. Don't forget the upscale stores and restaurants of San Diego. This diversity of people, culture, and experience is just one reason why Cartagena is a Unesco World Heritage

Dancers at the Independence festivities.

Site and a heavyweight-sized travel destination to this day.

A HISTORICAL OVERVIEW

As famous as the first Spanish explorers have become over the millennia, they were often found lacking when it came to navigation. Cartagena's full name is Cartagena de Indias as the earliest explorers thought they had found the Far East. Pedro de Heredia founded Cartagena in 1533, and it was built on an island just offshore, with marshes separating the city from the mainland.

Main Attractions

Getsemaní
The walled city
San Diego Quarter
Playa Blanca
Parque Nacional Natural
   Corales del Rosario y
   San Bernando

Map on page 184

⊙ Tip

Cartagena is hot all year round. That said, try to avoid August–November, which are the hottest and wettest months respectively.

Cartagena's position at the mouth of the Río Magdalena meant that it was the perfect trans-shipment point for merchandise coming from Spain and gold shipped back to the old world. For a while the Spaniards assumed they were safe from attacks as the city was built on the Bahía de Cartagena, a bay 15km (10 miles) long and 5km (3 miles) wide, dotted with small islands just offshore. However, these natural sea defenses didn't deter a number of attackers, including Sir Francis Drake, who briefly controlled the city in 1586.

Once the Spanish got their city back, they resolved to fortify Cartagena in order to protect their gold from future attacks. This is when the ramparts, which have become such an iconic part of Cartagena's identity, were first built. Forts were built as well, including three on the Puente Román, located in the southeast, which connects the old city with Isla Manga. Fortifications were also built on the mainland and in areas like Bocagrande, Tierrabomba, and Barú. The most muscular and dominating of the fortresses is

Castillo San Felipe de Barajas, located across from the Puente Heredia on San Lázaro Hill (see box). The others are San Sebastián del Pastelillo, which was built in the mid-16th century, and San Lorenzo. Fort La Tenaza protected the northernmost point of the walled city, which was vulnerable to attacks from the open sea.

The new fortress city seemed impenetrable, so the Spanish turned their sights toward integration. In 1650 they built the Canal del Dique, a 140km (87-mile) -long waterway connecting the Río Magdalena to the city, providing access for ships from upriver ports. Cartagena repelled more attacks, this time from the French. The city prospered in the 18th century, becoming a principal hub in the Viceroyalty of New Grenada. More attacks came, and the Spaniards built an underwater wall to block Bocagrande, thus cutting off one of only two sea entrances to Cartagena.

The 12-meter-high walls encircling the old city were completed in 1735. Besides the height, the Spanish

Iglesia de San Pedro Claver.

focused on density, making them 17 meters (56ft) thick and containing six gates. As with most historical fortifying walls, these were built to keep people in as much as they were to keep people out. The walls acted as a dividing line in the old city, with the lower economic classes living in the outer city, typically in Getsemaní, where you can still find colonial buildings today. The nobility, aristocrats, and high officials lived within the walls, in El Centro, with access to the lush plazas.

Cartagena declared independence from Spain in 1811. The city was a strategic strongpoint to a military genius like Bolívar, and when he arrived a year later he used Cartagena as a base for his campaign to secure the Magdalena region. After being retaken by the Spanish in 1815, patriotic forces retook the city in 1821, and that was the last time the Spanish held sway over Cartagena de Indias.

GETTING YOUR BEARINGS

Cartagena is divided up into multiple sectors, so it can be confusing to navigate the area upon first arrival. Colonial Cartagena is known as EL Centro, and it sits at the north end of Bahía Cartagena, surrounded by 12km (7 miles) of old ramparts. This is where many of the most idyllic plazas, parks, and upscale boutique hotels can be found. Budget hotels can be found in Getsemaní, which has a more working-class and bohemian feel to it. In this historic district, the streets have names instead of numbers, and they change from block to block.

The official downtown borders Getsemaní and doesn't go by centro, like many city centers do, but La Matuna. The city then continues for 10km (6 miles) north, south, and east, and traveling these extended routes will lead you around the bay, and to the access points for offshore islands, like Islas Rosario. Most churches in the historic districts of Cartagena typically have a 6:45am mass and a 6pm mass. If you need further assistance, be sure to stop by Cartagena's main tourist office, which is located in the **Casa del Marqués del Premio Real** on

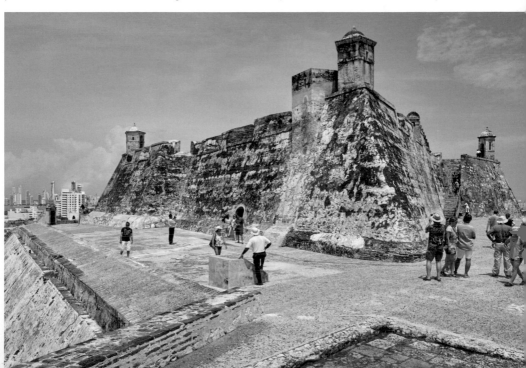

Castillo San Felipe de Barajas.

Local vendors sell fruit and baked goods.

the Plaza Aduana (tel: 5-660 1583; daily 9am–6pm).

WALKING THE RAMPARTS

One of the best ways to take in Cartagena is by walking one of its most iconic features: the ramparts that encircle the old city. Typically this route takes 90 minutes, but times vary depending on where you start and how often you stop. The best place to begin is the **Baluarte San Francisco Javier Ⓐ**, continuing around the Circuit to **La India Catalina Ⓑ** and on past the lagoons to the Puente Román. The circuit breaks, but its final section is along the **Calle del Arsenal** and finishes at the **Playa Barahona**, which is located by the bay. Sunset and sunrise are great times to go, but there's something about enjoying a sunset from the ramparts that makes the whole experience as delectable as can be. Feel free to hop down off the walls at any time and experience some of the famous sights detailed in this chapter. Also feel free to lose yourself in the old city's narrow streets and discover the highlights for yourself. Don't worry – the fact that every block has a different street name will make getting lost a particularly easy proposition.

THE OUTER CITY

A good anchor point for the outer city is the **Puente Román Ⓒ**, which leads from Manga Island to Getsemaní. Manga is known as a residential area

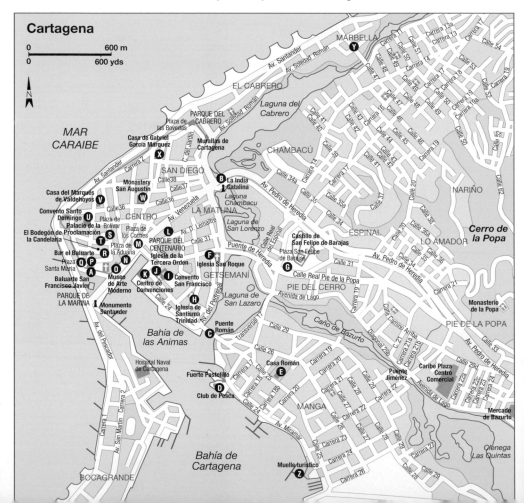

home to the **Club de Pesca**  (Fuerte San Sebastian del Pastelillo; tel: 5-660 5578; www.clubdepescadecartagena.com), a fishing club located on the ramparts that has a great seafood restaurant (and nicer view). On the island you can also walk to the **Casa Román** , a 19th-century mansion constructed in the Moorish style and home to Teresa Román Vélez, a local legend and celebrity chef in the country. The house isn't open to the public, but it makes for some nice photos.

Getsemaní on the northwest end of the bridge and is known as the bohemian area of the city, and is home to Cartagena's many artisans. Many of the single-story *casas bajas* (low houses) are being refurbished and renovated while keeping their colonial style. They are hot property at the moment and many have already been turned into boutique hotels, cafés, and restaurants. Many of the budget lodgings are here, which means streets like Calles 25 and Calle del Espiritu Santu (Calle 30) are bustling with travelers most nights. Some notable landmarks include the **Iglesia San Roque**  (Church of San Roque; Calle del Espiritu Santo and Carrera 10c), a 17th-century hermitage and hospital that was built during a great plague. Right here is the **Puente Heridia**. Cross it, heading east, and you'll immediately reach the **Plaza San Felipe de Barajas** . To the north of here is the start of the downtown sector, La Matuna, where a selection of mid-range hotels can be found between.

Back in Gesemaní there is another historic house of worship, **Iglesia de Santísma Trinidad**  (Church of Santísma Trinidad; Carrera 10 at Calle del Guerrero). This Holy Trinity church, located on the Plaza de la Trinidad was completed around 1643. Outside this canary-yellow building is a statue of Pedro Romero, who lived in Cartagena at no. 10 Calle del Guerrero. Romero emerged from his house in 1811 and decried, "Long live liberty!" which became the rallying cry to kick off the revolution. Along Calle 25, toward the entrance to the old city, is the **Convento San Francisco** , a monastery

Plaza de los Coches.

founded in 1555 but sacked by the French in 1559 before being rebuilt in 1590. It 1610 it became the first seat of the Spanish inquisitors, and it's on the front courtyard where a determined crowd declared independence from Spain on November 11, 1811. Today it's mostly a commercial center, but there are some beautiful galleries around the internal courtyard.

Nearby, on Calle 25 is the **Iglesia de la Tercera Orden** ❶ (Church of the Third Order), a whitewashed colonial church featuring a single steeple with twin bells. Both this church and the **Convento San Francisco** are just south of the **Centro de Convenciones** ❸ (Calle 24, no. 81-344; tel: 654 4000), which is Cartagena's main convention center. Built in 1972, the center seats around 4,000. If there isn't an event scheduled, see if you can find a guide to show you around. At night, near the arches leading into the walled city, vendors set up stands selling shrimp cocktails (known as *ceviche* in Colombia, unlike in Peru). There is a month-long Feria Artesania (craft fair) held

the in **Parque del Centenario** ❶ each year, but the month in which it is held changes from year to year. For more details, see www.artesanosdelparque centenario.blogspot.co.uk.

THE WALLED CITY

Walk through the Puerta del Reloj from Getsemaní and you'll arrive at the **Plaza de los Coches** ⓜ. This is one of Cartagena's most iconic plazas in the old city, but it has a dark past. Originally it was the site of the slave market, but then it became a sort-of transportation hub for embarking carriages. The long galleries here, at the base of the colonial buildings, offer much-needed respite from the sun's relentless assault. Inside them you'll find the Portal de los Dulces, a confectionery store selling cookies, *dulce de coco* (coconut brittle), and much more. There are also a number of fine bars with seating inside as well as patio tables. Sit outside during the day or night and you may well be treated to an impromptu music or dance performance.

Horse-drawn carts and taxis head toward the Naval Museum.

Just south and around the corner from Los Coches is the **Plaza de la Aduana** N, which features a large white statue of Christopher Columbus surrounded by flower bushes. Behind the plaza are the **Palacio Municipal** and the **Casa del Marqués del Premio Real**, which was the onetime home of the King's representative from Spain. On the corner is the **Museo de Arte Moderno** O (Museum of Modern Art; tel: 5-664 5815; www.mamcartagena.org; Mon–Fri 9am–noon, Sun 4pm–9pm; free last Sun of month), a two-story museum focusing mostly on Latin American art from the 1950s onward.

A 17th-century Jesuit church and monastery, the **San Pedro Claver** (Mon–Fri 8am–5.30pm, Sun 8am–5pm) is located near the museum at **Plaza San Pedro**. It is named after a local monk, Peter Claver, who was known as El Apóstol de los Negros (The Apostle of the Blacks) as he lent his lifelong energies to the neglected and the oppressed, and supported the liberation of slaves. Often he would go door-to-door begging and give the money he received to the African slaves traded in Cartagena. Claver died in 1654 and was canonized in 1896 by Pope Leo XVIII. His body is kept over the altar in a glass coffin. Upstairs rooms form a museum featuring items used by Claver, including maps and furniture.

The **Baluarte San Francisco Javier**, a fortification at the southwest end of the old city, is worth a visit even if you aren't into climbing up old walls. This is probably the best place for a relaxing sunset drink in all of Cartagena, so pull up a patio table there at **Bar el Baluarte** P (www.baluartesfj.com) and wash away the day's heat with a luxury cocktail. Nearby, at the **Plaza Santa Maria** Q is the **Museo Naval del Caribe** (Calle San Juan de Dios, no. 3–62; tel: 5-664 9672; www.museonavaldelcaribe. com; daily 8am–5pm), which features old nautical maps from the colonial

era, armaments, indigenous artifacts, and much more.

Also nearby, at the corner of Calle Ricaurte, is the old **Convento Santa Teresa**, a convent founded in 1609 for Carmelite nuns. The building has had many uses since, acting as a prison, a school, a barracks, and, in the 1970s, a police headquarters. The Banco Central purchased the building and it has since been turned into the Charleston Santa Teresa Hotel. Non-guests are allowed to enter the hotel's public areas.

Other sites worth visiting in the old city include **El Bodegón de la Candelaria** R (Calle Las Dama, no. 3–64), a restored colonial house that's over 300 years old, with white balconies and yellow walls. Supposedly a priest who lived in the home during its earliest days saw an image of the Virgin Mary, and there's a shrine in the room where the vision occurred. The green and leafy **Plaza de Bolívar** S is located one block away and features an equestrian statue of the Liberator. As you've surely gathered by now, you won't find

Museum of Modern Art.

> **Tip**

Colonial homes aren't known for their density, so expect the walls in most colonial accommodations options in the walled city to be on the thinner side. The exceptions are the most luxurious of refurbished hotels.

a Simón Bolívar statue anywhere in Colombia that doesn't exude valor and stateliness. Impromptu shows often occur here, and if you're lucky you may see some cumbia dancers moving to the rhythms from the Palenque region just south of Cartagena.

On the west side of the plaza is the **Palacio de la Inquisición** (Mon–Fri 9am–6pm), the premises where the Inquisition set up shop. The tribunal's jurisdiction included all of New Grenada, including Venezuela, Panama, and Nicaragua. The current building dates from 1706 and, all told some 800 people were sentenced to death on this site for 'Crimes against the Christian Faith.' It operated until revolution broke out in 1811, and was eradicated altogether when the new country was formed in 1821. The well-preserved stone door is the most ominous thing about the exterior of the museum, and the rest is a rather pleasant example of colonial Baroque complete with whitewashed walls and wooden balconies. However, the various torture and execution implements on display inside

Alfresco dining, Plaza de Santo Domingo.

serve as a reminder of the building's violent past.

Opposite the Inquisition museum is the **Museo del Oro Zenú** (Tue–Sat 9am–5pm, Sun 10am–3pm; free), another satellite branch of the national Museo del Oro, this one featuring pre-Columbian gold artifacts and pottery from the nearby Zenú indigenous region, which is located south of Cartagena at the marshlands of the Sinú, Magdalena, and San Jorge rivers. From the 2nd to the 10th century, these areas enjoyed the densest population of indigenous, and many of the artifacts on display are from this time period. At the northwest corner of the park is the **Catedral de Cartagena**. This church has been through a lot: it was completed in 1612 after being nearly destroyed by Sir Francis Drake. It was renovated twice in the 20th century and is fairly humble by Colombian colonial church standards, although the interior features a marble pulpit and gilded altar.

Across the street from the plaza is the long, white **Palacio de la Proclamación** ❶, which is named after the proclamation of the declaration of independence and was once a governor's residence. Nearby is the **Convento Santo Domingo** ❶, regarded in some circles as the oldest church in Cartagena, with constructing beginning around 1551. The present monastery replaced the old one in the 17th century, and today the outside of the church is beginning to look its age. Inside the church, behind a Baroque 19th-century altar, there is a 16th-century carving of Christ. Adjacent to the church is the **Plaza Santo Domingo**, which might just be the busiest section of the old city. There is no shortage of places to eat and drink here. The Botero sculpture on the plaza, *La Gorda*, is a delightfully corpulent alternative to the colonial surroundings.

North of Santo Domingo is the **Casa del Marqués de Valdehoyos** ❶ (Calle

de la Factoría, no. 36–47), a picture-perfect mansion that was once home to the Marquess of Valdehoyos, a slave-holding sugar magnate. Inside is great woodworking, from the chandeliers to the balustrades. Northeast of here you'll find **Plaza Merced**, which is bordered by a church and convent of the same name. The church was founded in 1618, and is now the **Teatro Heredia**, an opulent concert hall. Walk east two blocks and you'll arrive at Calle de la Universidad, at the end of which is the **Monastery San Augustín** , which was completed in 1580 but has been the home of the Universidad de Cartagena since 1828.

Walk along Baudillo (Carrera 7) and you'll arrive at the **Iglesia Santo Toribio de Mogrovejo**. It has a Baroque altar and, interestingly, you can still see the damage caused by a cannon-ball that went through the church in 1741 and lodged in the west wall. Last but not least, book lovers will want to visit the **Casa de Gabriel García Márquez** ✪ (located behind the Santa Clara Hotel), on the corner of Calle del Curato. This was the Cartagena home of Colombia's favorite son, and it only makes sense that the born Costeño made his home in the historic heart of the Colombian coast.

THE SAN DIEGO QUARTER

No matter where you stroll in Cartagena's historic districts, you won't be found wanting for restaurants. Even so, the San Diego quarter, located in the north of the walled city, is known for its large and varied selection of truly quality eateries. Ground zero for exploring this area is the intimate **Plaza Fernández de Madrid**, with its statue of the statesman, scientist, and former president of New Grenada in the early 1800s. There are good restaurants around the plaza, but head north and you'll find some real gems.

BOCAGRANDE

Bocagrande is where colonial Cartagena ends and the modern metropolis takes over. The area is less than one kilometer (just over half a mile) from the walled city, yet it feels a

> **Fact**
>
> East from the walled city, 150 meters up at Cerro La Popa, is the Convento La Popa (daily 8.30am–5.30pm). It was founded in 1607 by the Augustine Order of Fathers. In the complex, you'll have access to the Augustine church as well as the restored convent. You can arrange for a tour up the hill through a hotel or hostel, or pay a taxi driver around US$12–15 to take you up and back.

View towards Bocagrande.

million miles away. This southern part of Cartagena is unmissable: shimmering apartment buildings, hotels, and condominiums jut into the sky, and tower cranes are ever at work erecting new homes for Colombia's privileged elite. Locals come here for the beach, but, as with most beaches flanking the city, the water is nothing to write home about. However, it does get better farther south, toward the Hilton. On the southern tip of the area is the Fuerte Castillo Grande, which was built to protect Cartagena's inner harbor. To get to Bocagrande take a bus heading south from the entrance to the walled city, the Puerto del Reloj.

MARBELLA AND THE NORTH

Marbella ⓨ is a beach used mainly by locals, roughly one kilometer north of the walled city, past Plaza Las Bóvedas, which is a structure dating to 1799 with 12-meter high walls. At the base of it are a number of stores that used to be dungeons. During the week Marbella Beach is quieter than

Bocagrande, although it often isn't great for swimming due to strong currents. Just beyond, the promontory is lined with new high-rise hotels with private beach access.

Beyond that is the route to Playa Manzanillo, a remote beach about 10km (6 miles) from Cartagena, located in the tiny town of Manzanillo. This is a great place to come get away from the city and have whole stretches of coastline to yourself.

ISLA DE TIERRABOMBA

In the south, between Bocagrande and Barú Island is **Tierrabomba**, an island that acts as a natural barrier between Cartagena and the open sea. Fuerte San Fernando overlooks the bay from the southern tip of the island, and nearby Isla de Barú has the Fuerte San José. At one time these two forts were connected by chains in order to dissuade pirate attacks. Bocachica Beach is the main strip of sand here, but the water isn't the cleanest. Boats leave for Tierrabomba from the **muelle turistico** (tourist pier) ⓩ.

Fuerte de San Fernando on Tierrabomba Island.

ISLA DE BARÚ

When tourists and locals want a quick escape to typically beautiful Caribbean beaches, they come to **Isla de Barú**. It is the closest island to Cartagena, and one that is linked via road as well as by waterways. The tourist boats stop at **Playa Blanca**, the most famous beach in the area. Its pristine white sands and crystalline waters are the reasons people come here. There are some fish restaurants here, the most notable of which is **Gabriel** (open daily). Take caution when swimming, as some have reported careless jet-skiers speeding too close to shore and frightening the bathers. There are some lodging options here as well as hammock rentals and camping. If you come in the morning you'll find the beach can be quite crowded, but it calms down once the last arrival boats have left in the early afternoon.

To arrive at Playa Blanca by car, you can take a shared taxi for US$7 per person. Alternatively, take a bus from Cartagena's center to Pasacaballo and then a ferry across the Canal del Dique (the waterway separating Barú from Cartagena). Faster boats depart from the **Mercado Bazurto** between 7am–9.30am daily.

To the far southwest is an archipelago of some 30 islands that fall under the purview of Cartagena. These also make up the **Parque Nacional Natural Corales del Rosario y San Bernardo**. These coral islands are located 45-minutes from the Bay of Cartagena and are characterized by low-lying and densely vegetated terrain with the occasional narrow stretch of sand peaking out from the water. This is another of Cartagena's star beach getaways, and many head straight for **Isla Grande**, the biggest and most protected of the islands, with plenty of avian and aquatic life on display. There are also a number of islets that make for excellent snorkeling. Day tours to the island leave from la Bodeguita tourist pier in Cartagena between 7am–9am and return at 4–5pm. The tours include round trip tickets and lunch on the island.

Isla de Barú.

📷 COLONIAL ARCHITECTURE IN CARTAGENA

Cartagena is a popular tourist attraction today precisely because of its well-preserved colonial architecture, which transports the visitor back in time.

Cartagena de Indias was one of the first municipalities founded by the Spanish in Colombia, back in year 1533. Originally conceived as a humble port town, it grew quickly to become a seat of power in the New World and a key player in the expansion of the Spanish Empire. Nearly all the gold that was shipped back to Spain from Colombia passed through Cartagena, so designing it as a fortress city secure from invasions and attacks was a necessity.

It is for this reason that the architecture here stands out from other well-preserved colonial areas in the country. Military structures exist here alongside homes and religious institutions of the colonial era. In the walled city alone there are some 12 different religious buildings dating back to the 16th century.

To stroll the streets of Cartagena is to walk through history. Spend even a couple of hours here and it's not difficult to see why, in 1984, Unesco named Cartagena de Indias a World Heritage Site. It's possible to walk along the wall and visit the forts. From the various ramparts on the west you have a good vantage point to look into the walled city on one side, and see the Caribbean Sea on the other.

Colorful houses in the old city.

A colorful Cartagena street.

Clock tower at the entrance to Cartagena's old city.

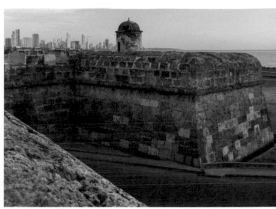

La muralla, the wall that surrounds the old city.

The walled city

A 4km (2-mile) wall, *la muralla*, surrounds Cartagena and took over 100 years to build. The Spanish Crown ordered it to be built to protect against incoming attacks and enemies of Spain. However, the wall also existed to maintain the social status quo. The aristocracy lived within the walls in the old city, while the artisans and workers lived just outside in Getsemaní. The walls acted as a barrier to keep the poor and working classes from offending the upper classes with their presence.

However, the wall wasn't Cartagena's only defense. It was supplemented by fortresses such as the Castillo San Felipe de Barajas and the Fort San Fernando, which were built around the late 16th century. In the early 17th century the walls were reinforced and a damn was built between Tierrabomba and Cartagena, effectively cutting off one of the two principal waterways leading into the city.

Within the walls of the old city you can still see these old great houses and places of worship once used by the aristocracy. The houses line the cobblestone streets and are notable for their wooden balconies and white-washed exteriors. These homes typically consisted of multiple stories and were located around a central courtyard.

San Felipe de Barajas fort.

Casa de la Aduana and San Pedro Claver church reflected in the Bahia de las Animas.

Peeering into the old city at dusk.

CARIBBEAN COAST

At the north of Colombia, where the land meets the sea, you'll find endless stretches of pure Caribbean coastline, which is home to some of the most romantic destinations in the country.

The roots of Colombia as a nation can be traced directly to its Caribbean coastline. It was on this area of South America's coastline that the first Spanish explorers arrived, and it is at modern day Santa Marta where the first official settlement was founded. It was from these shores that Spanish armies first moved down the Magdalena River toward the Andes, in search of gold and the famed lost city of El Dorado. It was also here that the Spanish built a great fortress city to protect their spoils, Cartagena de Indias. When revolutionary fever swept the country, some of the most critical battles, power grabs, and gambits played out in the theater of the Caribbean.

To say that Colombia began with the first European arrivals would be a misnomer. As a society, Colombia started some 10,000 years ago with the earliest hunter-gatherer tribes, migrants from Mesoamerica, who made their way to the front door of the continent, Colombia's Caribbean coast, before continuing southward along the same bodies of water later traveled by the Europeans. These early Caribbean people were known as the Kalina, and through the years they evolved into agrarian societies until their descendants, the Tairona, had established nothing short of an empire in and around the Sierra Nevada de Santa

Marta mountains. At the height of their power they were one of the most highly populated indigenous groups in the country, aside from the Muisca of the Andes. The Tairona and the Muisca both spoke a language called Chibcha, which was the principal linguistic group in the country at the time.

As the Tairona people lived in some of the most remote and inaccessible parts of the coast, they were able to preserve their bloodline despite the best attempts by Spanish authorities to eradicate them. Today the

Main Attractions
Santa Marta
Ciudad Perdida
Quinta de San Pedro
  Alejandrino
Rodadero
Parque Nacional Tayrona

**Maps on pages
196, 198**

Barranquilla Carnival.

descendants of the Tairona are the Kogi people, and they still reside in the Sierra Nevada de Santa Marta and have autonomous control of their land. Various national parks and NGOs are here, including the Tairona Heritage Trust (www.taironatrust. org), and they exist to preserve the culture of Colombia's Caribbean peoples as well as the coastal environment. It was the Tairona who believed – as the Kogi believe today – that the earth is the true mother of us all, and that to pollute or defile land is to blaspheme against God.

THE CULTURE

Just as the Bogatanos and the Caleños have their own pronounced culture, so do the Costeños. Eight of Colombia's 32 departments can be found along its 1,760km (1,094 miles) of Caribbean coastline, and some 10 million people reside here. That's a lot of culture, and these people stand out, demographically speaking, from other areas of the country. Predominantly Costeños make up a group referred to as *pardo*, a mix of European, indigenous, and Afro-Caribbean heritage.

New ethnic and cultural influences were introduced when a wave of immigrants from the Middle East arrived on the Colombian coast from places such as Turkey, Lebanon, and Syria. All of this co-mingling of different peoples over hundreds of years has benefited the culture of the coast greatly, and it can be seen, heard, and tasted in the area's art, music, and food.

BARRANQUILLA

Barranquilla ❶ was founded as a humble port city on the west bank of the Magdalena River, and it retains that distinction even today, except on a much grander scale. Barranquilla is a thriving port that is ever growing and ever expanding, with new shopping malls and apartment towers perpetually in construction in the affluent north of the city. To the east you'll discover working-class industrial neighborhoods where the congested streets are lined with factories, auto repair shops, bars, and motels. This central area near the river is quite run down, but

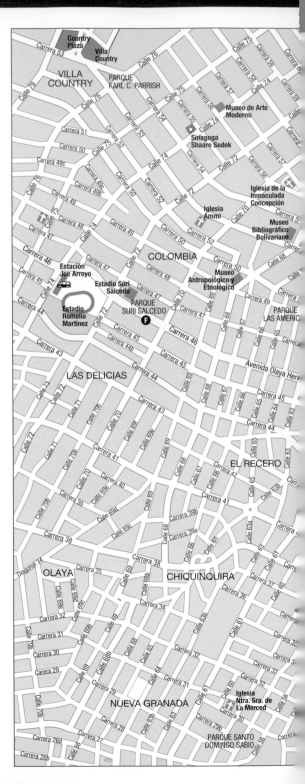

Barranquilla

0   500 m

0   500 yds

Caribbean Coast

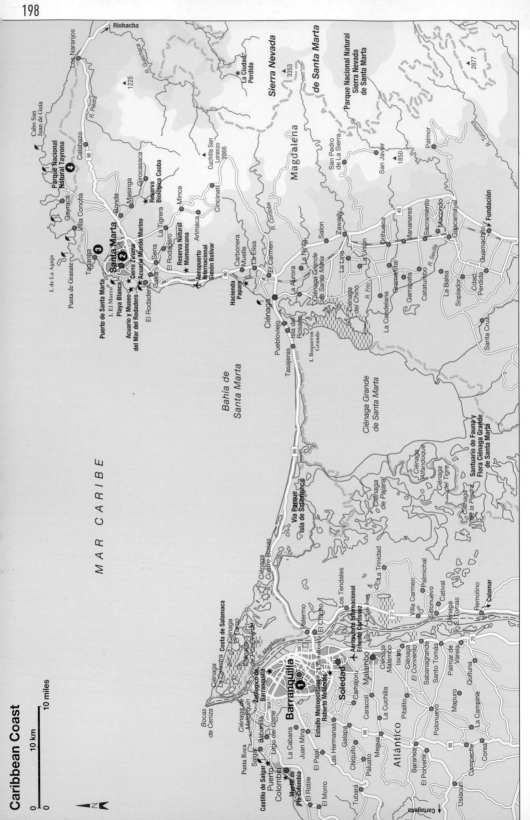

Caribbean Coast

0 — 10 km
0 — 10 miles

N

MAR CARIBE

Bahía de Santa Marta

Sierra Nevada de Santa Marta

Parque Nacional Natural Sierra Nevada de Santa Marta

Magdalena

Parque Nacional Natural Tayrona

La Ciudad Perdida

3353

2877

2866

1225

1850

Riohacha

Los Naranjos

Cabo San Juan de Guía

Punta de Granate

I. de La Aguja

R. Piedra

R. Guachaca

Calabazo

Guaracá

Villa Concha

Masinga

Bonda

Gairaca

Girocasaca

Reserva Biológica Caoba

Minca

Cuchilla San Lorenzo

Cincinati

Arimaca

Tagaraja

Santa Marta

Puerto de Santa Marta

I. El Morro

Playa Blanca

Acuario y Museo del Mar del Rodadero

Cerro Zizuma

Acuario Mundo Marino

El Rodadero

Gaira

Sena

La Tigrera

El Rodadero

Reserva Natural Mamancana

Aeropuerto Internacional Simón Bolívar

Carbonera

Muelle

La Elisa

El Carmen

Ciénaga

Hacienda Papare

Puebloviejo

Isla del Rosario

Tasajeras

I. Boquerón Grande

La Aurora

La Ninfa

Salon

Ciénaga Grande de Santa María

Ciénaga del Chino

La Caldelaria

R. Frío

R. Córdoba

La Unión

La Lira

Zawagí

R. Sevilla

Orihueca

Guamachal

Garrapata

Catatumbo

Guacamayal

Mananares

Sacramiento

Macongo

Guacamayal

La Balsa

Sopiador

Ciudad Perdida

Santa Cruz

Fundación

Palmor

San Pedro de la Sierra

San Javier

San Juan

45

Ciénaga Grande de Santa Marta

Santuario de Fauna y Flora Ciénaga Grande de Santa Marta

Vía Parque Isla de Salamanca

Ciénaga del Tigre

Ciénaga Alfandoque

Ciénaga de Pajaral

Ciénaga de la Piedra

Remolino

Calamar

Ciénaga de los Torvas

Ciénaga El Convento

Ciénaga Malambo

Sitionuevo

Palmichal

Villa Carmen

Catival

La Trinidad

Los Tendales

Palermo

Aeropuerto Internacional Ernesto Cortissoz

Los Reyes

Soledad

Malambo

Barranquilla

Zoológico de Barranquilla

Estadio Metropolitano Roberto Meléndez

Isidro

Sabanagrande

Santo Tomás

Palmar de Varela

Ponedera

Ciénaga de la Piedra

La Cuchilla

Carracoli

Megua

Pitalito

Polonuevo

Mapuro

La Campina

Corea

Campeche

Quituna

Usiacurí

Baranoa

El Potvenír

Sabanilla

Costa de Salamaca

Bocas de Ceniza

Punta Roca

Salgar

Puerto Colombia

Castillo de Salgar

Muelle de Pto Colombia

El Roble

El Morro

Juan Mina

La Cabana

Las Hermanas

Galapa

Chiquito

Paluato

Tubará

Atlántico

Ciénaga de Mallorquín

Ciénaga Cuatro Bocas

R. Magdalena

Cartagena

27

25

90

90A

90

this is where the real Quilleros (those from Barranquilla) live and work. Culture can be found here in the form of outdoor markets and museums.

Most visitors to Barranquilla are simply passing through via the international airport, which offers slightly better fares than nearby Cartagena. Barranquilla has played an important part in Colombia's history, represented by the stately Republican architecture found in the homes lining the streets of the old district. Also, it is in Barranquilla where Colombia holds its own version of Carnival – second only in size and scope to those in Brazil. 40 days before Easter, at the end of February or the beginning of March, this city becomes the scene of the country's biggest party (see page 202). In 2003 Unesco declared the Barranquilla Carnival a "masterpiece of the oral and intangible heritage of humanity."

GETTING YOUR BEARINGS

With over a million inhabitants, Barranquilla is hardly a tiny hamlet. Since most the suburban neighborhoods

outside of the center can seem difficult to differentiate from one to the other, it's best to have at least a general idea of the place by the time you arrive. If you are arriving by land then you will likely find yourself at the **Terminal de Transportes Metropolitano** (Carrera 14, no. 54–98; tel: 5-323 0034; www.ttbaq.com.co), the bus terminal located in the far south of town. To travel locally by bus, you can take the Transmetro, which runs north through the center and into the north of the city along the river. Another is Ruta 90/ Carrera 9, which runs east, crossing the Puente Pumarejo over the Magdalena River (great views over the bridge) and continuing through mangrove forests along the coast until you reach Santa Marta. Route 90 also heads west to Cartagena.

CENTRAL BARRANQUILLA

In the center you'll find the historic heart of Barranquilla, the **Plaza San Nicolas Ⓐ**. There's a statue of Christopher Columbus here, but the real standout is the **Catedral San Nicolás**

Bicycle rickshaw in Barranquilla.

de Tolentino (Carrera 42, no. 33–45), which sits at the west end of the plaza. The facade of this early 17th-century neo-Gothic church rises intimidatingly, with its twin steeples stabbing at the sky. The imposing design is softened by the church's cool white paint job with bright red trim, as well as soft arches hugging yawning windows and tall carved-wood doors. The interior keeps to the same color scheme, with more arches lining a long nave leading to the pulpit.

A few blocks north of the Plaza de San Nicolás is the **Paseo Bolívar** , a wide pedestrian-only throughway along Calle 34. Here, and extending west along Calle 45, you'll find the city's main commercial districts. At the end of the Paseo Bolívar at Carrera 46 is the **Parque Cultural del Caribe**, a modern green space that is home to the **Museo del Caribe** (Calle 36, no. 46–66; tel: 5-372 0581; www.culturacaribe.org; Tue–Thu 8am–5pm, Fri 8am–6pm, Sat–Sun 9am–6pm). This blocky grey monolith is a multistory introduction to the culture

of the coast. It features items from indigenous times, including ceramics and woven baskets, and the exhibits continue through the Spanish colonization and into more recent times. There are also audiovisual displays and video presentations. However, the text accompanying the exhibits is in Spanish only.

A few blocks farther west, along Carrera 43, you'll find another landmark in the city. Bar Restaurante La Cueva is a local institution, an upscale café famous as the preferred watering hole of rowdy Costeño journalists back in the 1950s, one of which was a young Gabriel García Márquez. The café has an attached store/foundation (fundacionlacueva.org) that sells books and promotes cultural events.

WEST OF THE CENTER AND FARTHER NORTH

Just northwest of the Paseo Bolivar is the **Plaza de la Paz Juan Pablo II** (also known as the Plaza de la Paz). This plaza is known for being home to the other of the two most famous

Barranquilla's main beach.

churches in Barranquilla, the **Catedral Metropolitana María Reina** (Carrera 45, no. 53–140; tel: 5-385 4689), which looms over the plaza's west end. Completed in 1982, it's a newer alternative to the Catedral San Nicolas Tolentino, but just as grand. The Modernist building is an architectural marvel of the city due to its large and rectangular front facade, which features seven dominating stained-glass windows in the shape of diamonds. Inside, the stained-glass mosaics really comes to life, flooding the room with color and complimenting a pyramid just at the top of the building, which also features intricate glass images on pious themes. Also inside is a flowing sculpture of Christ hanging over the pulpit, which could only be the work of famed Colombian sculptor Rodrigo Arenas Betancourt. Even if you don't go in, swing by at night and you'll likely be treated to a show when they light up the entire building.

A dozen or so blocks to the northwest from the Catedral Metropolitana you'll find one of the true gems of the city, the **Museo Romantico 🄴** (Carrera 54, no. 59–199; daily 8am–5pm). The museum is housed in a lovely old Republican mansion that was donated by a wealthy family, and features various items detailing the history of Barranquilla, including a number of Carnival costumes. There's also a room dedicated to García Márquez that features some of his notes, first editions, and typewriters. In truth lack of funding has taken a toll on this museum, and it is struggling – which is all the more reason to make a visit.

To the very northwest of the city, where the Pacific Ocean mercifully becomes visible, are upscale suburbs teeming with shopping malls, boutiques, and fancy bars and restaurants. These areas include El Prado, Altos del Prado, and Ciudad Jardín. One lovely park around here, located at Calle 72, is **Parque Tomás Suri Salcedo 🄵**.

AROUND BARRANQUILLA

The city of Barranquilla may not offer the pristine beaches of other coastal areas like Santa Marta or Cartagena, but head just a few kilometers outside of the city and you'll find stretches of sand worth the effort. One such option is **Puerto Colombia** (www.puertocolombia-atlantico.gov.co; buses leave from the Paseo Bolívar), which is located about 19km (12 miles) to the west of Barranquilla. The historical legacy of the beach was that it was the original ocean port of Barranquilla, and the pier that juts out from its shore was built in 1900. It's a nice beach for relaxing, but don't expect clear water. If you really want to kick back and enjoy life here, hit up the beach bar at Hotel Pradomar and sip a fruity cocktail under a *palapa*. Good surfing can be found here from February through May, when the waves are at their peak. Continue traveling northeast back toward Barranquilla and you'll hit some other good beach spots, like **Salgar**, and closer to the river you'll find **Los Flores**, both of

Catedral Metropolitana María Reina.

BARRANQUILLA CARNIVAL

"Quien lo vive, es quien lo goza!" ("Those who live it are those who enjoy it") – the official slogan of the Carnaval de Barranquilla.

When we think of the great carnivals and parades in the Western hemisphere, Rio de Janeiro's Carnival and New Orleans' Mardi Gras instantly come to mind. Although those two juggernauts have rightly earned their place on the Mount Olympus of revelry, other carnivals exist and they're just as worthwhile. The most dedicated of partiers will want to head to a coastal city in Colombia for the Carnaval de Barranquilla (www.carnavaldebarranquilla.org).

THE PARTY BEGINS

Carnaval de Barranquilla kicks off on the Saturday before Ash Wednesday and features many hours of float processions led by the Carnival Queen. Officials describe the entire event as a folkloric and cultural celebration. Like other carnivals, the Carnaval de Barranquilla is a group effort, with community members working throughout the year making costumes

La Marimonda, a popular carnival character.

and choreographing the activities that make up the celebrations. The first such carnival took place in the 19th century, evolving from humble beginnings as a slave holiday. It has been going strong ever since, evolving into the world's second largest carnival outside Rio de Janeiro.

MUSIC AND DANCE

The music and dance of Barranquilla's Carnaval has influences in Africa, Spain, and Europe, and this is most apparent in the drum-heavy cumbia heard throughout the festivities. However, a variety of Caribbean music is celebrated here, including *porro*, *puya*, and *merecumbés*. The costumes, parades, and dances are elaborate. Some even take the name of various animals. One example is a popular song and dance performed during the carnival called *El Torito* (little bull), which originates from Spanish folk and Christmas songs.

THE CHARACTERS OF CARNAVAL

It's not uncommon to see the dancers wearing tribal masks indicative of the fauna of the region. Animals from donkeys to dogs to bulls are represented in these masks. One of the most popular characters is *La Marimonda*, a colorful hooded mask denoted by a comically oversized nose and big floppy ears. Out of all the characters in the carnival festival, this one's origins are wholly Colombian. The *Marimonda* was invented in Barranquilla as a type of harlequin character to symbolize merriment and mischief.

THE PARTY WINDS DOWN

Sunday sees the Great Parade, and Monday is filled with music from Caribbean bands and orchestras. The Tuesday before Ash Wednesday is the last gasp of Carnaval, featuring the symbolic burial of the character Joselito Carnaval, who represents the joy of the occasion. The next day is Ash Wednesday, the official start of Lent.

The Barranquilla Carnival is a truly epic party. However, first-timers should pace themselves. This is an event that requires stamina – it's a marathon, not a sprint. Also, be prepared for the most common of Barranquilla Carnaval traditions – revelers spraying one another with cans of foam.

which have no shortage of great seafood shacks and restaurants.

There are some little-discovered gems of towns the more you travel south along the Magdalena River from Barranquilla. One such option is **Soledad**, a little colonial town notable mostly for its center cathedral with multiple red-painted domes. In a way this church is reminiscent of the Catedral San Nicolás in Barranquilla, but this version is smaller and with gold trim around a white facade instead of red. Continue south and you'll arrive at **Santo Tomás,** where you'll want to go on Good Friday if you enjoy the spectacle of processions of locals flagelating themselves with whips.

A national park worth pointing out in the area is **Via Parque Isla de Salamanca**. This island southeast of Barranquilla and just across the Magdalena is mostly made up of mangrove swamps. Initially it was created to protect these mangroves after the construction of the highway running from Barranquilla to Santa Marta destroyed much of the ecosystem. There isn't much tourism infrastructure here, but it's a decent place to see wildlife, including some 99 species of reptiles and 199 species of birds, and in 2000 it was named a Unesco Biosphere Reserve.

SANTA MARTA

Santa Marta ❷ is the place where Europeans first arrived, and the same place where death took hold of the man who gave Colombia its independence. Today, Santa Marta is the capital of Magdalena Department, and most of it is working-class residential neighborhoods and budget shopping districts, where local Samarios (residents of Santa Marta) pack the streets day-in and day-out. The road from Barranquilla to Santa Marta passes along beaches and mangroves home to shantytowns and all but abandoned fishing villages. When you do arrive at the picturesque heart of Santa Marta, on the bay, colonial buildings replace the shanties and vacationers outnumber the destitute. It's hard to imagine such

Holy week celebrations in Santo Tomás.

⊙ Fact

Santa Marta is officially the first Spanish settlement in Colombia, having been founded by the conquistador Rodrigo de Bastidas back in 1525.

The beach at Santa Marta.

a tiny place being home to so much storied history, the scene of so many happenings that all led to Colombia becoming Colombia.

Up until the early years of the 16th century it was only the peaceful Tairona people who occupied this stretch of the coast, trading between tribes and living in harmony with the earth. Then, when the Spanish did arrive, they found a native people adorned in gold and a land location within close proximity to the Magdalena River, thus providing a route inland. No wonder they decided to stay and form a settlement. Of course the Spanish never reaped their instant riches, and by the end of the century relations with the natives had become somewhat contentious. Some of the Tairona managed to escape to the hills, where they were able to preserve their bloodline, and their descendants, the Kogi people, still occupy the same area today.

Santa Marta continued to thrive, despite more than a few raids by British, Dutch, and French attackers. However, it was nearby Cartagena de Indias that the Spanish Crown made their principal seaport, and they fortified the city accordingly. With no real stores of valuables, and precious little sea traffic, Santa Marta would slowly decline in importance over the centuries, to the point it became nothing more than a charming colonial coastal town. Still, it is a very well preserved one, and many old buildings dating back to the 1500s populate its historic center. All in all there's a lot to see in this Caribbean colonial marvel, but luckily the town is small enough that visiting its myriad museums and sites means never walking more than a few blocks. Conveniently, the town is a perfect jumping off point to what might be the most beautiful national park in the entire country, the Parque Nacional Tayrona.

FINDING YOUR WAY INLAND

Santa Marta is located on an ocean bay, but it also lies at the mouth of the Río Manzanares, which runs southeast through town. This river is one of many that drains the Sierra Nevada

de Santa Marta mountains. Standing at Carrera 1, which runs north and south along the waterfront, you'll be able to see the tall green cliffs that hug both ends of the bay. Between Carrera 1 and the water is a seafront promenade, which is probably the most attractive part of town, especially at sunset. Here you'll find plenty of upscale restaurants and nightlife options, but this area is much better for a casual stroll or picnic by the water than it is for revelry.

Walking the promenade you'll also notice that the city hasn't forgotten its indigenous residents. There are various statues by the water celebrating Tairona heritage, including one on the south end of town, at Carrera 1 and Calle 22, called *La Herencia Tairona*, which features a proud indigenous couple holding court over their place in the world. The best place to get your bearings around here is at Carrera 1 and Calle 15. This is the center of Santa Marta, and if you head east on Calle 15 you'll pass right along Plaza Bolívar.

THE CENTER

This is where you'll find all the grand plazas, old colonial buildings, and rich museums for which the city is famous. Just know that perpetual work is required to maintain many of these old buildings, so if luck isn't on your side you might be turned away at a museum due to renovation. Still, the expansive and leafy **Plaza Bolívar**, complete with an equestrian statue of the Liberator, will in all likelihood remain open now and forever. This plaza is also a good base for exploring other parts of the city.

Nearby is one of the oldest buildings in Santa Marta, the **Casa de la Aduana**, which is now the **Museo del Oro** (Calle 14, no. 2–07; tel: 5-421 0251; Tue–Sat 9am–5pm, Sun 10am–3pm; free). This old colonial customs house dates back to 1531, but the museum it now houses was inaugurated in 2014. The museum showcases the history of Santa Marta through multiple exhibits over two floors. Like other gold museums, this one features pre-Columbian archeological finds, such as ceramics

Exploring Ciudad Perdida.

⊘ CIUDAD PERDIDA

The demographic growth of the indigenous Tairona people over the centuries before colonialism meant they needed developed areas where they could live in communities. Out of all of their villages, none are as famous as Ciudad Perdida (the Lost City). This 13-hectare (32-acre) city was located in the Sierra Nevadas and at its height was home to up to 2,400 Tairona who lived in round houses set on stone-paved terraces. An even larger – although slightly less awe-inspiring – former city and archeological site, known as El Pueblito, exists nearer the coast and was probably home to around 3,000 Tairona. Today you can visit this archeological site by booking treks from tour operators in Santa Marta. The tours involve trekking four or five days through the jungle and typically cost around US$600.

and gold work produced by the Tairona people. In the building there's also a scale model of the Ciudad Perdida, Colombia's premier indigenous ruins. Before being converted to a customs house in 1776, the Casa de la Aduana was a church-owned residence, home to the Chief Justice of the Inquisition. Some say it was even the first brick building in Colombia.

Out of all the colonial churches in Colombia, the **Catedral Basílica de Santa Marta** (Carrera 4, no. 16–02; mass times: Mon–Fri noon and 6pm, Sun 7am, 10am, noon and 6pm) might just be the most impressive. This isn't because it's the biggest or most ornate church in the country, although the domed roof and massive corner bell tower radiate a brilliant bright white in the afternoon sun, but because it sits on the former site of what is said to be the first Catholic church in Colombia. Some even believe it is on the site of first Catholic church on the continent, which was founded around 1531. However, the church that stands here today was finished in 1766. Inside it's

as virginal white as it is on the outside, with long, shrine-lined aisles leading to a grey marble altar, winged angels standing sentinel on either side of the pulpit and hoisting candelabras to the sky. The church held the remains of Simón Bolívar from his death in 1830 and until they were transferred to Venezuela in 1842.

Five blocks south of Parque Bolívar is the intimate and aptly named **Parque de los Novios** (also known as Parque Santander). It's a smaller park with a white gazebo and an imposing statue of Santander in the center. The area is fronted by whitewashed government buildings whose elegant colonial architecture stands out. On the south side is the **Palacio Justicia**, and to the east is the **Antigua Escuela Cuarto**, built in 1927 as a girls' school that was run by nuns and now part of the Palace of Justice. As for beach fun in the center, most locals just head to the **center bay**. You're flanked by shipping cranes to the north and the marina to the south, and everywhere along the beach you'll find street

Santa Marta's artisan market.

vendors selling everything from beer and shrimp cocktails to shaved ice and *chuzos* (meat skewers). Just back from the beach is a nice **mercado artesanal** (artisan market; daily 8am–9pm) selling good knit bags, clothing, jewelry, and handicrafts.

THE QUINTA DE SAN PEDRO ALEJANDRINO

The **Quinta de San Pedro** (Avenida Del Libertador s/n; tel: 301-241 5913; daily 9am–4.30pm; open later during high season), a small villa on a former 17th-century sugar plantation, is where the great Liberator, Simón Bolívar, spent his final days. The general who routed Spanish armies seemingly at will, who danced away the night before going to war the next morning, whose prowess on the battlefield was matched only by his zest for life and commitment to liberty, arrived here penniless and infirmed in 1830. At the end his body was racked with tuberculosis, having prematurely aged him decades beyond his 47 years. He died surrounded by a few close friends and associates; and on that day, December 17, 1830, Bolívar's dream of a united South America died with him.

The Museum itself is little more than the home with the room where Bolívar spent his final hours, and includes a few personal items. Paintings and memorabilia from the 18th and 19th centuries are also on display here. Also here is the **Fundacion Museo Bolivariano de Arte Contemporeano** (www.museobolivariano.org.co; daily 9am–5.30pm), a museum featuring contemporary works by Latin American artists. Enjoy a stroll around the expansive grounds of the villa, taking in the various monuments to Colombia's greatest hero, his only remaining contemporaries the old cedar and *saman* trees dotting the gardens.

RODADERO

Despite the tourist bars, nightclubs and restaurants, Santa Marta is more of a laidback colonial city. The more modern and vibrant **Rodadero**, located just 4km (2 miles) south of Santa Marta

Rodadero Beach.

⊙ Tip

The indigenous Kogi tribe (descendants of the Tairona people) still have authority over Parque Nacional Tayrona. Consequently, they typically close it once a year (usually February) for one month for spiritual cleansing purposes.

Taganga beach.

(minibuses run between Santa Marta and Rodadero, leaving from Carrera 1), is where you can find the hustle and bustle. The seemingly endless **Rodadero Beach** is lined with high-rise hotels and restaurants (all serving solid *pescados* and *mariscos*). Much of the beach is tree-lined, providing welcome shade, and street vendors roam the promenade selling drinks and seafood cocktails. At night you'll find people lining the embarcadero, blasting music, drinking, and co-mingling. It's a great time, but you should also look out for petty crime.

From the north end of the beach, head to the **Acuario Rodadero** (Aquarium; tel: 317-364 1113; www.acuario rodadero.co), where seals, sharks, and dolphins are on display, as well as myriad other aquatic animals. From here you can take a short walk north to **Playa Blanca**, another popular local beach, although much more secluded than Rodadero Beach. There are plenty of thatched-hut beach bars and restaurants here where you can enjoy some fried fish and ice cold beer.

TAGANGA

Located 3km (2 miles) north of Santa Marta is the picturesque fishing village of **Taganga ❸** (15 minutes by bus, leaving from Carrera 1 in Santa Marta). The pace of life is still slow here, but recently development and the tourism boom have knocked most of the sleepiness out of the village, as its streets are now prowling with backpackers and vacationers. However, Taganga still radiates a more relaxed vibe than Santa Marta, and the new tourism infrastructure means there are some good options for diving and fishing operators along the coast. Just north and around the corner from Taganga is **Playa Grande**, another quasi-secluded beach perfect for a day of lazing, drinking and eating. Watching the sun set over the Taganga's main beach, after all the tiny wooden fishing vessels have returned and tied up for the day, is still one of the most pleasant ways in all of Colombia to pass the time. Continue east along the coast from Taganga and you'll reach the stunning **Parque Nacional Tayrona ❹** (see page 209).

PARQUE NACIONAL TAYRONA

Parque Nacional Tayrona isn't just the beautiful Caribbean image you see on the postcards – it's a place of great spiritual significance to the indigenous cultures of today and generations past.

Spend just a few minutes on the coast of Parque Nacional Tayrona (park hours 8am–5pm) and you'll see why the indigenous peoples were so protective of their lands. To the south are the lush green mountains of the Sierra Nevadas, and in front of you, you'll see pristine white-sand beaches fronting aquamarine seas and crystalline lagoons.

The Tairona people (whom the park was named after) preserved these pristine lands in accordance with their earth god, and luckily for us it's still here to be enjoyed today. Sadly, though, increasing tourism hasn't always spelled good news for this part of Colombia and the residents who still occupy this area of the Sierras, the Kogi people.

THE PARK

Parque Tairona runs 85km (53 miles) north along the coast from Tagonga, just outside of Santa Marta. Most of this stretch is still undeveloped, and just offshore are any number of coral reefs. Snorkeling is good here, and the best spots are Cabo San Juan de Guia and the smaller La Piscina beach. El Pueblito is one popular inland attraction; it is here you'll find the ruins of an indigenous community. Many of the beaches are ideal for swimming, except Arrecifes. This is a picture-perfect stretch of windswept sand, but riptides are frequent.

CABO SAN JUAN DE GUIA

When you see pictures advertising Parque Nacional Tayrona, you're likely seeing images of Cabo San Juan. This windswept cove is home to one of the country's most beautiful beaches, the iconic boulders hugging the sand. Jutting out from the middle of the beach sits an equally iconic *mirador* that offers sweeping views of the Caribbean. There are a couple beach restaurants and bars here that serve food here, mostly fried fish and coconut rice.

GETTING THERE

Buses leave every 15 minutes or so from the Mercado Publico (Calle 2, no.8–81) to the El Zaino entrance of Parque Nacional Tayrona. However, most people choose to book a package to the park through local providers, because once you arrive it's still a long way to the nearest beach. If you choose to take another bus from the entrance, they'll drop you off near to Cañaveral Beach. Here you'll see the famous 'ecohabs' (www.ecohabsantamarta.com), individual thatched-hut accommodations that overlook the water.

WHAT TO KNOW

Some of the bays in the western end of the park, closest to Santa Marta, are easily accessible by road. These include Villa Concha, just 5km (3 miles) east of the city, Neguanje, and Playa Cristal. Just take one of the buses leaving from the Mercado Publico every day at 7am (return at 4pm). Camping is available in the park, including at a site near Cabo San Juan, which is usually crowded due to its gorgeous views. Prices are around US$5 per night for tents, and you can rent a hammock for around US$7 per night.

Cabo San Juan del Guia.

📷 CARIBBEAN BEACHES

Forget Barbados, Grand Cayman, and the Bahamas – there are Caribbean beaches in Colombia that are in a different league altogether.

If you've only seen the Caribbean Coast from the ramparts of Cartagena, the chances are, you aren't too impressed. However, venture out of the cities and you'll find some fantastic beaches that rival anything found elsewhere in this much-romanticized part of the world.

Colombia's most famous beach, Playa Blanca, is located near Cartagena. Its idyllic white sands and crystalline waters could have been lifted straight from the pages of a travel magazine.

Parque Nacional Tayrona might be the greatest option for excursions along the Caribbean Coast. This national park, which is still under the purview of the Koji indigenous people, offers camping and plentiful coves to explore.

The island of San Andres is great for beach lovers, snorkelers and divers alike. Don't miss the beautiful Johnny Cay, with its fantastic beaches.

If you venture beyond the municipality of Santa Marta you'll find some great beaches too. Playa Cristal is one such option, and the waters are as clear as the name suggests.

If you head farther east from Santa Marta, into the Guajira Department, you'll arrive at the little village of Palomino, and one of the finest stretches of sand in the country. That said, the currents are often too strong for swimming, so exercise caution.

The iconic Cabo San Juan de la Guia.

On the beach at Palomino.

Red flag indicating that swimming is forbidden.

Looking out over the Caribbean Sea from under a tree in Sapzurro, near Capurganá.

Remote Capurganá

When people think of the Colombia's Chocó Department, they tend to think of the Pacific Coast. However, this area extends north around the southern borders of Panama – including on the Caribbean Sea. One of the great beaches here is in Capurganá, a village of around 1,500 people in the Acandí municipality of the Chocó Department. Despite being remote and expensive to get to (it's accessible only by sea or air), it is becoming increasingly popular among travelers and wealthy Colombians on vacation.

It's not difficult to see why this beach is so popular. It's surrounded by lush jungle on three sides and coral reefs offshore allow for excellent diving. There are two principal beaches here. La Caleta is at the northern end of the village, which has golden sands and is ideal for swimming. Playa de los Pescadores is ringed with palm trees and is more lagoon-like. Both make for an unforgettable day at the beach.

Playa Blanca.

Johhnny Cay, San Andrés.

Beach bar on Capurganá Beach.

VALLEDUPAR

Located just off the heavily trafficked tourist route is a city known for its warm culture, cool rivers, and one of the best music festivals in the country.

The city of Valledupar is located on a fertile plain in the northeastern part of the country, right between the Sierra Nevada de Santa Marta and Sierra de Perijá Mountains. Officially it is both the capital of César Department and the birthplace of vallenato music. To the uninitiated, vallenato is one form of *música tropical*, northern hybrid music that combines various styles to create something that is wholly unique and undeniably Colombian (see box). On most weekends, local Vallenatos (residents of Valledupar) play their namesake music loudly and proudly, helping them to wind down after a week filled with work and, more often than not, sun and heat.

HISTORY

The city of Valledupar has its roots in agriculture. It was originally founded for its potential as a farm and cattle-raising center, but there are also many coal mines in the area. In fact, this is the last of the northeastern fertile plains before the topography turns into the arid desert of Guajira. Its position between mountain ranges and near to the coast means that natives from different regions often passed through or made their homes here.

The area's dominant indigenous tribe, the Chimilia (a Chibcha-speaking people) were conquered by the

Iglesia de la Inmaculada Concepció.

Spanish in 1532, and a conquistador by the name of Hernando de Santana founded the city of Valledupar in 1550. The Chimilia didn't go without a fight, though, and such was their legacy that even the Spaniard founder officially recognized them, naming the city Valle de Ubar, after a famed Chimilia leader named Ubar. Over time the name of the city was shortened to Valledupar.

During colonization, not only did the city become an agricultural hotbed but it was also a center for imports for the entire Caribbean region, including

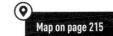

Main Attractions

Vallenato Festival
Galería Popular
Balneario Hurtado
Balneario La Mina
Balneario El Mojao

Map on page 215

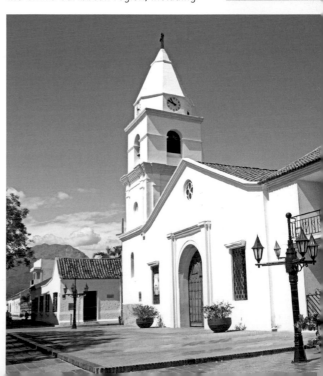

European cattle. As farming and cattle-raising continued to thrive in the area, the native population dwindled further. Once ideas of revolution began being whispered about, it was Valledupar that became one of the first cities to revolt against the Spanish Crown. In 1813 Valledupar proclaimed its independence.

In recent times Valledupar has suffered some tragic reversals. Despite rapid economic growth in the 1970s, the 80s were known for a period of political instability in the region. Some politicians, such as Juvenal Ovidio Ricardo Palerma, the leader of the leftist Patriotic Union (UP), headed for the hills and joined up with rebel groups like the FARC. This tragically led to mass murders and kidnappings, and since the 1980s thousands of people have been displaced due to violence and drug trafficking, with most of the rural farmers have relocated to the city. The United Self-Defense Forces of Colombia (AUC), made up of victims and landowners in the area, rose up to counter the attacks of the rebels, and

Vallenato statue.

this group did succeed in taking the region from guerrillas. The trade-off was that Valledupar was now in the hands of an unelected paramilitary force. In 2006, the AUC in the area of Valledupar demobilized. Since then the city has been on a tenuous road to peace and safety.

Overall Valledupar makes for a great stop during any Colombian journey. Mass tourism hasn't yet fully taken off here, and there seem to be live music concerts happening all the time, including the famed Vallenato Festival. There's also a well-preserved colonial center that features some great eateries and bars.

THE CLIMATE OF VALLEDUPAR

Like anywhere else in Colombia, altitude principally determines Valledupar's climate. The municipality sits low enough – 180 meters (600ft) above sea level – that it enjoys some of that Caribbean lowland heat, and its position between mountain ranges means much of that gets bogged down in the city. Daily average temperatures

⊘ VALLENATO AND VALLEDUPAR

Getting to know Colombia's various styles of *música tropical* is a real joy – a glimpse into the various cultures that have congregated here over the millennia. One iconic and indefatigably popular genre is vallenato. It not only has its roots in Valledupar, but still defines the city to this day. Hearing it for the first time, you'll note its two most prominent instruments: the *acordeón* (accordion), and the *guacharaca*, a percussion instrument, made from the trunk of a small palm tree. When a player scrapes the instrument with a metal fork it produces the unmistakably vallenato beat, often accompanied by a *caja vallenta*, a drum that was first introduced to the area by African slaves.

Like many northern Colombian musical styles, vallenato has many influences. Its roots are in cumbia, still a popular genre in the country and one that itself originated from *cumbe*, a style from African Guinea. Back then it was a courtship dance popular amongst the slaves, but over the years influences from European and indigenous instruments mixed together, and a new genre was born. Colombian cumbia was used as a rallying cry during the War for Independence. Being in Valledupar for the annual Fiesta de la Leylenda Vallenata (www.valledupar.com/festival), held every year at the end of April at the Parque de la Leyenda, is one of the great musical experiences Colombia has to offer.

are around 86°F (30°C), but the city's low altitude means that nights are often cool and refreshing. During the rainy season (February through April), Valledupar sometimes catches tropical storms moving in off the coast.

THE CITY OF VALLEDUPAR

The **bus terminal** (Carrera 7, Avenida Salguero, no. 44–156; tel: 5-571 6209) is located about 10–15 minutes south of the center, but a taxi shouldn't cost more than US$2–3. The best place to be based is around the **Plaza Alfonso López Ⓐ**, as it's located in the colonial heart of the city. Here, and the area immediately surrounding it, is where travelers will undoubtedly spend most of their time. A lovely mango tree sits on the south side of the expansive plaza, offering much-needed shade on the hotter days. Around the plaza locals sell drinks, ice cream, and *chuzos* (meat skewers) from carts.

A jutting statue, *La Revolucion en Marcha*, by Rodrigo Arenas Betancourt, dominates the entire area. Two nude figures in bronze soar toward the sky from cement pillars jutting out of the ground at a 30-degree angle. The expressionist work was commissioned by Governor Paulina Mejia Castro Monsalvo in the 1970s to commemorate Dr Alfonso López Pumajero, a progressive local politician. As Colombia's president from 1934–1938, López Pumajero ushered in a period of new agricultural and industrial policies, transformed university education, healthcare, and the tax system, improved workers' conditions, and introduced a social security initiative that modernized the country's economy. These measures also helped transform Valledupar from a sleepy village to a modern city with a thriving, diversified economy. The statue symbolizes the ascension and realization of the "Revolution in Progress," which was also the motto of López Pumajero's political campaign. Travel far and wide enough around Valledupar and you'll be treated to many other statues, many of which celebrate the culture and heritage of vallenato music.

On the northeast corner is the **Iglesia de la Inmaculada Concepción Ⓑ**

La Revolucion en Marcha statue.

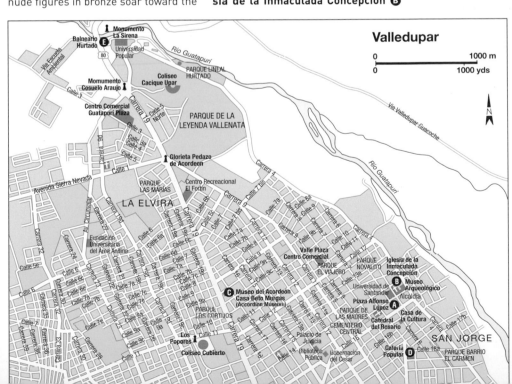

⊙ Tip

If you're planning on bathing in one of Valledupar's famous rivers, but it has been raining, be sure to wait at least a day. The day after rain, the rivers are often too muddy to be enjoyable.

(Church of the Immaculate Conception; www.diocesisdevalledupar.org; mass Mon–Fri 6:30am and 6pm, Sat 6:30am and 5pm, Sun 7am, 10am, 5pm, and 7pm), an 18th-century, whitewashed colonial church with white trim and a single corner bell tower. Nearby is the unmistakable white gallery of the **Casa de los Maestre Pavajeau**, which is worth a look. On the southeast corner is a fine restaurant called **Compae Chipuco** (Carrera 6, no. 16–05; tel: 5-580 5635; daily 8am–9pm), which also doubles as a cultural center and bookstore. The photographs on display here detail the city's history, the vallenato festival, and also include images of Gabriel García Marquez. There's also an exhibition here detailing the life of Consuelo Araújo Noguera, a journalist and one of the founders of the vallenato festival, who was killed by the FARC in 2001.

If you want to get a feel for one of the musical instruments that helps provide the pulse of this city, you can head a few blocks west of the plaza to the **Museo del Acordeón Casa Beto Murgas**

Locals by the Río Guatapurí.

(Accordion Museum; Carrera 17, no. 9a–18; tel 0-836 8877; www.museodelacordeon.com; Tue–Sat 9am–noon, 3–6pm, Sun 9am–1pm, closed Mon).

THE GALERÍA POPULAR

Those who want to explore other areas of town besides the colonial center should head a few blocks south to the **Galería Popular** Ⓓ (Mon–Sat 6am–6pm, Sun 6am–2pm), which is the largest and most bustling commercial area and market in the city. Even the few blocks leading up to it is an assault on the senses, as indoor/ outdoor retail stores peddle their wares – you've never see so many shoes for sale in your life! Also around the market are seemingly innumerable street vendors selling delicious iced juices like orange, watermelon, and *limonada*. The gallery's **food court** is one of the best dining options in the city, one approved by the locals who eat here every day. If this is your first taste of real Costeño food, expect lots of fried fish, beef, chicken, and pork.

BEATING THE HEAT ON THE RIVER

When locals want to go for a dip, they head to the north end of town where the Río Guatapurí cuts through the outskirts of the municipality. Just past the **Parque de la Leyenda** – the site of the vallenato festival, with capacity for 40,000 people – the bridge passes over the water and the **Balneario Hurtado** Ⓔ. This is one of the most popular sites in Valledupar as it is the best place to take a dip in the river. On sunny days the waters are clear and refreshing.

AROUND VALLEDUPAR

The outskirts of the city make for some of the finest excursions. The crown in jewel of tourism in the area is the town of **La Mina**, whose **Balneario La Mina** is a popular destination point for tourists and locals alike. Located 40km (25 miles) north of Valledupar, the *balneario* is a natural rock phenomenon on the Rió Badillo.

The snowmelt from the Sierra Nevada de Santa Marta feeds the river, and at this particular point it cuts through a network of prodigious grey-white stones, creating natural pools, spas, and mini-waterfalls with just enough current to allow for some easy body surfing. The sheer size of the stones – looking as they do like the partially submerged, calcified remains of mythical giants – also allows for some good diving in spots. Be sure to always test the depth of the water before diving in.

Just down from La Mina is another natural spa, **Balneario El Mojao**. Here you'll find some more waterfalls and natural pools. Part of the fun of coming to both El Mojao and La Mina is the palpable sense of community here. As tourism in Valledupar is not as developed as it is in established destinations like Medellín, Cartagena, or Bogotá, most of the bathers here are locals. They're laborers on a break, cooling off in the fresh mountain waters; young people just out from school; families with young kids in tow; or teenage boys who have come to show off to the girls.

The small town of **Atánquez** is located to the west of La Mina. It's a mountain town, sitting at approximately 2,000 meters (6,560ft) above sea level, and is inhabited mostly by the Kankuamo indigenous tribe, a Chibcha speaking people. It was founded in 1781 and outlasted the Spanish, but like many areas in and around Valledupar in the late 20th century, it suffered violence at the hands of rebel groups, like the FARC, and narcos in the area. Estimates place the death toll of Kankuamo people in Atanquez from 1986 to 2003 at 197. Making the worthwhile trip to La Mina is a perfect excuse to travel a bit farther and spend some time taking in the local indigenous customs.

The town also holds a Corpus Christi festival, a catholic ritual adapted by coastal Caribbean indigenous peoples, such as the Kankuamo. The celebration, which takes place on a Thursday in the last half of June, features music, elaborate costumes, and dances that represent the battle between good and evil. Locals dress as devils and Cucambas (birdlike representations of God). There are many great handwoven purses made by the indigenous for sale in this town – bags that can sell for hundreds of euros in the boutiques of Milan and Paris, but can be bought for around US$40 here.

A few kilometers east of La Mina, at the border of Guajira Department, is the village of **Patillal**, a great place to visit for those who want to learn a little more about Valledupar's rich musical heritage. In this little village, some of the great vallenato composers of the region were born, and they are commemorated here in the form of gold coins complete with birthdate and date of death. The memorials are located near the town church, and some notable composers include Rafael Escalona, Octavio Daza and José Hernandez Maestre.

A local dressed as el Diablo (the Devil) takes part in the Kankuamo festivities in Atánquez .

Deserted beach near
Punta Gallinas.

GUAJIRA

In the far northeast of Colombia, where the point of the country meets the sea, green turns to desert in the land of the indigenous.

You'll know you've arrived in Guajira when the green of the Sierra Nevada de Santa Marta Mountains gives way to desolate expanses of land home to no other plantlife than cacti and the stout *trupillo* tree. Guajira extends to the self-named peninsula, which marks the northernmost tip of South America. As with Tierra del Fuego in southernmost Argentina, arriving here feels not just like you've encountered the end of a continent, but the end of the entire world.

There's very little plant life in Guajira, and aside from the flocks of flamingos and other birds it can seem like the harsh terrain's sole purpose is to beat back any signs of life. However, what does exist here – and who have for centuries – are the Wayúu people, Colombia's largest indigenous group with the best preserved of all the native cultures. For most of their existence they managed to live apart from most Colombian culture, speaking their own language (*wayuunaiki*, which is in the Maipurean family of languages) and forming their own local governments on the peninsula. Despite being at near-constant war with the Spanish since their arrival, the Wayúu were never subjugated. Today, other than the harsh elements, the indigenous have to contend with man-made obstacles to health and prosperity (see box).

Fishermen in Punta Gallinas.

THE HISTORY OF GUAJIRA

Despite its remoteness, Guajira's position on the Colombian coast means it was discovered by colonisers around the same time as other explorers were first setting foot in nearby parts of the country. A Spanish explorer named Juan de la Cosa was the first to touch down on the coast of Guajira, in 1499. Back then the area was home to various indigenous groups; however, as the Spanish multiplied in numbers and created more and more settlements, the numbers of the indigenous began

Main Attractions

Palomino
Santuario de Fauna y
  Flora Los Flamencos
Cabo de la Vela
Punta Gallinas
Parque Nacional Natural
  Macuira

Map on page 221

◎ Tip

Water from the local wells is not safe for outsiders to drink. The locals have acclimatized to the water here, but if your body is unfamiliar with it, drinking from the wells will make you sick.

Young boy working in a salt mine.

to dwindle. The village of Riohacha, which would eventually become the capital of the department, was founded in 1535 at Cabo de la Vela (later relocated to its current location), around the time Colombia's other major cities and towns were being created.

The region was officially part of Magdalena Department until 1871, when it was separated and became a new Colombian territory. In the 1930s, Guajira saw an influx of immigrants from the Middle East – people from Lebanon, Jordan, Palestine, and the countries Ottoman Empire – and they predominantly settled in the border city of Maicao, which is home to the third-largest mosque in Latin America. La Guajira officially became a Colombian Department in 1964. In the intervening years Guajira was neglected, but today, it remains one of the most remote, fascinating, tragic, and beautiful areas of the country.

THE ECONOMY

Aside from Chocó Department, Guajira is one of the poorest regions in the country, and most of its residents live well below an already rock-bottom poverty line. The biggest industry in the region comes in the form of the open-pit coal mine located in Correjon, southern Guajira, which produces some 25 million tons of coal for export each year. There is some contention about the mine, as it sits near the principal water source in this parched region of Colombia, the Río Rancheria. This north–south-running river delivers much-needed water to the residents in the north, but many say the mine is appropriating too much of it before it gets to the indigenous people. Natural gas and salt mines are major economic sectors in the area as well.

RIOHACHA

Travel 160km (100 miles) east from the colonial town of Santa Marta and you'll arrive in what feels like fishing village, yet just happens to be a department capital. **Riohacha ❶** may not look much on the surface but on weekends, when its people come out to play, it becomes a lively city. Most important is

◎ INDIGENOUS UNDER THREAT

Over the year, the Wayúu people have somehow managed to survive in some of the harshest conditions in Colombia. Life in the arid desserts of Guajira is unforgiving, but they've adapted and thrived over time, becoming accustomed to a life of hardship. After having survived colonization by the Spanish, the Wayúu are under threat yet again. In 2011 the government initiated a truly epic failure of a civil-engineering project: the Cercado Dam. In theory the dam was supposed to mitigate the effects of regular droughts in the region, but so far all it has done is impede the water flow. Little water makes it past the cattle ranches and coal mines to the middle of the province, where most Wayúu live. As a result, they have been forced to search for alternative water sources, such as faraway wells, which are often polluted. It's been estimated that as many as 5,000 Wayúu children have died in the past six years due to a lack of clean drinking water. A glimmer of hope arrived in the form of the Inter-American Commission on Human Rights, which demanded that the Colombian government protect the health of its indigenous population. As a result, the government built wells and desalination plants in the region, which has eased some of the suffering.

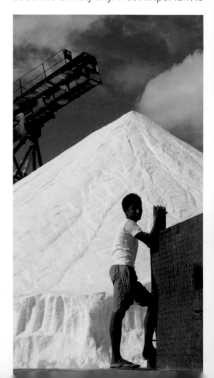

that this city is a gateway to the Wayúu culture, which is one of the richest in the country.

As with many places in Colombia, greed is what attracted the first visitors to Guajira. Riohacha, where it currently sits, was founded in 1544 by Nicólas de Federmán, and it quickly became famous for its pearls. These natural jewels were so popular, in fact, that pirates periodically attempted to sack the town until the 18th century, when pearling ceased. Once pearls ceased to be a factor, Riohacha ceased to be a destination point for outsiders.

Today Riohacha is mostly known for its long wooden pier that divides the town's two principal white-sand beaches. The water here may look dirty, but it's just the silt kicked up by the waves. A couple of blocks from the shore is the **church**, where a local-born hero of the revolution, José Prudencio Padilla, is buried. In 1823 he led the fleet of Republican ships that defeated the Spanish at the Battle of Lago Maracaibo. In the **central park**, you'll see a statue of him. While you're in Riohacha you should make time to visit the town's old **municipal market** (Mon 6am–6pm, Sun 6am–noon), located in the center, and the more **modern market**, located in south Riohacha. Most people who come to Riohacha will likely be passing through on their way to the northern coast, or even on into Venezuela. This is as good a place as any to stop and take a breather before continuing your travels.

⊘ Tip

Try reserving all tours and excursions to the Guajira peninsula from Riohacha. After Uribía, tourist infrastructure and transportation become increasingly scarce.

Try to visit on a weekend, when more life fills the city, and lively bars playing atmospheric music spring up seemingly out of nowhere.

TO AND FROM RIOHACHA, AND PRACTICALITIES

If you are arriving in Riohacha for the first time, you will want to get your bearings. Guajira not only borders the Caribbean Sea to the north, but to the south lies the Gulf of Venezuela. If you are planning any excursions in the area, it is best to make all arrangements in Riohacha, but it's also possible to organize trips from Bogotá. For reliable arrangements outside of Guajira contact **Colombian Highlands Travel Agency** (see page 133) located in Villa de Leyva.

Transportation is shoddy and sporadic in Guajira, which is why it's best to arrange excursions within the region. There are more buses to/ from Riohacha in the morning than the afternoon, although there are private transportation options for excursions to Cabo de la Vela and farther north. Be warned that

On the beach at dawn near Palomino.

any excursion to the remote parts of Guajira can be a time-consuming proposition. Taxis can take you as far north as the outposts of Uribía and Manaure, and from there its dirt roads all the way to Cabo de la Vela and beyond. It's best to take a tour to these areas, and they typically last three days.

WHEN TO GO

September through November is the rainy season in Guajira, so try to avoid the area during this period. If planning a trip to Cabo de la Vela, you will want to avoid Christmas and Easter as well, since the cape is filled with visitors and there are vehicles everywhere. It's best to go when there are as few people around as possible, as the emptiness and tranquillity are part of the experience.

PALOMINO

Palomino ❷ may be small, even tinier than the fishing village of Taganga, outside of nearby Santa Marta, but it is exploding in popularity as much as any other coastal hotbed in Colombia. New hotels and hostels are being built all the time in order to keep up with the influx of visitors. It's not difficult to see why people flock here: it's tranquil, there's a river running right into the ocean, and it affords great views of the Sierra Nevada Mountains, including Pico Bolívar.

Mostly people come for the beach. It has become very popular in recent years with visitors on the hunt for Colombia's lesser-known, drop-dead gorgeous Caribbean Coast beaches; this one has earned a spot on the list. It's long and inviting, and not nearly as crowded as anything you'll find near Cartagena and Santa Marta. There are strong currents here, though, so watch out for red flags on the beach denoting riptides.

SANTUARIO LOS FLAMENCOS

Some 25km (15 miles) west of Riohacha, the national park of **Santuario de Fauna**

y Flora Los Flamencos ❸ covers 7,000 hectares (17,300 acres), most of which is made up of mangrove swamps. These are separated from the Caribbean by sandbars, and various streams feed the sanctuary's two largest lakes, Laguna Grande and Laguna de Navío Quebrado. The saline vegetation here is an attractive spot for flamingos, and whole colonies of these birds have made it their home. Despite the wet and dry seasons, many flamingos stay here throughout the year, while others migrate here during the wetter months from Venezuela and as far away as Florida.

Just beyond the Laguna de Navío Quebrado's sandbar is a long stretch of coastal Caribbean beach that is nicely tucked away off the well-beaten tourist track. Here you can stroll along the white sands, with gentle aquamarine waters lapping at the shore, for hundreds of meters without passing anyone other than the occasional local. There are some beach bars and restaurants here run by local families that offer hammocks, meals, drinks, and rooms for the night.

The area is dotted with indigenous Wayúu communities, and the park guides all come from these villages. It's possible to arrange nature tours through local hostels, for around US$5 and lasting roughly one hour. The guides will typically point out the unique flora and fauna in the park, singling out various trees that possess medicinal qualities. The Wayúu rely on the plantlife in the area for a number of purposes, including everything from soap and shampoo substitutes to cholesterol-lowering wonder cacti.

ARRIVING AT SANTUARIO LOS FLAMENCOS

The sanctuary is located near **Camarones**, which is 3km (2 miles) outside of Riohacha. You can take a shared taxi for US$1–2 from near the old market to Camarones, and then a taxi 3.5km (2.5 miles) to the park entrance at Guanebucanc. There's a **visitor center** at the north end of Laguna de Navío Quebrado, and some cabana lodging options here (http://ecoturismosantuario.weebly.com) called Los Mangles

Flamingos near Punta Gallinas.

⊙ Where

Cabo de la Vela is *the* place to go for kitesurfing in Guajira, maybe even in all of Colombia. The conditions are perfect just off the cape and ensure that you can skim along the water all day long.

(open Feb–Mar). They also arrange birdwatching boat trips on the lake throughout the year for about US$7, lasting up to 3 hours.

URIBÍA

Riohacha may be the capital of the department, but **Uribía** ❹, located where the mangroves and lakes east of Santa Marta finally give way to the parched desert of the northern peninsula, is the indigenous capital of the country. The 14,000 residents of the town are mostly all of Wayúu descent, as are the nearly 100,000 that live in the areas surrounding Uribía. When you arrive here you'll note a marked change in the weather: the wind is furious. Many older residents of northern Guajira wear the effects of the elements, with weatherbeaten and sunscorched faces.

For most travelers, Uribía serves merely as a transition point between Riohacha and the northern coastal areas like Cabo de la Vela and Punta Gallinas. Transportation leaves from the central **Plaza Bolívar**, across from

Playa del Pilon, Cabo de la Vela.

the cemetery, and seats in a four-wheel-drive jeep from Uribía to Cabo de la Vela can be purchased for around US$7 (one way). It's best to leave for the coast in the morning, but there are transportation options all day.

One reason outsiders should come to Uribía specifically is to enjoy the biggest indigenous festival in the country: The Wayúu Festival. This occurs in May and locals celebrate their heritage with dance, song, and plenty of authentic food. The people couldn't be friendlier, but ask their permission before taking a photograph. For more information, see www.colombia.travel/en/fairs-and-festivals/wayuu-cultural-festival.

CABO DE LA VELA

In **Cabo de la Vela** ❺, on the northern Guajira coast, turquoise waters lap at a scorched desert shore, making the cape at once beckoning and forbidding. Even the harsh breezes can't drive away the fun; in fact, they facilitate it. Offshore winds form the perfect conditions for kitesurfing, and it's the premier activity in this little town of 1,800. There are some great operators here, and some say amateurs can learn the ropes in a single afternoon of training – although you might want to plan on spending a day or two learning the fundamentals of proper balance and kite manipulation. Either way those with a few days to spend will be zipping across the surface of the sea in no time.

The town is small enough that you can traverse it end-to-end, seeing everything there is to see in about 30 minutes or so. In the center are mostly *hospedajes* that double as restaurants, and there's a great place to grab an *empanada* and iced fresh *mandarina* or pineapple juice at the small stand called **El Yovas**, located at the east end of town. At the most easterly end of the cape, past Refugio Sau Ipa, is a lookout point topped by a wooden cross. It's a great and quick hike to the top, where you can survey all of Cabo de la Vela to the west.

PUNTA GALLINAS

Many people make the trek from Uribía to **Punta Gallinas** ❻ to spend time at this unique spot, which is the northernmost point on the South American continent. There is little here except scattered indigenous communities and some of the most striking landscapes on the planet. There are few places in South America where you'll feel closer to the end of the world; but when you leave the beach and dive into the perfectly warm ocean, you'll never feel closer to it.

Tours can be booked to and from Punta Gallinas from either Uribía or Cabo de la Vela, and includes a tour of the coast, including stops at the official northernmost point, as well as a cape featuring steep sand dunes and great swimming. It's possible to book overnight stays here through Hospedaje Alexandra, the only lodging option with infrastructure to handle visitors. Buses leave in the morning from Uribía to Punta Gallinas; 5am from Cabo de la Vela.

PARQUE NACIONAL NATURAL MACUIRA

Colombia is such an appealing country because it contains just about every kind of topography, including tropical jungle and desert, and this is perfectly illustrated at the **Parque Nacional Natural Macuira** ❼, where you can find tropical jungle and desert – in almost exactly the same place. This natural phenomenon is known as the Serranía de Macuira (named after the Wayúu's ancestors, the Makui) and was subsequently been turned into the Parque Nacional Natural Macuira. It resembles a mirage, that lush green vision desert wanderers see when they're suffering from exposure, but this is the only real 'mirage' in the world.

It exists in large part because of geography unique to this one specific point in Guajira. The 250 sq km (96 sq mile) area that comprises the park is set in one of the only mountainous zones on the peninsula, and it sits at

Wayúu people living on the Guajira Peninsula.

around 550 meters (1,800ft) above sea level. The highest point is Cerro Palúa, at 865 meters (2,838ft), and there are two other mountains, each sitting at around 750 meters (2,460ft). High levels of humidity here form the conditions necessary to produce lush vegetation and elfin cloud forest. This is only seen elsewhere in the country in the Andes *páramo*, which begins at heights above 2,700 meters (8,860ft). A technical term many scientists have given this ecosystem is a 'Biogeographical Island'.

WHAT TO KNOW

The park is open to the public, but parts of it, including the elfin cloud forest, are restricted. To access these areas, be sure to enter the park with a guide. It is possible to consult the friendly local indigenous members in the surrounding settlements, such as Nazareth, and hire their services. You'll soon find that all the park officials are locals. There's a park-information cabin in Nazareth, which also has a camping space just large enough to fit five or six tents. Some Wayúu in the surrounding settlements will let you hang a hammock on their property, and some of the settlements offer basic food. However, it's best to stock up on provisions in the last real town, which is Uribía.

Be sure to talk to your guide and explain the purpose of your trip; they will then give you a 30-minute induction before entering the park. Those who are planning on renting a car in Guajira should not travel alone when trying to arrive at the park. Every year the rains of the wet season alter the dirt roads on the peninsula in some way, and getting stuck out in these remote areas near the park is a far from ideal scenario. Part of the Venezuelan border cuts through the southeastern part of the Guajira Peninsula. If you wish to access the park along the Venezuelan side, you will need a visa.

MAICAO AND CROSSING FROM COLOMBIA TO VENEZUELA

The Caribbean Coastal Highway 90 continues from Riohacha east to **Maicao ❽**.

Sand dune in Macuira National Park.

⊘ A UNIQUE CLIMATE

The microclimate in this oddity of a desert/jungle park is what allows the unique vegetation to flourish. Moisture comes in from the northeast, creating clouds at night that dissipate in the morning, resulting in about 450mm (18ins) of annual precipitation that feeds the rivers running through the park, and which all evaporate once they reach the desert sand. The climate also allows for other life besides vegetation. The park is a birdwatcher's dream, and many rare species exist here, such as the cardinal. There are also some 15 species of snakes, including the colorful but dangerous coral snake. Local guides will happily point out the flora and fauna of the area. Spending time with the local guides is also a great way to learn about Wayúu culture as well.

This paved road is in good condition and will get you near the Venezuelan border in about 90 minutes. You can also travel from Maicao north to the outpost of Uribía in about 40 minutes. There are various buses throughout the day servicing both locations.

As a city, Maicao doesn't exactly beckon travelers. It mostly acts as a transition and stopping point for those traveling to and from the Venezuelan border. The town's commerce is made up of mostly clothing and textiles, and after dark most of the activity ceases and the streets become unsafe. There is a large Middle Eastern population here, resulting from mass immigration in the 1930s. In 1997 they founded one of the largest mosques in Latin America: the Mosque of Omar Ibn Al-Khattab. Due to Maicao's proximity to the Venezuelan border, its fortunes have risen or fallen, more or less, in accordance with that country's economy. However, during the 1980s and 90s, Maicao also suffered some of the residual violence of the government's war with the guerrilla groups operating in the nearby Sierra Nevada de Santa Marta mountains. Kidnapping and assassinations were common, but today the threat is negligible or non-existent.

The Venezuelan border is located 8km (5 miles) east of Maicao at the town of **Paraguachón**. It's best to take care of all visa requirements at the Venezuelan consulate in Cartagena Bocagrande, (Carrera 3, Edificio Centro Ejecutivo, Piso 14 Of. 14–02; tel: 7-665 0353; www.cartagena.consulado.gob.ve; Mon–Fri 9am–noon, 1.30–4pm) or in Barranquilla (Carrera 52, no. 69–96. Edificio Concasa. piso 03; tel: 5-368 2207; barranquilla.consulado.gob.ve; Mon–Thu 8am–noon, 1.30pm–4pm, Fri 8am–noon). There is no Venezuelan consul in Maicao and there have been reports of unreliability at the office in Riohacha. If you are interested in a transit visa you will need to show proof of an onward ticket to a third country within three days. If you are a US citizen you must apply for a visa at a Venezuelan embassy in the United States before attempting to cross the border. At the border, Venezuelan immigration is open daily 6am–9pm, and Colombian immigration is open daily from 8am–5pm.

Transportation between Maicao and Maracaibo (the first main city in Venezuela) is unreliable. There are private taxis (known as *por puestos*) that make the trip for around US$10 per person, or there are infrequent buses that run at odd times or fail to show up at all. The Brasilia Bus Company has an office in Maicao, but they don't run to Maracaibo. If you are entering Colombia from Maracaibo ensure that the driver stops at the Colombian entry post for your entrance stamp. From the bus terminal in Maracaibo you can find minibuses leaving for the Colombian border during the morning only, or private and shared taxis leaving throughout the day. For other immigration formalities contact Migración Colombia in Riohacha (Calle 5, no. 4–48; www.migracioncolombia.gov.co; Mon–Fri 8am–noon, 2–5pm).

Wayúu children on a truck.

Johnny Cay.

SAN ANDRÉS

Some 770km (480 miles) north of Colombia is a remote archipelago, dubbed the 'Sea of Seven Colors' by locals. Its white-sand cays, coral islands, and colorful reefs make for an unforgettable Caribbean experience.

The 11km (7-mile) -long island of San Andrés may be small, but it has a rich history filled with slavery, swashbuckling, power grabs, and maritime border disputes. It seems at some point or another everyone has wanted a piece of this idyllic coral island. Christopher Columbus was the first to spot it, way back in 1503. Then British Puritans arrived and kicked out the early Dutch settlers during the early 17th century. English ship owners brought West African slaves to the island via Jamaica shortly after to work the cotton and tobacco fields. Soon the Spanish attacked and the pirates followed hot on their heels. San Andrés appealed to pirates because it made for a strategic base of operations from which to launch raids on mainland cities and settlements – as well as attacks on Spanish galleons, which were loaded with gold.

The British managed to hold the islands for a chunk of time in the 18th century. However, in 1802, in a strategic move, they requested the archipelago be placed under the purview of the Viceroyalty of New Grenada, as Colombia had not yet been formed. Then, in 1818, with revolution in the air, Simón Bolívar's pro-independence forces occupied the island. By the time Gran Colombia had drafted its first constitution in 1821 the writing was on the wall, and by 1822 San Andrés, neighboring Isla Providencia,

and the whole of the archipelago were part of the new republic.

The seeds for future territorial disputes were planted when Panama broke off from Colombia in 1903. In a not-exactly-wild coincidence, envoys from President Theodore Roosevelt's administration arrived by boat the very same year to request that the islands become part of Panama. The locals refused and declared their loyalty to Colombia. By 1928 treaties had been signed stating that certain countries – namely Panama and Nicaragua – would

Main Attractions

Johnny Cay
Rocky Cay
Hoyo Soplador
El Acuario
Isla Providencia

Maps on pages 231, 234

Diving off San Andrés.

keep their hands off certain Caribbean islands – namely San Andrés and Isla Providencia. This lasted until 2001 when Nicaragua decided that the treaty they signed in 1928, known as the Esguerra Bárcenas Treaty, was null. The Hague disagreed, and in 2007 the issue was finally settled in Colombia's favor. However, tensions still remain, and Colombia maintains a small offshore military presence as security.

All of this history has led San Andrés to become what it is today: a Unesco Biosphere Reserve that boasts some of the most stunning beaches anywhere in the Caribbean, as well as world-class diving off the third-largest barrier reef in the world. It's also a cultural hotbed, with about 50 percent of the 80,000-strong population representing immigrants from the mainland, while the remaining 50 percent are comprised of descendants of Jamaican slaves whose genealogy is a mix of early French, Dutch, Spanish, and English settlers. In fact, despite most of the British leaving in the 1600s, the original Creole English is still part of the

San Andrés hotel.

culture today. Many locals do indeed speak Creole, which should be refreshing to those American or British visitors whose Spanish isn't exactly up to scratch and who'd like to converse with locals in their native tongue for a while.

The unique and eclectic genealogical make-up of the islands has resulted in a distinct variety of musical influences, all of which can be heard on San Andrés. The rhythms of *soca* music, a form of calypso that originated in Trinidad and Tobago and is popular in Venezuela, are ubiquitous here. Also, various forms of polka, like *schottische*, as well as *quadrille*, are common and represent the island's diverse cultural heritage. Even gospel music can be heard at Sunday services at the first ever Baptist church built on the island.

HOW TO GET THERE AND WHEN TO VISIT

San Andrés has always been a popular vacation destination for many Colombians, although most previously lacked the funds to make their dream of a Caribbean vacation come true. However,

◎ PIRATES OF THE CARIBBEAN

As with most events concerning Colombia's early history, gold – or rather the desire for it – was an important motivation for the country's new arrivals. Of course back in the 17th century San Andrés wasn't part of Colombia, as Colombia did not yet exist as a country. Nor was gold ever actually found on San Andrés. However, that didn't stop the Welsh pirate Sir Henry Morgan from establishing a base here and ransacking every gold-carrying Spanish Galleon he happened across. When there were no Spanish ships left to pillage, or when Sir Henry simply got bored, he and his men would head over to the mainland and raid cities and settlements such as Santa Marta and Panama, relieving locals of their gold and other valuables. A life of piracy – sanctioned or otherwise – eventually took its toll on Morgan, and one day he decided to change his ways and leave his old life of crime and piracy behind him, purchasing three sugar plantations in Jamaica. Morgan managed to change his image so much that he was eventually made Lieutenant Governor of Jamaica. The gold he pilfered during his time as a pirate in the Caribbean was never fully accounted for. According to legend, it can still be found in an underwater cave off the coast of San Andrés.

since Colombia's tourism boom – plus the arrival of a national budget airline carrier and more frequent international flights to the area – it has seen an even greater influx of visitors. The island's long distance from Colombia means the only practical way to get there is to fly, and with VivaColombia Airlines (see page 279), it has never been cheaper to purchase tickets. Be aware that upon arrival at the airport all foreigners are required to purchase a tourist card for around US$33. Do not lose it, as you will need to present it on your return flight. The card is also required if you wish to travel to Isla Providencia. Inter-island travel from San Andrés to Providencia is relatively easy, with cargo ships leaving the main *muelle* (dock) at the north end of the island.

FINDING YOUR WAY AROUND SAN ANDRÉS ISLAND

You'll arrive in San Andrés at **Gustavo Rojas Pinilla International Airport ❶** on the north end of the island, about 1km (half mile) from the main town. Your appetite for beach fun will likely be whetted before you even touch down, as a daytime descent affords aerial views of the various shades of blue and green surrounding San Andrés pristine white-sand beaches. A taxi to town shouldn't cost more than US$3, and from here you'll have your pick of hotels, hostels, and restaurants. Most of these are in San Andrés' central commercial district, which is located on the **northeast peninsula ❷** of the island.

Head north on Carrera 5, which leads all the way to the beach, and then stretches eastward along the top of the island. There's also a **tourist information kiosk ❸** here (daily 8am–8pm). Looking out from here, you'll have a direct view of **Johnny Cay ❹**, which is one of the most popular playgrounds in the archipelago. Most people come to San Andrés because they want the pristine beach, and Johnny Cay is the most iconic atoll on the island, the one that you literally see on all the post-cards. Fast water taxis leave from the **Muelle Casa de la Cultura ❺** (Pier; Carrera 1, no. 21) and stop at the best cays: first to El Acuario and Haynes

Local woman serving food on San Andrés.

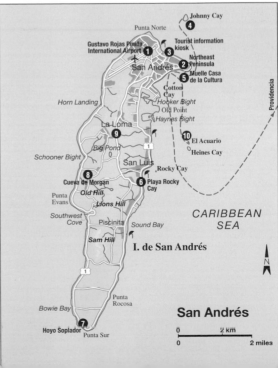

Cay, and then to Johnny Cay. The boats leave daily at 9am and 11am, returning at 3.30pm, costing US$10 for the round trip. Upon disembarking at Johnny Cay, you must pay an entrance tax of around US$3 to help maintain the island.

To the north of Johnny Cay is a rocky shore with plenty of tide pools. It's a great place to take solitary photos of the surrounding sea and nature, as most visitors head for the south of the island. It's at the south you'll find all the thatched hut restaurants, beach bars and friendly Creole locals selling food and drinks and renting umbrellas and beach chairs. The water here is as drop-dead-gorgeous blue as anywhere else in San Andrés, but offshore winds make for some decent-sized waves, so Johnny Cay is much better for bodysurfing than it is for snorkeling. Big weekly beach parties are held here on Sundays.

To the west of the pier is Calle 1, a promenade that runs along the water and alongside clothes stores, pharmacies, and restaurants. There are also any number of street vendors here serving refreshing tropical cocktails.

Tourists arrive at Johnny Cay.

Follow the promenade around the peninsula and you'll see plenty of shopping malls, restaurants, and cafés, all of which sit just behind palm-lined beaches dotted with outdoor bars. If you're lucky, you'll catch a Creole chef, often the mother or grandmother of the household, setting up pots and trays of fresh-cooked Creole-Caribbean fare on long tables in a buffet-style form of dining self-service. Delicacies include stuffed crab shells, fried breadfruit, conch, fresh island fish, and much more. This humble goodness might just be the best eating on the island.

As for transportation, there are plenty of places to rent golf carts, but most people choose to get around the island by motorcycle, moped, or public minibus. A single ride around the island costs around US$1.

THE EAST SIDE

Those who want to get away from the relative hustle and bustle of San Andrés' commercial district will want to head to the east side of the island. There are a number of cays located just offshore,

as well as the rusted out hulks of once-great tankers. There are some small, quieter towns here; while the beaches are just as stunning as anything you'll find on the north side of the island. There are also plenty of waterfront resorts for those who want to bask in the sun and enjoy the good life.

One great beach on the eastside is **Playa Rocky Cay** ❻, which is known for tranquil waters, as well as the tiny island of the same name that sits about 100 meters offshore. Everyday lines of people wade in single-files lines through the shallows of a submerged sandspit out to this cay. It makes for great photos, as a huge shipwrecks lies just behind the island. There are also a number of beach restaurants on shore that offer good meals (mostly fresh seafood, of course), at reasonable prices.

THE SOUTH AND WEST

Leaving the beauty and tranquillity of the east side of San Andrés may seem counterintuitive, but an interesting landmark can be found on the south side. **Hoyo Soplador** ❼ is a hole in the rocks at the southern tip of the island that forms a geyser when seawater rushes up below it. The jutting water, combined with the crashing offshore waves, makes a picture-perfect image.

As for the west side of San Andrés, there are a few beaches and reasons to visit. There is cave a called the **Cueva de Morgan** ❽, which, as legend has it, was a hiding place for lost treasure. Here you'll find an adjacent museum that recounts the history of the coconut.

THE CENTER

From the north, west, or east shore, you can take a bus to the center of the island. If you come from the west, you'll pass by La Laguna, a freshwater lake. In the center you'll find sleepy hillside towns made up of clapboard houses. **La Loma** ❾ is, at 120 meters (394ft) above sea level, the highest point on the island. Also here, on the town side, is

the famous **Baptist church**, which was the first one built on the island in 1847. Come for Sunday a service (10am–noon) and you'll be treated to gospel music.

In the center of the island you'll find palm groves, and often some industrious local is shimmying up the tall trunks to relieve the trees of their coconuts. At the base of the palms are seemingly endless groups of iguanas waddling around in the grass. It's no surprise that they congregate here, as the daily hordes of tourists keep them well fed and happy with free food.

EL ACUARIO

Those who want crystalline waters ideal for snorkeling should head to **El Acuario** ❿. This cay gets its name as it acts as a natural aquarium of sorts, and is the perfect place to spot white-speckled eagle rays and enormous mantas. Here you can also wade across the shallows to Haynes Cay, where there's a tiny outcropping of sand with a couple of beach bars and restaurants. One such eatery is Bibi's Place, which serves beer, cocktails,

Walking out to El Acuario.

and delicious giant platters of fresh fish for lunch.

PROVIDENCIA

These two islands may occupy the same archipelago, and they may be of similar small statures – Providencia is just 7km (4 miles) long and 3.5km (2 miles) wide – but culturally and economically they couldn't be more different. Where San Andrés is more developed, Providencia has blocked most mainland and foreign operators from building. Also, Providencia is volcanic in origin, whereas San Andrés is a coral island. This means there's more greenery on Providencia, as well as scene-stealers like waterfalls.

On Providencia, not only will you find a smaller local community than on San Andrés (around 5,000 residents), but fewer lodging options as well. That said, there is some infrastructure here, with most of the island's residents living in the town of **Santa Isabel** ⓫, on the north end of the island. The few hotels that do exist here can be found on the west side at **Bahia Augadulce** ⓬. As building upward is prohibited on

Providencia, all lodging options are no higher than two stories.

At the southwest end of the island you'll find its two most famous beaches: **Bahia Manzanillo** ⓭ and **Bahia Sur Oeste** ⓮. They are long, palm-lined beaches abundant in white sand and little else that are a far cry from the busier beaches of San Andrés. To the north, you'll find the famous **Isla Santa Catalina** ⓯, a former pirate hideout separated from the mainland by a narrow channel. There are boat trips around the island, but you can also walk to it via a 100-meter bridge called the Punete de Los Amantes (Lover's Bridge). There's also an ATM just before this bridge, which is worth taking note of. At the west end of Santa Catalina are the ruins of an old British defensive fort, **Fuerte de Libertad**, with the original cannons still intact.

Providencia is also famous for the mass migration of black land crabs, which takes place nightly during the wet season. Each night masses of female black crabs descend from the forests of **High Hill** ⓰ toward the shore,

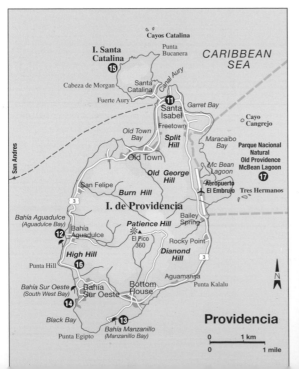

where they lay their eggs in the water. A month after the hatchlings are born, they make their way up to the forest. Because this migration involves the crabs traversing roads and beaches, the municipality has banned driving as well as eating crabs during this period. In spite of this, increased mainland immigration and tourism have contributed to dwindling crab populations.

For more information on conservation in the area, be sure to check out Coralina (www.coralina.gov.co), a government organization dedicated to preserving the abundant natural beauty in both San Andrés and Providencia.

OLD PROVIDENCE MCBEAN LAGOON

At the northeast side of the island you'll be treated to sweeping panoramas of incredible landscapes. On the east is where you'll also find Colombia's only national park on this archipelago, the **Parque Nacional Old Providence McBean Lagoon** ⑰ (www.parquesnacio nales.gov.co), which was created here in 1966. The park was specifically setup to protect the reef of the same name, which at 32km (20 miles) long, is the third-largest barrier reef in the world. At **Cabo Congrejo** (Crab Cay), you will be required to pay an entrance fee of around US$5. This idyllic little outcropping is a great place for snorkeling and swimming. Toward the southern end of the national park you'll find **Cayos Tres Hermanos**, notable for its surrounding light blue and crystalline waters.

DIVING SAN ANDRÉS AND PROVIDENCIA

On San Andrés Island you'll find good diving conditions, with depths ranging from three to 30 meters (10–100ft), and visibility from 30–60 meters (100–200ft). Some good sites here include Black Coral Net and Morgan's Sponge. For deep water diving, try the Pared Azul (Blue Wall). For Providencia, some good dive sites at Old McBean Lagoon include Manta's Place (filled with the titular mantas), Felipe's Place (where you'll find a well-preserved underwater statue of Christ), and Stairway to Heaven, famous for its large coral wall.

The view from Crab Cay.

Santuario Las Lejas, Ipiales.

CALI

As the Pan-American Highway descends south from the mountains of Antioquia, it drops right into the middle of the Valle Cauca, and finds a city filled with pulsing salsa and its residents dancing to its rhythms.

The city of Cali sits nestled between the mountain ranges of the Cordillera Occidental and the Cordillera Central. The earliest Europeans settled this green valley, and in less enlightened times landowners brought slaves here to work the cane fields. The Valle de Cauca is also fertile ground for growing pineapple, and an abundance of livestock graze these grasslands as well.

It's no wonder, then, that the earliest settlers valued this prized land with its warm but not oppressively hot climate. And they did show up early –Sebastián de Belalcázar founded Cali in 1536, which at the time was called Santiago de Cali. Before journeying north, Belalcázar had been with Pizarro's army in Peru, but left after the Inca Empire had been conquered in 1533. In 1534 he founded Ecuador's capital city of Quito, then continued north into modern-day Colombia and founded Popayán at the same time as Cali.

Left to his own devices Belalcázar would have continued on, founding cities until ripe old age, but north of the Valle de Cauca he encountered stiff indigenous resistance that halted his northward march. This kept him out of the Andes – but it left room for other conquistadors, like Jiménez, to come down from the coast along the Magdalena, conquer the Muisca, and found cities like Bogotá.

Sabor y Estilo Salsa Academy, Cali.

Cali was actually founded just south of its present location, around Ciudad Universitaria, but in 1539 it was moved north to where it sits today. Back then Cali was unrecognizable from the expansive department capital it is today. For a couple of hundred years it remained a sleepy colonial town of 20,000 inhabitants, dependent on its neighbor to the south. Today, Popayán has traded places with Cali and become the sleepy colonial town. Cali was also originally under the purview of Quito and Ecuador. Then, in 1900 a

Map on page 240

Main Attractions
La Ermita
Museo del Oro Calima
San Antonio
Popayán
Tierradentro

railroad arrived that connected Cali to the capital, opening up the whole southern region of Colombia. A boom in industry and commerce followed, and Colombia had full control of its connected south.

Cali's close economic ties with the rest of Colombia are no coincidence. Besides the Llanos, the Valle de Cauca has some of the most fertile land in the country, making it the breadbasket of Colombia. Aside from pineapples, sugar cane, and cattle, the valley also produces cotton, rice, and coffee. As with many cities around the world that were founded on fertile lands, Cali is a modern metropolis brushing up against *campesino* culture.

The 20th century saw Cali expanding consistently, becoming ever more interconnected in the process. Not only is Cali connected to Ecuador in the south by the Pan-American Highway, but it also connects to the biggest seaport on Colombia's Pacific Coast to the east, Buenaventura. Cali has a diverse cultural makeup, which includes a large Afro-Caribbean population, many of whom arrived in the city via this port over the years. Also popping up over the years have been industrial municipalities that border Cali to the north and south. Yumbo and Jamundí are two such examples that have contributed to Cali's growth and prosperity.

It's not always been bright and prosperous for Cali, a place that suffered through civil strife and narco-terrorism as much as any other place in Colombia during the darker years. The other famous group of Colombian narcos, the Cali Cartel, was made up of born and bred Caleños. They rose to prominence in the early 1990s as Pablo Escobar's operation was decimated. The two brothers who headed the cartel, the Rodríguez Orejuela brothers, couldn't have been more different from Pablo Escobar. Whereas Pablo relished his larger-than-life image and happily cultivated a reputation as a ruthless mass murderer, the Cali brothers were more subdued. They were wealthy by birth, not born into the ghettos like Pablo. Therefore they were more refined. They preferred nightclubs to machine guns and didn't need to pound

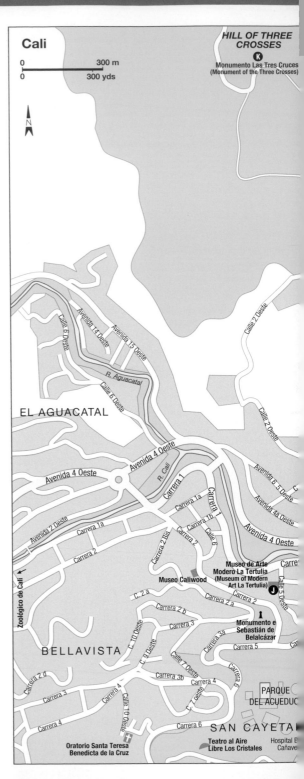

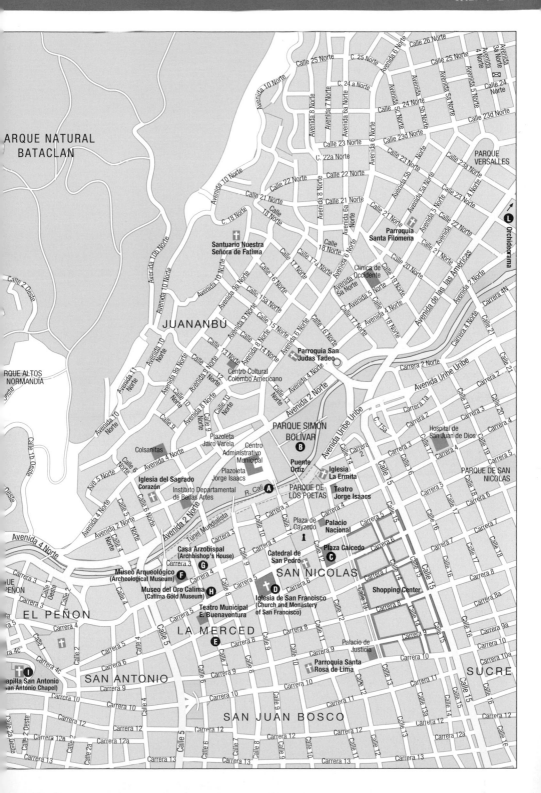

their chests to get attention – they were known as the 'Gentleman of Cali.'

They may have been savvy enough to sit back while Pablo warred with the Colombian government and reap the rewards of the fallout, but their place on the mountaintop didn't last long. By 1995, just a couple years after they had surpassed Pablo as *numero uno*, the brothers found themselves in a Colombian prison. By 2006 they were extradited to the US, finally bringing to an end the story of the Cali Cartel and the era of the narcos.

GETTING ACQUAINTED

Despite being a large, bustling city with a population of some 3 million people, and sitting at a high altitude of around 1,000 meters (3,280ft), Cali has its own culture and identity that is completely separate from Bogotá and Medellín. Here you'll find a milder tropical climate resembling that of a savanna. It's a large metropolis, but a relaxed one, not moving at the breakneck pace for which Colombia's capital is known. Unlike Medellín, Cali's central urban areas and suburbs are not dominated by shopping malls.

Cali is a located in the Valle de Cauca, west of the Cauca River. However, a tributary of the Cauca, the **Cali River** Ⓐ, runs west and northeast right through the city center. This body of water, with its green grassy banks lined with tropical trees, makes for a welcome change of pace from the surrounding concrete metropolis. It's also a good point of reference for those who want to get their bearings in the city. The river acts as a demarcation point: north of it Carreras become Avenidas and the suffix "N" is affixed to the front of all the street names. The city itself rolls out for another 15km (9 miles) south of the river, but the center is where visitors will likely spend much of their time. And it's easily navigable.

THE CITY CENTER

If the river is a point of reference, the **Parque Simón Bolívar** Ⓑ should be the anchor point for visitors to Cali. It is near to the colonial heart of the city and hugs the river. The area is home

⊘ CALI AND SALSA

To the typical outsider traveling around Colombia for the first time, it can seem like every Colombian, man and woman, knows how to dance perfect salsa. So when even Colombians tell you that Caleños are the most serious about this most sensual of musical genres, its surely cause to sit up and pay attention.

Cali has anointed itself the 'Salsa capital of Colombia,' and it's difficult to argue against it. The city is home to the largest salsa festival in the country (and indeed the world) – the Festival Mundial de Salsa. Caleños' love of this music isn't merely a once-a-year-proposition. Every night, once the sun goes down, the city of Cali thrums with the pulsing syncopations that are right at home in the sticky night, in the tropical climate of the savanna. Ask any Caleño where the best salsa spots in the city are and they're going to rattle off a dizzying array of options, all likely worthwhile. While the best options can be found around Barrio Menga or Barrio Juanchito in the northeastern part of town, there are some great individual spots all over the city. The main night to go out dancing is Thursday. For more local info on where to go, visit www.comoespahoy.com.co.

to tall palm trees, the blocky **Centro Administrativo Municipal building**, and the **Plaza de Alcaldia**. You can find your way anywhere around town using this park as your baseline. Also here is the lovely **Puente Ortiz**, a pedestrian bridge built in the 1840s that crosses the river, leading through the park and to Avenida 2 Norte. South of the river it turns into Calle 11. Near to this is bridge is a pedestrian-only throughway, the **Paseo Bolívar**, notable for a sculpture of 19th century romantic novelist Jorge Isaacs, as well as a bronze statue of the Liberator.

Plaza Caicedo ⓒ is located a couple of blocks to the south of Parque Bolívar. Centering the plaza is a monument to independence leader Joaquín de Caycedo y Cuero. Looming over it is the **Catedral Metropolitana**, built in the mid-19th century over the site of a former church, which was founded in 1539. The Metropolitana is expansive, featuring three aisles and some fine stained-glass mosaics.

Nearby you'll find one of the most impressive colonial sites in the city, the **Iglesia de San Francisco ⓓ** (Church and Monastery of San Francisco). The brick exterior dates back to the mid-18th century; however, the interior has been renovated a few times over the years, most notably in the 19th century and then again in 1926. The work seems to have paid off, as the church has a stunning ornate ceiling, surrounded by many carvings, images, and paintings dating back to its founding. Also inside the church is a chapel, the **Capilla de la Inmaculada** (Chapel of the Immaculate Conception), with a long nave lined with gold-topped columns. As for the adjoining monastery, it was built around the same time as the church and features a bell tower reminiscent of stacked blocks called the Torre Mudéjar. The word Mudéjar is fitting here, as it denotes a part-Gothic part-Islamic style of architecture found in Spain between AD 1100 and 1400.

Cali's oldest church is **La Merced ⓔ** (Carrera 4, no. 6–117; tel: 2-880 4737). This house of worship was erected in 1545 in what was a symbolic location of the founding of Cali nine years

View of the city of Cali from the Church of San Antonio.

earlier. Its rustic and classical appearance shines through today due in no small part to a renovation project paid for by the Banco Popular. Next to La Merced two art galleries are housed in a former convent: the **Museo de Arte Colonial** (actually part of the church; Mon–Fri 9am–12pm 2–5pm, Sat 9am–12pm), which features a collection of 16th and 17th century paintings, and the **Museo Arqueológico ⑤** (Archeological Museum; Carrera 4, no. 6–59; tel: 2-885 4675; Mon–Sat 9am–1pm, 2–6pm). Here you'll find interesting collections of pre-Columbian pottery from the Calima indigenous group. The courtyard features a replica of a tomb in Tierradentro. Nearby, across from La Merced, is the **Casa Arzobispal ⑥** (Archbishop's House; corner of Carrera 4 and Calle 7), is the oldest surviving two-story home in Cali – and it once hosted Bolívar in 1922.

Over by the river, at the intersection of Carrera 1 and Calle 13, is one of the standout churches in the city, **La Ermita** (mass: Mon–Sat 7.30am and 5pm, Sun 10am and 5pm). Neo-Gothic churches evoke a sense of awe, but when they're painted blue and bright white, as this one is, it's almost as striking as a celestial vision. The original church that sat on this site was built in 1602, but it was mostly destroyed in a 1925 earthquake. The design of the new building was influenced by the cathedral in Cologne, Germany, and was finished in 1942. Inside are rows of grand arches, above which you'll see narrow stained-glass mosaics. The pulpit forgoes the gold-painted décor that is common in Colombian churches in favor of an 18th-century marble altar brought over from Italy. It even boasts a musical clock imported from Amsterdam. One item that survived the 1925 earthquake is a typical Caleño painting called *El Señor de la Caña*, which sits over the altar and features a bleeding and crowned Christ holding the fruit of the Valle de Cauca's earth, sugarcane.

La Ermita sits on the pleasant **Plaza de los Poetas**, where you'll find life-size statues of famous Caleños, and once again Jorge Isaacs makes an appearance. From here you can cross Parque

La Ermita, Cali.

Bolívar north via the Paseo Bolívar or the Puente Ortiz. Crossing the river you'll notice many sculptures lining the banks, which were commissioned in the 1990s. One, the *Maria Mulata*, is a representation of a Colombian blackbird, and another is a great bronze piece called *El Gato Rio*, which features a cat with big bug eyes done by artist Hernando Tejada. Cali's also known for its exotic old trees, and you can find a prodigious *ceiba* north of the park at Avenida 4 Norte where it meets Calle 10.

Near to the Casa Arzobispal is the **Banco Republica building**, which houses the **Museo del Oro Calima** Ⓗ (Calima Gold Museum; Calle 7, no. 4–69; tel: 2-684 7755; www.banrepcultural. org/cali/museo-del-oro-calima; Mon–Fri 9am–5pm, Sat 10am–5pm; free). This is one of the satellite branches of Bogotá's Gold Museum, and, as with the main branch in the country's capital, the Cali version has an extensive array of pre-Columbian artifacts, including many gold pieces and impressive ceramics. Most of the exhibits are displayed behind the thick metal doors of a security vault, presumably to keep any modern-day conquistadors from getting any bright ideas.

The pieces in the museum represent over 9,000 years of history covering various periods dominated by distinct indigenous groups. The Museo Calima separates the later years of this history into three periods: the Llama, Yotoco, and Sonso. Most of the artifacts were recovered from the Calima region of Colombia, just north of Cali. Its temperate climate and proximity to the river and fertile lands meant it saw a lot of human traffic in the pre-Columbian era. Stone and bone tools used by the earliest hunter-gatherer tribes are on display here, representing the earliest artifacts from pre-ceramic times. Fossilized corn pollen found on items dates many of the artifacts used by these groups to around 5,000 BC.

The Llama period represents the point when the early peoples shifted to an agrarian society. The museum showcases pottery and ceramics dated from this period as far back as 1500 BC. There are also some interesting

Musicians playing on a street in Cali.

☉ Tip

Newbies to salsa dancing may want to take some lessons before diving straight in. Most hotels and hostels offer such services, and there are academies as well.

ceramic vases and masks that show evidence of a hierarchal society. Artifacts on display in the museum from the Yotoco period date back to the beginning of the Christian era and show that the indigenous cultures developed advanced gold-working abilities, evidenced in elaborate gold ornaments, headdresses, and sculptures. The Sonso period spans from around AD 800 until the Spanish conquistadors arrived in the early part of the 16th century and features burial items like a wood sarcophagus and late-period gold work ornaments and jewelry, notable for their elaborate shapes such as hoops and pectorals. Overall, the museum is well worth a visit.

SAN ANTONIO AND THE WEST

South of the river and to the west lies the neighborhood of San Antonio, which is regarded as the bohemian heart of Cali. Like La Candelaria in Bogotá, San Antonio is located in the hills. One of the most popular treks is to make your way up Carreras 5 and 10, through neighborhoods filled with lovely but ever-dwindling Colonial homes up to the **Capilla San Antonio** ❶ (San Antonio Chapel; 2-658 0022), a humble 18th-century church that appears little changed since it was founded in 1747. Most people come here for the view of Cali as seen from the park in front of the plaza. It's a popular spot on weekends when locals come to see a sweeping vista of Cali laid out before them.

North of San Antonio, before the river, you'll find the **Museo de Arte Modero La Tertulia** ❶ (Museum of Modern Art La Tertulia; Carrera 1, no, 5–105; tel: 2-893-2939; www.museola tertulia.com; Tue–Sun 10am–8pm, Sun 2–6pm), which has some 1,500 pieces of local and other South American art spread out over three floors. There are discounts for students and groups, and there's a salon featuring the occasional exhibition, which is always free. To the west of the modern art museum is the zoo, the **Zoológico de Cali** (tel: 2-488 0888; www.zoologicodecali.com.co; daily 9am–4pm), where you can see such South American animals as tapirs

Rear view of Cristo del Rey statue,Cali.

and llamas, together with animals from farther afield, like the Burmese python. A nice collection of birds and primates rounds out the exhibits, and the zoo efficiently incorporates the river. From here, head west for one of the best *miradors* (lookouts) in the city, the **Monumento Cristo Rey**, a Christ statue that could easily pass for the Cristo Redentor (Christ the Redeemer) of Rio de Janeiro. Sitting on a 1,470-meter (4,800ft) -high hill, it affords stunning panoramic views over Cali.

THE NORTH AND EAST

Another great *mirador* in Cali is located in the northwest part of the city. The **Monumento Las Tres Cruces** ⓚ (Monument of the Three Crosses) is named for the three crosses sitting atop a 1,450-meter (4,757ft) hill. During Holy Week it's a traditional pilgrimage site that offers more great views of the city and Valle de Cauca. To the east is the **Orchideorama** ⓛ (Avenida 2 Norte, no. 48-10; 665 8358; www.caliorquideas. com; Mon–Fri 8am–noon, 2–5pm), a garden that features an exotic flower much admired in Colombia, the orchid. The park cultivates various types of orchids, and its idyllic green grounds make it a popular spot for weddings. Some 4km (2.5 miles) east is a family fun center, the **Acuaparque de la Caña** (tel: 2-438 4812; www.acuaparquecali. com; Tue–Sun 9am–5pm), which has a waterpark and several rollercoasters.

AROUND CALI

POPAYÁN
When strolling the cobblestone streets of Popayán, it's easy to imagine it as the colonial powerhouse it once was, before the gas lamps and horse-drawn carriages gave way to electricity, automobiles, and skyscrapers. This city of around 250,000 people, to the south of Cali, still exudes the spirit of the Spanish colonial settlement that defined its earliest origins. Indeed it almost seems stuck in time – a bustling community frozen in the past and protected from the encroaching present by the Mountains of the Cordillera Central that surround it.

Eat
For the best places to eat in Cali, head to La Plaza de Mercado Alameda (Calle 8 at Carrera 26), which is located in the southwest of the city.

The colonial city of Popayán.

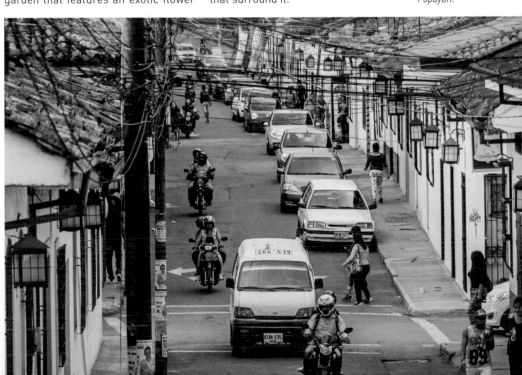

☉ Tip

Salsa dancing isn't the only fun activity in Cali. In the surrounding Valle Cauca are some great sites for paragliding; inquire at your local hostel or hotel.

The Spanish viewed Popayán as an important strategic point in the New World. To them it represented a vital link between Quito and Lima in the south, and Bogotá and Cartagena in the north. These days it makes for a relaxing excursion from Cali and a good spot to relax after all that partying in the city's *salsotecas*. It's also a good base for excursions to the archeological site of Tierradentro.

HISTORY, TRAGEDY, AND PERSERVERENCE

It's hard to imagine that this well-preserved marvel ever suffered any kind of debilitating damage. However, in 1983 that's exactly what happened. The 5.5-magnitude concussion toppled many buildings and resulted in the death of 267 people. However, the city, which was first founded in 1537 and prided itself on its colonial heritage, wasn't about to give up easily. Popayán had survived previous earthquakes – and even volcanic eruptions – and they were determined to survive this natural disaster as well. They mounted a vigorous reconstruction project, and managed to rebuild many of the buildings. The only remnant of the previous tragedy is the occasional empty lot where colonial-era buildings once stood.

The whitewashed buildings that remain are dazzling in their brightness, and there are few more pleasant ways to spend a few hours here than strolling along the narrow streets, between the colonial homes and relaxing in the old plazas. Spend enough time here and it's easy to lose yourself in the colonial spirit that the area exudes.

This city is also home to a modern university scene and has a large student population. Popayán has produced many presidents over the years. Some, like Tomás Cipriano de Mosquera, who served from 1845–1849, date from the New Granada era, while others, like Guillermo León Valencia served in more modern times, from 1962–1966. Popayán has also produced many notable painters, composers, and writers. Edgar Negret, a sculptor and painter, is considered one of the all-time great sculptors in the geometric form.

Parque Caldas, Popayán.

AROUND THE CITY

Popayán is the capital of the Department of Cauca, and surrounding it are the green mountains of the Cordillera Central. These look down from the south, north, and east of the city. Toward the southeast it's possible to see the top of Volcán Puracé, which stands at 4,650 meters (15,256ft). The Río Cauca rises at Puracé and passes Popayán toward the north. A tributary of this river, the Molino, passes through town, and there are lovely bridges over this body of water that are just as romantic (if not more so) than any cobblestone street in town.

The **Catedral Basilica Nuestra Señora de la Asuncíon** (Cathedral Basilica of our Lady of the Assumption; Calle 5 at Carrera 6; daily 8.30am–6pm) is one of the most iconic buildings in the city, and it's as virginal snow-white as many of the houses in the historic district. It sits on the south side of the **Plaza Mayor** (Parque Cladas) and has a long and storied history. The original chapel on the site, which was made from adobe, was inaugurated in 1537 but was replaced by a thatched-roof cathedral in 1558. In 1594 this was replaced by another cathedral, which was subsequently destroyed in 1784 by an earthquake. The latest iteration of the cathedral was completed in 1900 and restored again after the 1983 earthquake. The church is in neoclassical style and there's a marble Madonna behind the altar. The building itself is topped by a stately 40-meter (130ft) -high dome.

Popayán is not at a loss for churches. Some other impressive houses of worship in the area include **San Agustín** (Carrera 6, no. 7–54; mass times: Mon 7am, Tue–Sat 7am and 6pm, Sun 7am, 11am, and 6pm), which is located two blocks south of the cathedral. It was founded in 1881 and features a statue of Christ kneeling on a globe. One block east of the cathedral is **La Encarnacíon**, which was built in 1764 and used for religious music festivals today. The **Iglesia Sant Domingo** (Church of Saint Domingo; Calle 4, no. 4–15; mass times: Mon–Sat 7am and 5pm, Sun 10:30am, noon, and 5pm) is another whitewashed church with domed towers. It was

Puracé National Park.

ⵔ PURACÉ PARQUE

Travel about 30km (20 miles) southeast of Popayán and you will reach the Parque Nacional Puracé. Covering over 86,000 hectares (212,510 acres), Parque Nacional Puracé is home to Volcán Puracé, which stands at 4,646 meters (15,243ft) above sea level. It also includes the Pan de Azúcar at 4,670 meters (15,322ft) above sea level, and a line of volcanic craters called the Volcanes los Coconucos. You can hike up to the summits of these peaks. Be warned though: it's a challenging two-day expedition that should only be attempted by the physically fit. However, those who do make it up to these high altitudes may just be treated to a sighting of the spectacled bear or mountain tapir.

originally created as a convent in 1552 and has been rebuilt over the years. Inside are some interesting woodcarvings. **La Ermita de Jesús Nazareno** (Calle 5 at Carrera 2; mass times: Mon–Sat 5pm, Sun 9:30pm and 5pm) is the oldest church in the city, dating back to the founding of Popayán. **The Iglesia San Francisco** (Church of San Francisco; Carrera 9, no. 3–74; mass times: Mon–Fri 5pm and 6pm, Sat noon, 5pm, and 6pm, Sun 10am, 4pm, 5pm, and 6pm) is located about two blocks east of the Plaza Mayor and is a nice Baroque cathedral dating from around 1775. It has been partially restored after earthquake damage.

Culture aficionados should head to the **Museo de Historia Natural** (Museum of Natural History; Calle 2, no. 1a–25; tel: 8-209 800; Mon–Sun 9am–11am, 2–4pm), which has eight rooms featuring educational displays on the natural history of the area, including geology and archeology. There are also exhibitions covering insects, reptiles, birds, mammals, and sea life. Other museums include the **Casa Museo**

Negret (Calle 5a, no. 10–23; tel: 2-824 4546; Mon–Fri 8am–12pm, 2–6pm), which celebrates a single subject, one of the city's most famous residents, the artist Edgar Negret. The museum contains some of his artwork, sculptures, and photographs, plus some other works by Latin American artists. The **Museo Nacional Guillermo Valencia** (Carrera 6, no. 2–69; tel: 2-820 6160; Tue–Sun 10am–noon, 2–5pm; free) is the birthplace of the poet and diplomat Guillermo León Valencia; the **Museo Casa Mosquera** (Calle 3 Norte, no. 5–14; tel: 2-820-9800; Tue–Sun 9am–noon, 2–6pm) is the home of the former president of Colombia, Tomás Cipriano de Mosquera y Arboleda. There are six exhibition rooms here featuring some 711 historical and cultural items.

If you're up for a walk you can head east along Calle 5 from the Plaza Mayor, past La Ermita, to the **Iglesia de Belén** (mass times: Mon–Sat 4pm, Sun 11.30am–4pm), a pleasant chapel on a hill overlooking Popayán with great views of the city. From there you could continue on to the **Morro de Tulcán**, which also overlooks the city center and has an equestrian statue of the founder Sebastían de Belalcázar. Next to here is the **Ríncon Payanes** (also known as Pueblito Patjo), which features nice colonial buildings and stands selling local handicrafts.

TIERRADENTRO

Anyone with even a passing interest in pre-Columbian history will want to make Tierradentro a firm fixture on their itinerary. It's one of the most interesting archeological sites in the country due to its ancient man-made *hypogea* (burial caves) that were created between the 6th and 10th centuries. These were built as tombs, not for ordinary members of Tierradentro society, but for the elite. The burial areas, which range in size from small and shallow to about 8 meters (26ft) deep, feature spiral staircases and walls

Iglesia San Francisco.

decorated by the builders with black, white, and red geometric patterns. The various ancient sites, as well as the stunning views of the surrounding Cordillera Central, are why Tierradentro is a Unesco World Heritage Site.

Tierradentro is located in Inza, Cauca Department, which is a relatively quick 100km (62-mile) -trip northeast of Popayán. It's something of a rough road from the capital of the department, but the spectacular mountain scenery makes it all worthwhile. The scene is set right when you arrive in Inza, as the main plaza here features indigenous stone statues. About 9km (5 miles) outside of Inza is El Cruce, the intersection where a road turns off for the 20-minute drive to the village of San Andrés de Pisambalá, at the edge of the archeological site. The park administration office is also on this road.

There's an **archeological museum** on the road to the park (daily 8am–noon, 2–6.30pm), which offers a unique overview of the site in the form of a scale model of the region. There are also exhibits detailing the Paez, the indigenous people responsible for the sites, and whose descendants still live in the surrounding indigenous villages today. The helpful staffers provide useful info about the area.

You can leave for the sites from the museum or village on horseback, although a guide is required. Hiring a guide and horse for the day will cost roughly US$15–20. You can also walk – again from either the museum or the village – but be sure to take plenty of water, sunscreen, and a hat. There are five principal burial sites of note: Segovia, El Tablon, El Duende, Alto de San Andrés, and El Aguacate. Segovia can be reached via a 15-minute walk from behind the museum, and it has about 30 tombs. Be sure to look at tombs 9, 10, and 12, as these have the most interesting wall designs. Beyond Segovia, 15 minutes up a hill, is El Duende, which has four tombs. From El Duende it's a 40-minute hike along a road that descends to San Andrés, and then another 30 minutes downhill to El Tablón, which has eight stone statues. El Alto de San Andrés is 20 minutes

Tierradentro Valley.

beyond the village. Beyond El Alto, it's around 90 minutes up and down various hills to El Aguacate. There are around 30 tombs here but only one is properly maintained. Either way you'll be treated to some great views around Aguacate.

PASTO AND THE FAR SOUTH

The capital of the Department of Nariño, some 388km (240 miles) south of Cali, is Pasto, which was founded in 1539 by Lorenzo de Aldana. It's a robust city of some 500,000 inhabitants sitting at 2,527 meters (8,290ft) above sea level on a high plateau. To get here from Cali involves traveling along the Pan-American Highway, where you'll be treated to stunning scenery all along the way. Many visitors pass through here on their way to Ecuador, as the border is only 88km (55 miles) away, but it's a worthwhile destination in its own right, with fine architecture and, a couple hours away, one of the most amazing hillside colonial churches in the world.

As with many areas in southern Colombia, Pasto is a center for cattle ranching. It's also had its fair share

of earthquakes, but most of the colonial buildings still stand despite other buildings being destroyed over time. It is noteworthy as a historical center, because for many years during the Independence Wars it was a stronghold of the Spanish forces, and was the last Colombian city to fall to the patriots. Overall the setting here is a very attractive one, helped no doubt by the presence of the Volcán Galaras, which overlooks the city from the west.

The main plaza here is the **Parque Antonio Nariño**. The **Gobernación building** is a fine example of historical architecture. Also here you'll find the **Iglesia de San Juan Batista** (Mon–Fri 7.30am–11am, Sat 3.30–6.30pm, Sun 7.30am–1am), which, founded in 1537 is the oldest church in Pasto. The outside is blocky and slightly forbidding, but the interior is ornate and cavernous. Other churches worth exploring nearby include the **Cristo Rey** (Calle 20, no. 24–64) and **La Merced** (Calle 18 at Carrera 22).

Another branch of the Gold Museum, the **Museo del Oro Nariño** (Calle 19,

Burial cave, Tierradentro.

no. 21–27; tel: 2-721 9100; Tue–Sat 10am–5pm; free) can be found here in Pasto. It has exhibitions showcasing artifacts from the indigenous communities of Southern Colombia, as well as a library and an auditorium. Also in the city center is the **Museo Alfonso Zambrano** (Calle 20, no. 29–79; tel: 2-731 2837; Mon–Sat 8am–noon, 2–4pm; free), which has a nice collection of colonial and indigenous art, with a particular focus on Quiteño (those from Quito) pieces.

TOWARD THE BORDER

Those heading south to Ecuador will stop in at **Ipiales**, the last major town before the border. It's about a 2-hour trip, and nearby is one of the most striking churches anywhere, **Santuario Las Lejas** (7km/4 miles from Ipiales; www.santuariolavirgendelaslajas.com). Its origins are mystical, even by church standards. In 1754 a woman, Maria, and her deaf-mute daughter Rosa were traveling between Potosi and Ipiales and stopped at a cave near the Guaitara River. Rosa entered the cave and when she returned, she had the powers of speech. Days later Rosa went to the cave again where she encountered the Mother Mary and Baby Jesus. Later, Rosa fell ill and died, and the Mother Mary resurrected her. People began to visit the cave in droves, and that same year a priest built a straw church at the site. They first began the church as we know it today in 1899, and it wasn't finished until 50 years later. The church, located on the side of a gorge, is one of the greatest examples of Gothic Revival architecture in Colombia, maybe even the world.

Ipiales is 2km (1 mile) from the Rumichaca Bridge, which crosses the Río Carchi, and forms the border with Ecuador. Buses and *colectivos* run from Calle 14/Carrera 11 in Ipiales to the border, for around US$1. A taxi should cost between US$5–7. For visa issues contact the **Ecuadorian Consulate** in Ipiales, located in the **Oficina Migracion** (Carrera 7, no. 14–10; tel: 1-773 2292; www.ipiales.consulado.gob.ec; Mon–Fri 9am–noon, 2–5pm).

Santuario Las Lejas.

Beach at Nuquí.

CHOCÓ

Much of Colombia's little-visited Pacific Coast may be remote and borderline inaccessible, but it holds myriad rewards for those who make the pilgrimage to its pristine beaches and sleepy fishing villages.

There are a couple reasons Colombia's Chocó Department remains the least visited area of the country. One of these has to do with its location. In the south of Colombia, Chocó stretches 400km (250 miles) west from the Cordillera Occidental to the port city of Buenaventura and the Pacific Coast. The coastline continues north over 1,400km (870 miles) from the Valle de Cauca to Panama. In this northern region you'll find the only break in the 48,000km (29,825-mile) -long Pan-American Highway. From Alaska to Tierra del Fuego, the only place where this network of highways doesn't exist is in what's known as the Darién Gap, a 160km (100-mile) -long rainforest area in southern Panama's Darién Province. Construction has been impeded here due to the fact that this area of the department receives a staggering yearly rainfall of some 3,000mm (118ins). Where this area meets Colombia is where the Chocó begins.

CHOCÓ'S CHECKERED PAST AND TRAGIC PRESENT

The other reason Chocó isn't more popular is to do with crime. In the 1990s and 2000s, when the rebel groups were forced out of the cities by Colombia's military, they fled to the remotest parts of Amazonas: the Llanos and Chocó. These areas appealed

to rebel groups who wanted to continue their cocaine production operations in little-developed areas with a negligible or non-existent military presence. The guerrillas therefore settled near to trafficking routes and under cover of dense rainforests. In doing so they seized land from local *campesinos*, poverty-stricken families and other residents of these areas, forcing the mass migrations that continue to plague the country.

Today, Colombia's refugee crisis is of harrowing proportions. Out of all

Main Attractions

Fiesta de San Pacho
Nuquí
Parque Nacional Natural Utría
Bahía Solano
Isla Gorgona

Map on page 258

Fishermen near Utria National Park.

⏺ Fact

If you travel up to the municipality of Lloró, in the Chocó Department, at the border of Panama, you will arrive in a place that holds the record for Highest Average Annual Precipitation, with a massive 13,300mm (523.6ins) per year. According to the 2012 World Almanac, that officially makes Lloró the wettest place on earth. Such high levels of precipitation and heavy rains often results in flooding, landslides, and overflowing rivers, which displaces entire communities and even causes deaths.

A canoe on the Atrato River.

the countries in the world, Colombia is believed to have the second-most internally displaced persons (IDP). Since 2014, nearly six million people have been registered with the govern ment as having been internally placed. These are predominatel poorest people from the poorest of the country, many of whom are Colombians from the Chocó De ment, a region where over 65% people live well below the povert So long as Colombia is at wa rebel groups, the country will a have a refugee problem.

In the last few years the Department has been the s ground of the kidnapping of a Colombian General by FARC rebels, an armed attack by National Liberation Army (ELN) that forced the closure of the road between Medellín and Quibdó, and, in 2014, the kidnapping by ELN rebels of a Dutch man, who was released one year later. Until recently Buenaventura, Colombia's southern Pacific port city, was ranked as the most dangerous and violent in the nation.

Per State Dept – Don't travel to Choco –

LOOKING TO THE FUTURE

However, Chocó's violent past and present economic problems are no reason to bypass this section of the indeed ventura an infurom the rnational it up to d States. veen the t Colomstem the r future. ss – only d there is still no paved roadway from Medellín to Quibdó – means you will doubtless find untouched landscapes and idyllic hidden beaches.

The nature here is just as stunning as any other place in Colombia. In the northern Chocó are the Serranía de los Saltos and Serranía del Baudó mountain ranges. These majestic monoliths seem to rise straight out of the Pacific Ocean, reaching heights

of some 500 meters (1,640ft). Cutting through the tropical green rainforest that blankets their surface are a number of cascading white waterfalls, the sight of which will transport you to a lost world. Whale watching is one of the principal tourist activities here, and you'll want to be in Nuquí during the June to October season, when it's not uncommon to see pods of humpback whales breach the jade waters off Colombia's Pacific Coast.

SAFETY CONSIDERATIONS

Despite Chocó's status as being a region that is ever opening up to tourism, it's always wise to exercise caution. Check with local authorities before venturing either to Buenaventura or Quibdó to check on the current situation. Other good resources include the UK's Colombia travel advice section of the foreign travel information page (www.gov.uk), and www.visitchoco.com, which is run by the Chocó Community Tourism Alliance.

TRANSPORTATION WITHIN CHOCÓ AND GETTING YOUR BEARINGS

As it stands, the only road services in the Chocó exist from Medellín to Quibdó. The bus company Rapido Ochoa (tel: 574-444-8888; www.rapidoochoa.com) runs a service from Medellín to Quibdó for around US$25 and the journey takes about 7 hours. However, portions of the road leading into Chocó are unpaved, which makes for an arduous and uncomfortable journey. Instead, it is recommended to fly from Medellín to Quibdó. Satena (tel: 571-605 2222; www.satena.com) and Aerolineas Antioquia (www.ada-aero.com) offer one-way tickets for around US$60. You can then connect onward to Nuquí (around US$40), or Bahía Solano (US$60) with Satena. There are also direct flights from Medellín to Nuquí and Bahía Solano for around US$80–100 with Satena, and direct

flights from Medellín to Bahía Solano for around US$80–100 with Aerolineas de Antioquia.

Within Chocó overland routes are practically non-existent. Infrastructure projects aim to connect Quibdó to Nuquí and the port town of Tribugá by road and eventually train. However, these developments seem to be moving at a glacial pace, which is almost understandable when you take environmental conditions and funding obstacles into account. There's no telling when a road linking Quibdó to Nuquí might finally be finished. Instead transportation around the various coastal destinations in Chocó is usually done by water. Boats between Nuquí and El Valle run on Monday and Friday and cost about US$23 for the round trip.

It is possible to make the three-day overland trek through the jungle from Quibdó to the coast. However, due to safety concerns this is not recommended. In 2013 a former governor of Quibdó was kidnapped by guerrillas just outside the city, so the risks

Young boys in Bahía Solano.

⊘ Tip

The road from Medellín to Quibdó is rough and unpaved for the most part. It is wise to take a flight from Medellín to Chocó.

are very real. That said, upon arrival at the coast you can move freely back and forth between towns via water taxi with few security concerns. ATMs and currency exchange houses are a rarity here, so it's best to stockpile some pesos before you arrive in Chocó.

QUIBDÓ

Critics of **Quibdó** ❶ make a persuasive argument when they rattle off the reasons not to visit Chocó's capital city. There's no thundering Zona Rosa, like in Medellín's Poblado neighborhood, or hilly colonial enclave like Bogotá's La Candelaria or Cali's San Antonio.

If you're lucky you might find a small number of foreign travelers, but most of the few *extranjero* faces you're likely to see belong to volunteers or aid workers. You'll certainly be treated to a noticeable military presence when you arrive, as Quibdó is the typical embarkation point for anti-narco operations in the area.

However, to write off Quibdó altogether would be a mistake. Its location on the banks of the Río Atrato is pleasant, and the **Catedral San Francisco de Asis** (Carrera 2, no. 24a–32), which overlooks the water, is as striking as any other colonial church in the country. Its long, grey, sturdy exterior with twin towers and tall side galleries make it elegant and fortress-like all at once. Inside the church is very stately, with large white columns lining a long nave that leads to a pulpit sitting at the base of an impressive dome. This church acts as both a religious and cultural touchstone for the city – it's the start point for the famous Fiesta de San Pacho.

Then there's the **Malecón**, the waterfront promenade running along the edge of the river. At dusk, the birds return from their day's exploits for a good night's rest, and the locals come out here to take in the sunsets over the water. There's an expansive public space just below the church where you can enjoy sunsets, and this area often hosts outdoor concerts during festivals.

There's definitely something to be said for stepping out of your comfort zone and into an area mostly free of tourism. In Quibdó you'll find the locals to be warm and curious, eager to know more about you and your reasons for visiting their tragic, beautiful region. Of course Quibdó is also the transfer point from the rest of Colombia to Nuquí or Bahía Solano on the Pacific Coast. If you're not taking a direct flight to Nuquí or Bahía Solano, then you'll likely be flying from Quibdó.

THE FESTIVAL OF SAINT FRANCIS OF ASSISI (FIESTA DE SAN PACHO)

What's true for most of Colombia is true for even the most deprived parts of the nation: Colombians love a good party. Every year, the residents of Quibdó have a huge celebration, starting September 3. The Catedral San Francisco kicks off the month-long festivities with a Catholic opening mass. However, despite the influence of Rome, this is as much a celebration of Afro-Colombian roots and the religious heritage that comes with it.

After mass the church band kicks things into a higher gear with a performance of traditional *chirimía* music. It's a rollicking, get-up-and-move folk genre that features instruments from around the globe. These include horns, the *tambora* (two-headed drum made from local trees), and European cymbals. The result is a versatile kind of music that has absorbed many influences over the years, including versions of the polka and the Spanish Jota, and there are even hints of big band and Mardi Gras-style jazz. This music is constantly evolving with the people, and as for the singing, it often features plenty of African-inspired vocals. All of these influences combine to form something truly unique to the region. However, once the party leaves the church, and the musicians take to the street, and San Pacho becomes one giant party unrivalled anywhere, save for the great carnivals of the world.

Of course it wouldn't be a carnival without parade processions featuring dancers clad in colorful and elaborate costumes. During the month of San Pacho, each of Quibdó's 12 districts holds a mass in the morning followed by processions of dancers, musicians, and themed floats. On the morning of September 3, for example, locals bring an image of a patron saint down to the banks of the Río Atrato and sing hymns. The afternoon's processions mark the symbolic journey of the saint. Every neighborhood takes part, and as in New Orleans or Brazil, local

Quibdó's cathedral.

> **Tip**

One of the most popular tourist attractions in Chocó is whale watching. The season is relatively short, and only lasts from June through October, so be sure to make your arrangements during these times.

artists and artisans design the floats, decorations, and costumes while the younger generation learn the craft at their feet. Its then up to committees formed in various neighborhoods to organize events of San Pacho and promote the city's cultural heritage. The result is one big month-long party where everyone plays a role and everyone carouses until they can carouse no longer.

There are many reasons the Fiesta de San Pacho takes place every year, including heritage and tradition. Perhaps the occasion is stronger now more than ever for the simple reason that, in the face of great tragedy, loss and deprivation, there's nothing more cathartic than giving over to wild exuberance and musical expression as a way to reaffirm the beauty of life.

NUQUÍ

Many travelers who come to Chocó will likely be heading to **Nuquí** ❷, before possibly continuing to Bahía Solano. That's because, aside from the Parque Nacional Natural Utría,

Nuquí is one of the best places to spot humpback whales on the entire Pacific Coast. As a town, though, it will likely leave many visitors feeling underwhelmed, with just an airstrip where the flights arrive and a couple of stores. Most people will simply be passing through, headed for the famous Pacific Coast eco-lodges to the north and south of the town.

The fact that these lodging options are thriving is proof positive that the Chocó's safety reputation is improving, leading to at least minor gains in tourism. Many locals, in fact, would say that the gains are more than minor. There are various sustainable tourism initiatives in this area, and many of the employees report that during whale-watching season (from June to October) the areas of Nuquí, Bahía Solano, and the Utría Natural Park see up to a 50% increase in tourism.

Of course this leads to higher prices, and visitors who touch down in Nuquí and want to stay at one of the award-winning eco-lodges are going to a high price for the pleasure. Package tours can run well over US$500 for just a few nights' stay, and backpackers looking for budget options will likely be disappointed when they can't find a room for less than US$50 per night. Still, visitors can take solace in the fact their hard-earned dollars are not just going toward a great eco-tourism experience, but are helping to lift up local workers whose towns have been ravaged by deprivation and narco violence.

There's also reason to hope that the future interconnectivity of Nuquí to mainland Chocó could lead to lower prices in the future. The road and train project connecting the Pacific town to Quibdó and the port of Tribugá is still ongoing, and when it's completed, transportation, food, and lodging prices could be more attractive to the budget traveler.

Whale breaching the waters off Gorgona Island.

PARQUE NACIONAL NATURAL UTRÍA

Between Bahía Solano and Nuquí you'll find the **Parque Nacional Natural Utria** ❸ (boat from El Valle or Nuquí costs around US$25 return, reserve transportation at your hotel or eco-lodge). The park encompasses a portion of Chocó that is highly representative of the area's rich biodiversity, which is the key reason the park was created in 1987. It comprises some 54,000 hectares (133,437 acres) and preserves several aquatic and land species of animal. At the south end of the park visitors will find mountain walls descending at steep angles right into the ocean, and when viewed through the mist, the beauty of these mountains, carpeted as they are in a bright green rug, becomes even more enigmatic.

To the north is the *ensenada* (inlet) that is home to most of tourist activity in the park. There's an abundance of marine life that likes to congregate here, including two different types of whales as well as migratory turtles and many species of bird. However, the real stars here are the whales, and this is one of the prime viewing areas to catch a glimpse of these migrating animals as they move just offshore of Colombia's coast. To the locals, the arrival of the whales means good luck – and there are few better places to experience this luck than in the Parque Nacional Natural Utria.

About halfway up the inlet you'll find the national park headquarters. There's a visitor center here with friendly staff, maps, some exhibits of whale bones, and a restaurant. Here, you can inquire about volunteer projects such as clearing the nearby beaches of garbage. Paddling around in a kayak or canoe is the best way to explore this area, as motorboats aren't allowed past the headquarters. Here you can chance upon some secluded white sand beaches, as well as enjoy some more stunning coastal mountain scenery. It's possible to make arrangements to arrive at the park either in Nuqui or El Valle for a day trip, depending on weather conditions. If you ask the captain nicely, some water taxis running between El Valle and Nuquí will drop you off at a private island, Playa Blanca, just offshore from the park. It's a good spot for snorkeling and fishing. It's also possible to hitch rides with fishermen in this area.

You can find more information about the park, as well as inquire about safety concerns, at www.parquesnacionales.gov. co, or by emailing ecoturismo@parques nacionales.gov.co.

EL VALLE

50km (30 miles) north of Nuquí, and past the Parque Natural Utría, is **El Valle** ❹. Located on the coast, it's a rapidly developing hotbed of tourism, not least of all because it's got what's probably the best surfing in the entire Chocó. The conditions here are also great for bodysurfing or merely swimming, and the best part is that many of these beaches are of the secluded

Utría National Park.

⊙ Where

Transportation to Isla Gorgona can be reserved through Unión Temporal PNN Gorgona (tel: 321-768 0539; www.vivegorgona.com). The journey involves one boat from Buenaventura south to the town of Guapi (US$68 pp), then another boat from Guapi to the island (US$100 pp). They can also arrange flights from Cali to Guapi (US$170 pp).

A basilisk lizard, Gorgona Islands.

variety. One beach option that is generally regarded as the best is **El Amejal**, which is located to the north of town and is as wide as the day is long. Visitors can find sleeping options here in the form of *cabanas*. **El Tigre** is another isolated beach that's about a three-hour walk from town, or you can arrive by boat. If you do decide to hire boats around El Valle, be warned that currents in the harbor have been known to knock boats into the rocks. Make sure any boat you ride in has the proper safety equipment, such as life vests. Also, it's possible to hire local guides in El Valle for canoe trips up the Río Baudó.

One conservation project here that's popular with visitors is a *tortugario* called Estacíon Septiembre, located on a beach about 5km (3 miles) from El Valle. Run by the Fundación Natura (tel: 1-245 5700; www.natura.org.co), this project was founded in 1991 to help protect the offspring of various species of marine turtles. In September the turtles arrive at the beach and lay their eggs in the sand and the foundation protects these eggs from predators and then, a couple months later, the recently hatched offspring as they make their way to the water. Those who contact the organization can arrange a visit. Visit the website for more details.

BAHÍA SOLANO

There's a road that cuts inland from El Valle, heading north 18km (11 miles) until you reach the coastal retreat of **Bahía Solano ⑤**. Just before you reach the town you'll pass its small airfield. Bahía Solano is a young place, originally founded as an agricultural colony in 1935, before splitting off from Nuquí in 1962, when it formed its own separate municipality. The population is a respectable 10,000 people or so, and aside from the tourist lodges here there are few landmarks other than a charming Pentecostal church.

As remote as it is, this bayside town is one of the tourism centers of the Chocó. Vacationers from Medellín frequently make the trip here during the whale season, as you can see these majestic animals breaching the water from the shore. It's also not uncommon to see volunteers releasing baby turtles onto the beach near the water. Outside of the season Bahía Solano transitions into a sleepy fishing village. However, its location along the narco's smuggling routes means that every once in a while, a fisherman happens to come across a stray parcel of cocaine. The resulting windfall is equivalent to a lifetime's earnings, which means some of these guys hit the proverbial lottery.

Regarding activities, trekking, diving, snorkeling, whale watching, surfing, birdwatching and waterfall hikes are all popular excursions here. You can enquire about these activities at the Hotel Balboa Plaza. It's hard to miss this three-story lodging option, as its grand design and delusions of luxury are the stuff of narcos. Coincidentally – or maybe not considering the location – it was Pablo Escobar who built this sprawling pad back in the 1980s. As with many of Escobar's still-remaining haunts, the Hotel Balboa is a shell of its former glory.

BUENAVENTURA AND ISLA GORGONA

As mentioned earlier, the southern Chocó was for many years regarded as one of the most dangerous parts of Colombia. This extended to the port city of **Buenaventura ⑥**, which earned the distinction of being Colombia's most dangerous city, a hub for drug and human trafficking. Today Buenaventura is much safer (although the trafficking trade still exists here), and a strong military presence in the area means that visitors who spend a short time here likely won't face any real trouble. As a port it handles around 60 percent of Colombia's total exports, so its streets are always bustling. There isn't much to recommend in Buenaventura, and most likely travelers will be arriving here merely as a transition point for hopping one of the cargo boats up the Pacific Coast (see page 280).

Sadly, for a long time the danger of Buenaventura extended to **Parque Nacional Natural Isla Gorgona ⑦**, an island national park in Chocó's far south. Originally it was inhabited by indigenous groups and was first settled by the Kuna from the San Blas archipelago in Panama. The conquistador Francisco Pizarro arrived in 1528 from Peru and named the island *Gorgona*, after the poisonous snakes that were found here. It was these snakes, and the island's shark-infested waters, that dissuaded inmates from escaping Gorgona when it was an island prison. In 1984, the prison was shut down.

Gorgona boasts some picture-perfect deserted beaches that make great vantage points for witnessing whale migration. You probably won't get closer to the animals than by sitting on one of Isla Gorgona's white-sand beaches and simply waiting as entire pods pass by, mere feet in front of your face. There's also great snorkeling and diving here, but it's best to bring your own equipment from the mainland.

⊘ Fact

Isla Gorgona is a prime destination for birders, as the park protects various species on the island, including geese, cormorants, herons, and pelicans. There's also no shortage of monkeys and iguanas here as well.

Dolphins off the Gorgona Islands.

⊘ THE NEW AMAZON?

Each year tourists flock to Colombia's Amazonas Department to see that great stretch of river and catch a glimpse of the eclectic wildlife. However, more and more people are discovering that the Amazon isn't Colombia's only untamed jungle.

The flora and fauna of the Chocó region is not to be overlooked. Each year it's possible to witness sea turtles crawling onto the beaches of the Pacific coast in Chocó. Then of course there are the humpback whales that pass by the shores every year from June through October. Spotting them has become a popular activity in the region. Not forgetting, of course, the jungles and protected parks of the Chocó Department that countless species of insects and animals call home. All things considered, there's no better time to discover Colombia's Chocó region than now.

Hiking in the jungle at the
Amacayacu National Park.

AMAZONAS

At Colombia's southernmost tip, where the country meets Peru and Brazil, the world's largest river cuts through a jungle ecosystem that is home to a third of the world's wildlife.

Leticia, located in the Amazonas Department, enjoys a few distinctions that make it stand out from anywhere else in the country. Namely, it's the nation's southernmost town and is located right on the Amazon River, at the borders of Colombia, Brazil, and Peru. Also worth mentioning is its extreme remoteness: there are still no roads linking Leticia to any other city or town in the country, which means to get there you have to fly, or take a boat from Peru or Brazil.

Since the recent boom in tourism, **Leticia ❶** has seen more and more visitors from all over the world. Where there once were sleepy working-class neighborhoods, a few malls, and a couple of hotels and *hospedajes,* broken up by patches of dirt and tall grass, now you'll see a burgeoning metropolis pushing up against Brazil's own ever-expanding municipality, Tabatinga. Those who arrive by plane will see a scale model of the grand international hub that is due to replace the current humble airport sometime in the next few years, which spells further growth on the horizon.

Amazonas' history is an interesting one. Way before there were towns dreaming of expansion, there was the rubber boom. This took place in the late 19th and early 20th centuries

when Leticia was still part of Peru's Loreto Department. This period is regarded as the most ignoble era of the region's history. The governments of Brazil and Peru sanctioned the enslavement of thousands of local indigenous peoples to toil among the rubber trees, and many died as a result of backbreaking labor and extreme conditions. The Colombian author José Eustasio Rivera recounts the awful conditions in the Amazon Basin during this time in his novel *La Vorágine* (The Vortex, 1924).

Main Attractions
The Amazon River
Isla de los Micos
Puerto Nariño
Macagua
Museo Natütama

Map on page 266

Ticuna children, Puerto Nariño.

In 1922 Peru ceded Leticia to Colombia in exchange for rights to the land south of the Putumayo River. In 1932, however, Peru had a change of heart and sent 200 soldiers to occupy the town. The conflict became known as the Colombia-Peru War and was settled the following year by the League of Nations, who awarded the territory to Colombia. Tensions have been mostly stable from then until the present day, although not without Colombia maintaining a conspicuous military presence in town. In accordance with Colombia's constitution of 1991, some 52 percent of the Colombian Amazon has been set aside for indigenous peoples in the form of 121 *resguardos* (reserves) home to some 55,000.

PLANNING YOUR AMAZON ADVENTURE

Major advances in the region's tourism infrastructure means it's easier than ever to find cheap flights to and from Leticia. You can purchase tickets in Bogotá, or online in advance, through VivaColombia (see page 279), Colombia's only budget carrier. You'll want to make Leticia your base and organize all excursions from there.

Leticia's climate will dictate the clothing and supplies you pack. Average high temperatures hover in the 87°F (31°F) range, with humidity typically in the 60–90 percent range. Durable but light clothing is a must, but trekking boots are mostly useless if you're planning a hike through the jungle. Most tour operators will provide you with rubber hiking boots, which can stand up to the moisture. It's also worth noting that there isn't a rainy or dry season in Amazonas, but rather a high-water season and a low-water season, which denotes the water levels on the Amazon River. The high season is from December to May and the low season is from

⊘ AN AMAZONIAN VISION?

The North American indigenous have their peyote, the Bwiti people of Africa have their ibogaine, and the natives of the Amazon have ayahuasca. A medicinal herbal brew, ayahuasca roughly translates to vine of the spirit, and is made by boiling the vine and leaf of the *banisteriopsis caapi* vine. Also known as *yagé*, ayahuasca is the central component in many indigenous spiritual ceremonies in the Amazon. Drinking the potent mixture leads to altered states of consciousness, hallucinations, and can last between 4–8 hours. Therefore, these ceremonies should always be conducted under the watchful eye of an experienced guide, usually a spiritual shaman. Although not recommended, travelers can pay to take part in these ceremonies.

June to November. The recommended time to visit the area is during the low season, as high water levels make certain excursions difficult.

While the planning can be taken care of on a whim, taking the appropriate precautions might just mean the difference between the Amazonian experience of a lifetime and a few days sick in bed. There are countless animals in these jungles and many of them can make travelers quite sick. Insect repellent is a must, as Amazonian bugs love to feed on unsuspecting travelers.

The CDC lists environments in Colombia at altitudes below 1700 meters (5,577ft) as having a low but potential risk for malaria. This applies to Amazonas, where mosquito bites are frequent. Talk to any local and you'll be hard-pressed to find specific incidents of infection, and ex-Bogotá residents who have lived there for decades without taking medication have never had the disease. Still, travelers who want to err on the side of caution can invest in malaria tablets such as malarone, or a round of doxycycline. Consult your doctor before traveling.

The CDC also recommends that all visitors to Colombia (no matter the region) to get a yellow fever vaccination. As of early 2017 immigration wasn't specifically checking for yellow fever certificates or mandating shots, but this could change in the future – especially when Leticia's small airport finally gets its international upgrade. Travelers in Bogotá without their shots can go to the long-distance bus terminal, where a small medical clinic will administer shots for anyone, including foreigners, for free.

ARRIVING IN LETICIA

Anyone arriving in Leticia is subject to an entrance tax. As of January 2017, the fee is US$7. There's a **tourist information point** (daily 7am–noon, 2–5pm) in the airport baggage claim next to the entrance-tax payment kiosk. Despite being besieged by new arrivals, they'll answer questions and provide maps.

In town you'll encounter tour providers hustling for an honest living, but their persistence can be taxing. Many of these operators run acceptable tours

⊙ **Tip**

Although malaria is rare in Colombia, mosquitos are abundant in Amazonas. Check with your doctor before leaving for Colombia to see if a course of anti-malaria treatment is right for you.

Bridge between a lodge and the Amazon River.

⊘ Tip

Be sure to take care of all visa issues and exit requirements from Leticia, before you leave on any river trips. Failure to have the appropriate Colombian exit stamp upon arrival in Peru or Brazil means you will be sent back.

that are comparable from one to the next. However, it is still best to arrange a tour through the reputable companies listed in this book, or through your hostel or hotel. The commercial center, located on Calle 8 and between Carreras 11 and 6, is bustling, noisy, and lined with little other than souvenir shops, mini-markets, and discount retail outlets. However, this is the area to come if you are looking for faster-speed internet cafés, as the Wi-Fi in many hostels and hotels isn't exactly lightning fast.

AROUND TOWN

At the start of Leticia's downtown, at Calle 8 and Carrera 11, you'll find **Parque Orellana**. This may not be the town's main park, but it is still a good one. There's a large amphitheater in the center, which often hosts outdoor concerts on weekends, or holiday shows during the Christmas season. At the edge of the park, at the corner of Calle 8 and Carrera 11, you'll find some good street food in the form of *pinchos* (grilled, skewered meats), and

cold drinks and beer are on hand from the myriad food carts.

If you head a block west from the park on Calle 8 you'll reach the *muelle* (dock), the disembarking and departure point for all boats coming to and from town. Its adjacent waterfront walkway is about 100 meters long and is known as the **Malecón Turistico**, a type of promenade. Anyone booking an excursion to anywhere else on the Amazon will leave from this area.

Just above the docks you'll find the **mercado municipal** (Local Market; Mon–Sat 4am–7pm, Sun 4am–2pm), which is another in Latin America's great tradition of indoor and open-air municipal markets. The best of these are often a maze of produce and meat vendors assaulting your senses with fresh beef, fish, and produce. This mercado municipal is one such place, although its dingy concrete facade reflects the disrepair of the immediate surrounding area. On the ground level workers hack coconut and yucca while produce vendors hock a welcome variety of fruits and vegetables, like papaya, limes, grapes and mangoes.

Busy street near the river port in Leticia.

Upstairs, the entire floor is lined with humble, makeshift kitchens acting as mini-restaurants were folks can grab a cheap set-menu breakfast or lunch, often featuring just three options: meat, chicken, or fish. A *caldo* (soup) usually accompanies the meal.

Two blocks north on Carrera 11 is **Parque Santander**, the town's main plaza. On the way you'll encounter one of the stars of Leticia's flora, the *pomarrosa* tree. It produces a sweet fruit similar to an apple, and its lurid flowers shed their needles, coating the nearby ground in an impressive display of electric pink. In the park there is a central fountain as well as a small lake with an arching bridge. It's a good area to spot birds in the green *carbonero* trees, and there are plenty of birds to see here.

One of the most pleasant things to do in Leticia occurs every night at sundown when it's possible to climb up to the top of the bell tower in **La Catedral**, the cathedral on the east side of the park (US$1 to climb up). Here you'll witness the return of hundreds, if not thousands, of macaws to their homes in the park's trees, announcing in a dense cacophony their intention to get a good night's rest. It's the perfect environment to survey the country's southernmost city and take in the Amazonian frontier.

ISLA DE LOS MICOS

The idea of a mysterious Amazonian island ruled by a cabal of primates seems like the stuff of adventure fiction, but 35km (22 miles) northwest of Leticia, such a place exists. In reality, there is little that's mysterious about **Isla de Los Micos ❷**, a small island overrun by the *mico fraile* (squirrel monkey). The island is more a tourist attraction than a protected area, with visitors following professional guides around marked pathways and feeding banana pieces (the only food allowed) to the ravenous inhabitants.

There's no need to fear the primates either. The *micos* aren't ill-tempered Kong-like apes, but rather diminutive bundles of energy with a playful disposition and soft grey fur tinged with yellow. In fact, they are in such abundance on the island, that accidentally treading on them as you walk becomes a real risk. They're not afraid of human contact either, which makes for great photo-ops, of course, but be sure to keep your pockets zipped up and any small valuables out of reach of the thieving critters.

Many tour operators bundle a trip to this island in their package price, but you can go on your own via water taxi (US$5 each way) and pay the US$10 entry fee yourself. A trip to the Isla de Los Micos is great for families and kids. It's best complimented by a visit to the **Fundación Maikuchiga**, a primate sanctuary in nearby Mocagua that offers educational tours regarding the various primate species in the area, as well as information about conservation.

MOCAGUA

Mocagua is home to 800 members of the eponymous tribe that live in this area of the Amazon. It is about an hour

The market in Leticia.

and a half west of Leticia (US$8 by boat) and half an hour east of Puerto Nariño. This is one of many *resguardos* in the area set aside for indigenous groups, and the Mocaguas have created a thriving, modern community in an ideal location. The town is set on a section of high banks on the Amazon, which allows for breathtaking views of the river. Mocagua even has a 'disco', which is really just a terrace bar sitting on a hill that makes a great spot for a sunset drink as the last light of the day disappears over the jungle. There are a couple of *hospedajes* in town, which can be reserved through operators in Leticia and Puerto Nariño.

FUNDACIÓN MAIKUCHIGA

Aside from experiencing the local pace of life in Mocagua, another great reason to come to this area is to visit the **Fundación Maikuchiga** (www.monkeystory.org). This sanctuary focuses on community conservation, primate research, and the occasional animal rescue. Those who do come will enjoy a 30-minute tour that showcases the various primates in the area. There are

Banana vendor and boats at the fishing port, Leticia.

five principal species that live in the immediate area surrounding Maikuchiga, including the *mono auyador* (howler monkey), *mico* (squirrel monkey), *capuchin* (the aggressive thief of the jungle), and tamarin. The tour also includes a visit to the home of the fifth and most incredible of all, the *leoncito*, or pygmy marmoset – the smallest monkey in the world. A full-grown adult will fit in the palm of a human hand, and a child or adolescent can wrap itself around a person's finger. Here at Maikuchiga there are no captive pygmy marmosets, but the tour does include a visit to their home – a jungle tree. These species live in family *manadas* (troops) and typically inhabit a single tree. They're lemur-like in appearance and move at incredible speeds, zipping around vines and branches in order to avoid birds of prey. If you visit the marmoset tree house you'll notice small circular holes where these omnivorous rascals gnaw into the bark looking for tree gum. Aside from a benevolent giant offering them banana pieces, this is a primary source of nutrition for these tiny creatures.

Monkeys aren't the only stars of the show at Maikuchiga. The avian inhabitants of the jungle make for a fine sight as well. Colombia in general is a birders dream, as it is home to almost 2,000 different species of birds. Some of the most exotic species reside here in Amazonas, and in the area around Maikuchiga it is possible to see some rare and even endangered species, like the wattled curassow.

For all the wildlife attractions that abound in Maikuchiga, the principal role of the organization is one of conservation, and that is the dominant message. Sara Bennett, a US expat and director of the operation, has been working in the region since 1984. In that time she's witnessed changes in climate and tourism that threaten the fragile ecosystem of Amazonas. It's through a simple visit that the average traveler or tourist can

learn how they can do their part to preserve these surroundings for generations to come (see page 275).

PUERTO NARIÑO

Puerto Nariño ❸ is fast becoming
one of the most idyllic outposts on the
Amazon River, which has its positives
and negatives. The community itself
is an ideal to aspire to: some 1,200
people (many of them members of the
22 indigenous communities that live
in the surrounding areas) have created the smallest official settlement in
Colombian Amazonia, and it runs like
a dream. Everything here seems to
operate in perfect harmony, with community and commerce doing their best
to avoid exploiting the pristine environment surrounding the town. However,
ever-increasing tourism puts pressure
on a fragile ecosystem, and there are
already reports of dubious practices
like fishing out of season to provide
food for Amazonas restaurants.

Still, this town wears its ecological status on its sleeve. There are no
cars in Puerto Nariño, and the only

vehicle is a tractor used for garbage
collection. You'll see locals trimming
hedges daily and beating back the tall
grass that threatens to overtake the
populated areas, the jungle forcing
them to work overtime to protect their
little piece of paradise. How Puerto
Nariño evolves in the future will be
interesting to see, considering it is a
young settlement (founded in 1961),
with limitless potential.

ENJOYING THE TOWN

The only way to arrive at Puerto Nariño is by boat (US$10 each way from
Leticia; first boat at 8am and last at
3.30pm). You'll arrive at the long dock
at the town's entrance, and the first
thing you'll notice is that everything
is built on stilts, which is a safeguard
for the high-water season. There's a
tourist information point just west
of the main dock (8am–noon, 2–5pm)
once you get off the boat. Despite its
name, this isn't an ideal place to gather
information, as little English is spoken
here and they typically don't possess
as much knowledge of the area as the

Puerto Nariño.

local guides do. Best to reserve your Puerto Nariño excursion through one of these local operators before you leave Leticia.

Separating the town's front from the river is a well-manicured stretch of lawn dominated by a mini-stadium where locals get together and play basketball or soccer. There's no real weekend in Puerto Nariño, so locals tend to organize their recreational activities by the time of day rather than specific days. Rising up from the river, the town itself sits on small hills, with residential houses making up most of the structures.

Getting lost isn't an issue in Puerto Nariño, as the town is only about four square blocks. In the center you'll find kiosks selling beer, *pinchos,* and grilled river fish, as well as one of the town's two restaurants. Fish is the best option, but be sure to ensure that any threatened species, such as *pirarucu,* is in season before ordering. On the east end of town there is a line of homes that have been converted into small hotels, all with similar accommodations

Tourists on the river near Puerto Nariño.

(around US$10/20 for shared/private rooms) and all of good quality. There are mini supermarkets dotted throughout town and two or three small 'discos' on the waterfront where locals relax after a day on the river, with a dance and a drink. Those who want to give Colombian traditional dancing a try can arrange a visit through a local operator with Ronaldo, a local who offers dance classes in his house starting at 6pm every day. The styles are eclectic: salsa, cumbia, and the indigenous *danza de delfin enamarado* (dance of the love-struck dolphin).

MUSEO NATÜTAMA

The small Museo Natütama (Wed–Mon 9am–5pm) in Puerto Nariño, run by the Natütama NGO, is a great introduction to the flora and fauna of the region. The museum offers guided tours (Spanish only), which take about 30 minutes, with an additional 20 minutes of video nature documentaries, which are in English, and includes exhibits of aquatic animals including river dolphins, manatees, turtles and stingrays.

There are various sculptures on display here representing the spiritual connection between river animals and humans, done by local artists from the 7 de Augusto indigenous community.

EXCURSIONS FROM PUERTO NARIÑO

To fully experience the area surrounding Puerto Nariño requires more than a day trip. Reserving a package stay (three or four nights) often involves a number of activities, all of which are remarkable in their own right. Typically these include night walks through the jungle for insect, frog, and spider spotting. Caterpillars, scorpions, tarantulas, and poison dart frogs are all common sights. Other night excursions include caiman 'hunts,' which really just involves caiman-spotting on the river from a canoe, although the more fearless guides will try to catch younger caimans by hand in order to show them off to visitors.

Popular day trips include Amazon River swims and pink dolphin-spotting, although manatees and anacondas often prove elusive. Piranha fishing is another activity, as is a visit to local indigenous communities. Those who book their tour through Sergio Rojas' Amazonas de Turismo will enjoy a visit to his makeshift biosphere on the outskirts of Puerto Nariño. Here, in a manmade lake, caiman, turtles, dragonfish, and the largest scale fish in the world, the *pirarucu*, seemingly exist in perfect harmony. It's an amazing place to see various species of animal in one place, and the sight of a 3-meter (10-foot) shadow gliding beneath the water before a huge *pirarucu* breaches the surface will stay with you for quite some time.

AMACAYACU NATIONAL PARK

Near to Puerto Nariño, about 60km (40 miles) northwest of Leticia, is Colombia's first-ever Amazon protected area: **Parque Nacional Natural Amacayacu**

❹. Founded in 1975, it stretches some 100km (60 miles) from north to south and covers a whopping 3,000 sq km (1,158 sq miles). The park boasts various ecosystems, including river flood plains as well as *terra firma* rainforest. Needless to say, this allows for a rich diversity of wildlife.

The park is home to some 5,000 species of plants, 500 species of birds and 150 species of mammals. The greatest diversity of primates in the world is found here, with 12 different species represented; of course in the river you'll find pink river dolphins and manatees as well. Unfortunately, as of early 2017, the park is closed to visitors and there are no immediate plans to reopen it. However, visitors can visit the edge of the park and see and appreciate its diverse flora and fauna by making excursions from Puerto Nariño or staying in Macagua.

THE INDIGENOUS COMMUNITIES

There are three main indigenous groups in Puerto Nariño: the Tikuna,

⦿ Fact

The rich biodiversity of the Amazon Rainforest is well-documented, but did you know that experts estimate that there around 30 million species of insects in this region? Scientists have even found 700 species of beetle on a single tree.

Communal village of Tarapoto Laguna, close to Puerto Nariño.

Cocama, and Yagua. These three are collectively known as Aticoya. Many of these groups live in various *resguardos* stretching from Leticia to Peru. Many of these people have adapted to modern ways of life, but some cultures, like the Tikuna and Yagua have carried their ancient traditions through to modern times. Often this includes wearing traditional dress, living in thatched huts, and even hunting with poison-tipped blow darts.

Spending time in a local indigenous community is a popular excursion from Leticia and Puerto Nariño. This typically involves lunch and dinner (often *ajiaco* and river fish), and a stay overnight. It's worth noting that while these trips are enlightening, the indigenous aren't always enamoured with being treated as tourist attractions, and many just tolerate their guests without actively engaging. Having said that, their culture goes to the heart of the Amazon, and even today they set the tone for sustainable hunting and fishing practices in the area. For example, they don't hunt certain water animals like river dolphin, and most tribes adhere to a seasonal fishing plan so as not to diminish certain species.

TRANSPORTATION

All aquatic transportation leaves from the *muelle* (dock) at the river just below the Mercado Municipal. To journey into Brazil, you must first get your entrance stamp at the *polícia federal* (federal police station) in Tabatinga. To enter Peru you must get your entry stamp at the immigration office on Santa Rosa Island, a Peruvian community just offshore from Leticia.

TRAVEL TO BRAZIL AND PERU

There's no immigration control between Leticia and Tabatinga, which is the Brazilian town that borders Leticia to the east. As a result, visitors can travel freely between the two municipalities. However, those who wish to venture deeper into Brazil or Peru will first need to get an exit stamp in Leticia. This can be done at the immigration office in the airport (daily 8am–5pm). You then have 24 hours to exit the country.

On the Amazon River.

CONSERVATION IN AMAZONAS

Ensuring that Amazonas remains a viable tourist destination for years to come simply means enjoying this destination responsibly.

Colombia's tourism boom has had undeniable benefits for the country. Unfortunately it also has the potential to threaten certain of Colombia's more fragile ecosystems. This is especially true in Amazonas Department. As a city, Leticia is growing at geometric rates, and the increases both in size and human footprint since the mid-2000s has been striking. The potential of unfettered tourism to threaten local indigenous communities and smaller settlements, like Puerto Nariño, is very real. Climate change is also a problem, as the water levels of the Amazon River become ever more extreme and unpredictable. This threatens various fish species that are used to finding their food supply in regular locations throughout the year.

PUERTO NARIÑO AND THE RISE OF TOURISM

NGOs first arrived in Puerto Nariño around 2008 and informed the locals of the coming tourism deluge. In preparation, certain residents began training for jobs in tourism, and the best guides and tour operators (those listed in this book, like Amazonas de Turismo), got their start during this period. They are experts in local customs and heritage and also run the most efficient and comprehensive tours without placing an undue burden on the local infrastructure. In short, reserving through local experts means you'll have a more personalized, fulfilling, relaxing, and enjoyable experience, especially since it's typically done in smaller groups.

EATING RESPONSIBLY

Dining in the regions is also something that can either be done correctly or incorrectly. Even the indigenous groups don't eat certain river animals, including and especially dolphin. However, overfishing for scale fish is an issue and there are certain seasons in which to collect certain monsters of the deep, like the

pirarucu. Also, due to its prominence on nature shows, it's also become somewhat fashionable to eat the *mojojoy*, a fat white worm endemic to the region. Some restaurants will even sell the animal. However, to find it requires upending entire palm trees, which can threaten the growth of that tree. Generally, it's best to avoid it altogether.

A WORD FROM MAIKUCHIGA

Sara Bennett, of the Fundación Maikuchiga, has been working in Amazonas since 1984 and has some easy-to-follow guidelines for visitors who want to reduce their carbon footprint in the area and behave like responsible eco-tourists. First, make sure you arrange all tours locally, with local operators. Second, make sure the local community is personally involved, especially if it's an indigenous community. Third, always reserve your excursions in small groups, generally of fewer than 10 people. Adhere to these simple rules and it's all but assured you'll enjoy the experience of a lifetime.

Nukak man hunting for monkeys near Letica.

Cocoliso Isla Resort, Isla Grande.

COLOMBIA

TRAVEL TIPS

TRANSPORTATION

GETTING THERE

By air

Colombia is well serviced by many major airline carriers. Many international hubs that offer direct flights from outside the country include Bogotá's **El Dorado International** (tel: 1-266 2000; www.eldorado. aero), Cartagena's **Rafael Núñez International** (tel: 5-656 9200; www. sacsa.com.co), Medellín's **José María Córdova International** (tel: 4-402 5110; www.aeropuertojosemariacordova. com), Cali's **Alfonso Bonilla Aragón** (tel: 2-280 1515; www.aerocali.com. co), and Barranquilla's **Ernesto Cortissoz International** (tel: 5-316 0900). Other airports that also receive international flights include San Andrés' **Gustavo Rojas Pinilla International** (tel: 8-512 0020) and Pereira's **Matecaña International** (tel: 6-314 8151). Airfares will likely be more expensive when traveling in the high season (December–February), so those looking for cheap tickets will want to travel during the shoulder (March–September) or low (October–November) season.

From the United States

To Bogotá, United Airlines (tel: 1-800 864 8331; www.united.com) offers direct once-daily flights from New York, and twice-daily flights from Houston. American Airlines (tel: 1-800 433 7300; www.aa.com) also flies direct daily from Miami and Dallas to Bogotá, with other direct flights from Miami to Cali and Medellín. Delta (tel: 1-800-221 1212; www.delta.com) offer daily flights from Atlanta to Bogotá and sporadic flights from Atlanta to Cartagena. Budget carriers Jet Blue (tel: 1-801 449 2525; www.jetblue.com) and Spirit Airlines (tel: 801-401 2222; www.

spirit.com) fly direct daily from Fort Lauderdale to Bogotá, Cartagena, and Medellín.

Colombian national carrier Avianca (tel: 0810-333 8222; www. avianca.com) offers direct flights from New York to Bogotá, Medellín, and Cartagena, as well as weekly flights from Los Angeles to Bogotá.

From Canada

Air Canada (tel: 1-514 393 3333; www.aircanada.com) flies direct a few times a week from Toronto to Bogotá. Canada's budget carrier, Air Transat (tel: 1-877 872 6728; www.airtransat.com), flies once a week from Toronto and Montreal to Cartagena. United, American, Delta, and Air Canada also offer connecting flights from Vancouver, BC, to Bogotá.

From Europe

There are direct flights weekly from Paris to Bogotá with Air France (tel: 800-992 3932; www.airfrance. com). There are also weekly flights from Frankfurt with Lufthansa (tel: 800 645 3880; www.lufthansa.com). There are daily flights from Madrid to Bogotá with Iberia Airlines (tel: 800-772 4642; www.iberia.com), Air Europa (tel: 0871-423 0717; www. aireuropa.com) and Avianca. Iberia and Avianca also fly a couple times a week direct from Madrid to Medellín, and Avianca flies once a week direct from Madrid to Cali. KLM Royal Dutch Airlines (tel: 800-618 0104 www.klm.com) offers a few direct flights per week from Amsterdam to Bogotá.

From the United Kingdom

For many years travelers from the UK had to change planes in Europe or the US. However, Avianca (tel: 0810-333 8222; www.avianca.com) now offers direct flights from London to Bogotá once a day.

From Australia/New Zealand

Indirect flights to Bogotá from Auckland/Sydney are serviced by Qantas Airlines (tel: 0800-122-0337; www.qantas.com), which connects with Latam Airlines (tel: 0810-999 9526; www.latam.com) via Santiago or Lima. American and United flights connect via San Francisco, Los Angeles, and Houston.

From Latin America

Avianca is extremely well connected to most major hubs in Latin America. These include direct, often daily flights from Buenos Aires, Sao Paolo, Rio de Janeiro, Lima, Santiago, Caracas, Panama City, Mexico City, La Paz, Quito, and San José (Costa Rica) to Bogotá. Aerolineas Argentinas (tel: 0810-222 86527; www.aerolineas.com.ar) flies a few times a week to Bogotá, and Latam has daily flights from Santiago. Copa (tel: 1-800 359 2672; www.copaair.com), also flies direct from Panama City to Bogotá.

By river

In Amazonas Department, Colombia shares a border with Peru and Brazil at Leticia. Iquitos, located 365km (226 miles) to the west of Leticia, is reachable by either speedboat or slow boat. The fast boats are small, cramped, and oftentimes poorly ventilated, but they get you there in eight hours (US$85 from Leticia to Iquitos, leaves Tuesday and Sunday). The slow boats take about three days to make the journey; if you have the time, they are by far the better choice (Around US$25, including meals). The boats themselves are typically two-or-three-story powerboats with no cabins, meaning passengers must bring their own hammock in which to hang from ceiling beams on the lower decks. Vendors often sell hammocks outside the docks for between US$10–20. The conditions on board are somewhat rustic, but waking up in a hammock while motoring up the Amazon River, eating fresh fruit for breakfast and drinking coffee while looking out to the riverbanks, makes for an experience you won't forget in a hurry.

There are fast boats from Leticia to Manaus, Brazil, leaving Tuesday, Thursday and Saturday and cost US$173. Also slow boats take seven nights and cost around US$110. All meals are included.

By sea

One of the most popular international trips you can embark on from Colombia is the journey from Cartagena to Panama City by sailboat. This started out as pleasure-boat captains simply trying to earn an extra dollar by ferrying travelers back and forth between countries, and has now become a popular industry. Individual captains compete for passengers, and sometimes even companies run the boat trips. As a result, travelers have their choice of options, and oftentimes finding a boat can be as easy as checking the noticeboards in Cartagena hostels. One dependable option is Sailing Koala (tel: 312-670 7863; www.sailingkoala.com), which not only stops in the San Blas Archipelago, but also arranges dinner with an indigenous Kuna family. Another option is Blue Sailing (tel: 310 704 0425; www.bluesailing.net). Most boats charge around US$550 for the charter, and food is included. The trip itself takes about five days and passes through the San Blas Archipelago. Day three is when you'll arrive at the coral islands, and most boats will stop here for some snorkeling and a beach BBQ. Members of the Kuna tribe will also likely pass along in canoes, eager to sell handmade garments and spiny lobsters.

For those traveling on a budget, it's possible to haggle a lower price with private captains, or find a cheaper boat, but the quality of the journey will suffer as a result. Those who want to try their luck petitioning boat owners directly can head to the Club Nautico (Yacht Club; tel: 5-660 4863; near the Puente Román). Here you can engage ship captains about charter opportunities to Panama or many other locations in the Caribbean. There are often opportunities to work on boat crews in exchange for passage as well.

By bus/road

There are a few overland routes into Colombia from other countries. These include the southern Colombia-Ecuador crossing at Ipiales–Rumichaca. The main Colombian–Venezuelan crossings are at Cúcuta–San Antonio and, from Maracaibo at Maicao–Paraguachón. However, due to Venezuela's ongoing economic crises, there's high likelihood of border crossings between the two countries to be restricted or even prohibited.

GETTING AROUND

Despite many of Colombia's cities and towns being separated by various topographies, and many sitting at different altitudes, the country is surprisingly well connected via roads, highways, and airline routes. A sophisticated network of long-distance buses links all major cities in the country (although travel times can be extensive, especially when traveling between Bogotá and the coast), with minibuses and vans often connecting the smaller towns within the various departments. Travel within major cities is increasingly easy these days, as most have implemented some form of metro system, with the Medellín metro being by far the most impressive and efficient in the country.

Even better, Colombia's well-established national airlines are competing more and more, meaning

Cartagena airport.

travelers now reap the benefits of low prices. It seems that every year it's increasingly more cost-effective to fly between major cities than to take a bus. When it comes to arriving at various airports/bus terminals, Colombia's current economic situation means it won't break the bank to take a taxi. Otherwise, public transportation is a great way to get between transportation hubs and city/town centers. Journey times often vary, with little traffic in smaller towns making for uninterrupted journeys. However, during rush hour in the major cities be prepared to sit in traffic.

As for traveling on foot, despite Colombia being a welcoming country whose residents are almost universally eager to help an *extranjero* in need, hitchhiking isn't really a part of the culture, especially if you have limited Spanish. It is best to avoid hitchhiking altogether.

Air

Colombia has a good network of budget domestic airlines that make it cost efficient to fly between cities. No other carrier represents this more than VivaColombia, the country's premier budget airline. In recent years this airline has opened up major routes across Colombia, charging rock-bottom prices for their services. As with many budget airlines, the sheer amount of restrictions and conditions in order to secure a cheap ticket can seem overwhelming. If you don't want to pay hefty extra fees, be prepared to print out their boarding pass and only bring one piece of carry-on luggage.

List of Colombia's domestic airlines

Aerolineas Antioquia. www.ada-aero. com. This regional airline offers attractive prices but very limited services.

Avianca. tel: 0810-333 8222; www.avianca.com. Colombia's premier airline offers cheap domestic and international flights as well as a solid miles/ rewards program.

Copa Airlines tel: 1-800 359 2672; www.copaair.com. This Panamanian air carrier also owns Copa Airlines Colombia, which has offices throughout the country. It's a reliable option for domestic flights as well as travel to Panama City.

Satena. tel: 571-605 2222; www. satena.com. This government-owned airline has reasonable prices but its destinations are limited. Satena is best for those traveling to and from Chocó.

VivaColombia. tel: 1-844 569 7126; www.vivacolombia.com. This is Colombia's best choice for budget air travel between most major cities. However, out-dated check-in and baggage policies mean you many have to jump through a few hoops to get your cheap ticket.

Airports

Despite varying in size, Colombia's international airports provide similar services, such as food courts, left luggage amenities and, more often than not, tourist information points with English-speaking staff. The only exceptions to this are the smallest hubs, such as **Alfredo Vásquez Cobo International Airport** in Leticia, Amazonas Department.

Most foreign travelers will be flying into **Aeropuerto Internacional El Dorado**, or BOG (Calle 26, 1103–9; tel 1-266 2000; www.eldorado.aero), which is located 13km (8 miles) northeast of Bogotá's city center. The airport underwent a full renovation and upgrade in 2012, adding a second terminal to the structure. It is now comprised of terminal 1 (domestic and international flights) and terminal 2 (formerly known as *Puenté Aereo*, which is operated by Avianca and offers domestic flights only).

In terminal 1, travelers will find everything they need to hit the ground running in the capital city. There are various *casas de cambio* (currency exchange windows) both inside and outside the terminal, with many staying open 24/7. There are also duty free stores inside, but the products aren't exactly sold at bargain-basement prices. Outside the terminal are a number of ATMs, including Banco de Bogotá and Citibank, both of which accept Visa and MasterCard. Also outside is a left luggage station (US$4 per bag per 12-hour period), and on the third floor is a giant food court with sit-down restaurants and fast-food options.

Tourism offices are located in terminal 1 just outside baggage claim as well as on the second floor (both open 6am–9.30pm daily). The English-speaking staffers are extremely helpful. Currently El Dorado charges foreign travelers an airport exit fee of US$37 per person. Outside, new arrivals can catch minibuses to the north of the city. No. 26 goes direct to La Candelaria (US$1). Taxis are plentiful here and a trip to the center will cost about US$10.

By sea

In Colombia, water travel is mostly done between countries from Leticia to Brazil and/or Peru. However, a boat trip that is getting increasingly popular is the route from Buenaventura to Bahía Solano, in the Chocó Department, along Colombia's Pacific Coast. Cargo boats leave from the main port every Tuesday night at high tide (leaving for the return trip Saturday at noon), and the journey takes anywhere between 18–24 hours. It costs around US$50 and includes a cramped bunk as well as three meals.

By rail

Like many South American countries, Colombia developed an extensive railroad network around the turn of the 20th century. However, most of these tracks are out of service today. One sad example in recent times of just how futile Colombia's railroad aspirations are involves the town of Aracataca, the birthplace of Gabriel García Márquez. In 2007, with an aim to boosting tourism (a goal that still hasn't materialized) the town municipality launched the 'Yellow Train of Macondo,' a rail route that was to offer services over the 85km (53 miles) from Santa Marta to Aracataca. The line was christened with much fanfare, drawing reporters from across the nation as well as the UK and the United States. Gabo himself, and his wife, rode on the maiden voyage and great crowds of people gathered to witness the arrival of their hometown hero. However, despite the hype and fanfare, regular services are still yet to materialize.

These days most of the rail journeys in Colombia are of the touristic variety. One of the most famous examples is Bogotá's tourist train (www.turistren.com.co), which is a 53km (33-mile) line running from La Sabana station in downtown Bogotá (Calle 13, no. 18-24), stopping in Usaquén and continuing northeast to Zipaquirá, where visitors can visit the famous salt cathedral. Trains run every couple of hours on Saturday and Sunday from 8.15am to 4.40pm and tickets cost around US$17 return.

By bus

Inter-urban buses

The best method for getting around large cities in Colombia is via their metro lines. For example, Bogotá has the Transmilenio (www.transmilenio.gov.co/en), which is the most efficient way of moving quickly around that sprawling metropolis. Rides cost around US$0.75 and are paid for by rechargeable cards, which can be purchased from station tellers (US$1).

For long-distance services from the capital, Bogota's main hub is the **Terminal Central Salitre** (Diagonal 23, no. 69–60; tel: 1-423 3630, extension 145; www.terminaldetransporte. gov.co). This bus station is located on the west side of town, a couple of kilometers from the airport. It's also just about as big as El Dorado, considering it boasts some five different entrances, all of which make getting lost in the terminal a distinct possibility. However, there is a tourist information point (Mon–Sat 7am–7pm, Sun 8am–4pm; English spoken) inside the terminal at entrance 5, which is very helpful. Also in the bus terminal, between entrance 4 and 5, is **Hospital Fontibón** (Mon–Fri 7am–7pm, Sat–Sun 7am–1pm, 2pm–7pm), a small clinic that gives free yellow fever shots to all.

Long-distance bus travel

Prices for these trips are reasonable, but be prepared to experience an uncomfortable journey. Those traveling the main routes, such as from Bogotá–Cali–Medellín–Cartagena,

Medellín metro line.

should find it to be smooth sailing all the way. However, minibuses in the various rural departments and mountain areas have adopted a 'whatever works', approach, and it's not uncommon to find yourself speeding through the hills at breakneck speeds, passing other vehicles on blind curves. That said, at least there's never a dull moment.

By road

Colombia is thankfully blessed with a well-maintained system of highways. Other than in underfunded Chocó Department where the few roads that do exist are unpaved for long stretches, you'll find the roadways in most parts of the country to be in good condition. However, it is wise to be on the lookout for landslides in the wetter and more mountainous areas. They are also relatively easy to navigate across long distances. A couple of roads connect Bogotá with Medellín and the coast, and to the northeast roads run from Boyacá Department to Santander, passing through Bucamaranga and continuing toward Santa Marta, Barranquilla, and Cartagena. Roads also branch off at Bucamaranga and head to Cucuta, at the Venezuelan border. There are also routes from Bogotá over the cordillera to Valle de Cauca and Cali, and all the way down to the border with Ecuador.

The Pan-American Highway is part of this network of roads as well. This is the stretch of pavement running from Alaska down to Tierra del Fuego, broken only by the Darién Gap in Panama. It picks up again in Colombia at Turbo, in the Gulf of Urabá, and connects Medellín and the Zona Cafetera, continuing south to Cali, Popayán, and finally to the border with Ecuador. Anyone bringing a car into Colombia will be required to present proof of ownership or rental, as well as a valid tourist card. Keep all papers you are given, as you will need to present them on your exit. For drivers from Europe and the UK, Colombian authorities should accept a Carnet de Passages as a valid identification of your motor vehicle.

On major roads there are toll stations (*peajes*) every 50–100 km (30–60 miles) or so, and depending on the area the average fee is around US$3. For detailed information on tolls and prices, see: www.viajeporcolombia.com. For a good route-planning tool, check out www. rutascolombia.com.

At the time of writing, January 2017, gas prices are as follows: US$3 per gallon for regular, US$2.50 for diesel.

Car rental

All in all this interconnected nature of Colombia means road trips are a great way to see a country filled with stunning natural landscapes. Most visitors will likely be renting their vehicles, and there are good deals on economy-size cars averaging around US$30–40 per day (often better deals can be found on fare aggregator websites like www.kayak. com). However, a mid-size vehicle isn't always the best option for traversing some of Colombia's more rugged topography. For mountain and jungle journeys, a four-wheel drive vehicle with high ground clearance is ideal, and these often cost over US$100 per day to rent. Various car rental agencies can be found at most airports in Colombia, as well as throughout major cities and towns. They will require the renter to present a passport and driver's license, and often a credit-card deposit is needed to complete the transaction. Basic car insurance likely won't cover natural damage, such as flooding, so it's always best for those thinking about going on a country road trip to inquire about extra coverage. Also make sure the renter provides detailed records of any current damage to the vehicle, such as scratches and dents, before you rent.

By taxi

In major cities, radio taxis are abundant. They are typically bright yellow with the company information written in black on the side. Only take official metered taxis with the driver's info clearly displayed. Note that in smaller cities and towns some drivers may not use meters, charging a flat fee instead.

What first-timers to Colombia will likely notice right off is that taxi meters don't display exact prices. Instead, they display units, and each unit represents around 82 Colombian centavos (US$0.3). Once you get in a taxi, the meter starts at 28 units (close to US$1) and every 30 seconds (or 100 meters) it increases one unit. Taxi fares increase after dark.

Cycling

Colombia's mountainous terrain and stunning landscapes make it an increasingly popular destination for long-distance cyclists. Riders and adventure-sports enthusiasts flock to Santander Department – especially San Gil – to partake in cycling excursions around the mountains. However cycling is popular in the cities as well, especially in major cities like Bogotá, Medellín, and Cali, where *ciclovía* occurs every Sunday from 7am–2pm. During this time certain streets are closed to vehicles and cyclists have control of the roads. Newcomers who really want to get to know a city on two wheels should sign up for a group bike tour, as the operators know the best and safest routes.

On foot

The best places for a stroll in Colombia are the smaller colonial cities and towns. There's nothing like walking the ancient ramparts of Cartagena's walled city. While it can be nice to get lost wandering the bigger cities, in places like Bogotá you run the risk of wandering into dangerous neighborhoods after dark. Moreover, the altitude of Bogotá leaves most new visitors short of breath, so long-distance walks aren't practical, at least for the first month. Avoid walking alone in any big city after dark; hitchhiking between cities and towns isn't recommended.

A – Z

A

Accommodations

Over the last 10 years or so, as Colombia has earned a reputation as a safe country to visit, new accommodations have been popping up regularly. There are more lodging options than ever before, and this is evidenced by the international hotel chains that have a presence in the big cities as well as the abundance of hostels throughout the country. In fact it's hard to believe that as recently as the 1980s few, if any, hostels existed in Colombia. Hostel prices tend to be comparable throughout the country, while hotels range from low to mid-range and high end. Outside of cities and towns you can sometimes find *fincas* (farmhouses) that have been converted into guesthouses, similar to a bed-and-breakfast. Usually this involves sharing space with the owner(s) of the *finca* (often a family), and breakfast is typically included. The same is true of *hospedajes* (often converted homes run by a family). Those visiting the Zona Cafetera can choose to stay on a working coffee farm, which is experience in itself and highly recommended. The high season for all accommodations is December–February, so plan on paying higher prices during this period. Making reservations through websites like www.booking.com and www.kayak.com is common and efficient.

Addresses

Colombia's address system can throw anyone off. It is similar to many other countries in South America. It works like this: street-crossing-house number. Or, using a real-life example, you'll likely encounter: Carrera 11, no. 15–23.

Calles and carreras are streets and avenues, and they are typically numbered. In this instance 15 would be a calle. In Colombian addresses, typically Carreras cross calles and vice-versa. You are just as likely to see an address like 'Carrera 11, no. 15–23' as you are 'Calle 15, no. 11–23'. Which comes first depends on which block the building faces. The final field represents the building or house number.

Colombian addresses can include letters (Carrera 10a, or Calle 5b), as sometimes there can be more than one of the same number calle or carrera. Add to that diagonals, transversals, and circulars, and you've got something of an eclectic postal system. It may seem overwhelming, but in time you'll get used to it. It's also worth noting that most cities and towns are set up on an easy-to-navigate grid system, so using Google Maps can really help cut through the confusion and help you get the lay of the land, wherever you may be in Colombia.

Admission charges

Most of Colombia's museums charge around US$2–5 for entrance. However, many are free on Sunday. For example, all of Bogotá's museums are free on Sunday, which means you can enjoy some of the country's best culture for nothing. But be warned: because the entrance is free on Sunday, crowds are even bigger, so expect the Gold Museum to be even more hectic and crowded than it usually is.

As for transportation, most cities have a metro system, and rides are typically purchased on a pre-paid, rechargeable card. These usually cost around US$1 to purchase.

For discos, often a small cover charge (sometimes including a free cocktail or beer) will be required at the door. This can range anywhere between US$2–10 depending on the size and quality of the disco. For regular bars, there is typically no cover charge to enter.

Age restrictions

The legal drinking age in Colombia is 18, as with most Latin American countries, the scrutiny over drinkers' age has been lax. However, new laws have been passed intended to crackdown on underage drinkers. Being served alcohol anywhere shouldn't be a problem, as long as you have proper ID. Usually a passport copy will suffice for this purpose. To rent a car in Colombia, the renter must be at least 21 years of age and possess a valid driver's license from their home country.

B

Budgeting for your trip

Average prices when traveling around Colombia:
Beer: US$1.50
Glass of house wine: US$ 2.50
Main course at budget restaurant: US$3
Main course at a moderate restaurant: US$5–8
Main course at an expensive restaurant: US$10+
Reservation at a cheap hotel: US$15–25 per night
Reservation at a moderate hotel: US$25–60 per night
Reservation at an expensive hotel: US$80+
Average taxi fare around most large cities: US$5–8
Average taxi fare around smaller cities and towns: US$2–4
Average price of a city bus ticket: US$0.75

Average price for a metro ticket: US$0.75

Overall Colombia's economy is stable. However, it is subject to fluctuations, particularly when global gas prices go down. The currency devaluation of 2014/ 2015, is an example of this.

C

Children

Like many Latin American countries, Colombia is very family-oriented as a culture. It's not uncommon for families to go out for meals in big groups with their children, so you will have no problems doing the same. Often hotels and other establishments will make accommodations for children, and kids usually receive reduced-price admission at places like museums and theme parks, provided they are aged under 12 or thereabouts. Often children under three can receive free or reduced-fare bus and airline tickets if they share a seat with a parent. Many of the higher end hotels offer baby-sitting services, but finding this in mid-range and budget lodgings isn't likely. Regardless, those traveling with children will likely find themselves engaging more with local Colombian families, which is always a good thing. Also, officials are likely to be even more willing to accommodate a traveler when they see they have children with them.

Climate

Due to Colombia's position near the equator, it doesn't enjoy seasons in the strictest sense of the word. Temperature variations in the country depend on location and altitude: the coast is always hot and humid; Bogotá is mostly drizzly, overcast, and chilly during the nights. The higher (or lower) you travel in terms of altitude determines the various climates you'll experience. Wet and dry seasons exist in most areas of the country, with precipitation levels varying between locations.

Central Andes (Bogotá)

April to October is considered the rainy season in and around Bogotá. The best time to visit is between December and February, and this is a general rule of thumb for all cities and towns in the country. The average high temperature in Bogotá is around 66°F (19°C) and the average low is around 41°F (5°C). Often the climate here is sunny or partly cloudy during the day, while at night temperatures fall to the point that warm-weather clothing is required.

Caribbean lowlands (Cartagena)

Expect the Caribbean coast to be very hot. The average high temperature in Cartagena is around 86°F (30°C) all year round, and the average low is 77°F (25°C), with high humidity. Temperatures can get even higher the farther east from Cartagena you travel, such as in Barranquilla and Santa Marta.

Southern Colombia (Cali)

There are few temperature variations in southern Colombia due to its proximity to the equator. Cali's average high temperature is 77°F (25°C) and the average low is 65°F (18°C). Due to Cali's altitude and its tropical-savanna climate, the days can be quite warm.

Antioquia (Medellín)

Much of Antioquia sits at altitudes well of over 1,000 meters, so most of its cities and towns enjoy a perpetual spring-like climate, especially Medellín. Average high temperatures here are 71–74°F (22–23°C) throughout the year, and the average low temperatures are 53–55°F (12–13°C).

Zona Cafetera

Like Antioquia, the cities and towns in the Zona Cafetera are at altitude, so the higher temperatures are mitigated by low humidity. The average high temperature in Armenia, for example, is 80°F (27°C) all year, and the average low is 59°F (15°C).

Amazonas

Rather than wet/dry seasons, Amazonas Department has high-water/low-water seasons denoting the level of the Amazon River at the time. The high season is December– May and the low season is June– November. The average temperature in the Amazon is 80°F (27°C) year round with high humidity.

Northwest Colombia (Chocó)

This region is one of the wettest in the world. Precipitation here averages between 600-800mm (23– 31ins) per month, all year round. The average low temperature throughout the year is 71°F (22°C) and the average high is 86°F (30°C), with high humidity.

Crime and safety

For a country that has dealt with internal armed conflict for over 50 years, Colombia has made great strides in terms of safety. As of early 2017, the government is on the verge

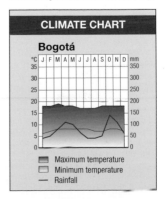

CLIMATE CHART

Medellín

°C J F M A M J J A S O N D mm

Maximum temperature
Minimum temperature
— Rainfall

CLIMATE CHART

Cali

°C J F M A M J J A S O N D mm

Maximum temperature
Minimum temperature
— Rainfall

CLIMATE CHART

Bogotá

°C J F M A M J J A S O N D mm

Maximum temperature
Minimum temperature
— Rainfall

of a peace deal with the country's largest guerrilla group, the FARC. Moreover, their operation, and those of other rebel groups, such as the National Liberation Army (ELN), has been significantly degraded, and they've been forced out of most major urban areas into the remote countryside or jungle. Now more than ever, Colombia is regarded as a generally safe destination for tourists. Tens of thousands of US citizens visit the country every year without incident.

However risks do exist. Violence and guerrilla activity continue to plague certain parts of the country, like Chocó Department. As long as there is no peace deal, terrorism will always be a possibility. Also, because some 80 percent of the world's cocaine production occurs in Colombia, narco-trafficking is also a very real reality. Therefore no traveler should leave their bags unattended in transportation hubs, and never agree to carry someone else's bag for them.

Petty crime also remains a problem throughout Colombia. There have been reports of foreign travelers being mugged or even robbed at gunpoint. These incidents occur in various locations across the country, including city streets, taxis, and public transportation. Often the assailants are only interested in money, so if this happens, it's best to oblige them without resistance. Most important is to avoid traveling alone, always travel in clearly marked taxis, avoid areas in large cities that are dangerous at night, such as public parks and the downtown neighborhoods, and take the usual precautions: don't leave valuables lying around your hotel or hostel room, avoid wearing flashy jewelry and general displays of wealth. If a member of the police or military approaches you asks for ID, always be polite and produce it for them. A paper copy will often suffice.

For (mostly) up-to-date safety information, including a list of Colombian areas generally considered to be safe for travel, see: www. travel.state.gov and www.gov.uk. Both of these resources acknowledge that it's possible for the security situation in Colombia to change on short notice, so you should always pay attention to the warnings issued by local authorities. You can also get more specific safety information by calling 1-888 407 4747.

Customs

Customs checks occur at airports and land and river crossings between Venezuela, Brazil, Ecuador, and Peru. Due to the drug trade, customs checks at airports can be extensive, and sometimes there are military checks on long-distance bus routes where passengers are asked to produce ID. Always monitor your baggage at airports and bus terminals, and never carry firearms or drugs when traveling.

When entering and exiting Colombia, travelers are allowed the following: 200 cigarettes, 50 cigars, and fewer than 50 grams of tobacco; two bottles of alcoholic beverages; and a reasonable quantity of perfume. Currency import regulations state that amounts exceeding US$10,000 or equivalent currency must be declared on arrival. All vegetables, plants and food of animal origin is prohibited from entering or leaving the country. Passengers arriving to Colombia with cats or dogs must first get authorization and approval from the Colombian Agricultural Institute (ICA; Bogota, Carrera 41, no. 17–43; tel: 1-332 3700; www.ica. gov.co; Mon–Fri 8am–5pm).

As of January 2017 there is an airport embarkation tax of US$37.

D

Disabled travelers

Disabled travelers to Colombia will find a country that, in some areas, accommodates their needs, yet is woefully underdeveloped in parts. For example, new hotels and lodging options are required to provide disability access, and most live up to this standard. However, in certain older neighborhoods and towns, especially the colonial ones, old buildings and streets may not be suitable for disabled travelers. As for transportation, the modern metro systems in the big cities offer disability access, but local minibuses are typically small and unmodified, which may present problems to mobility-impaired travelers who want to travel to certain local areas.

The best way to view Colombia is that it is an imperfect country where it concerns the needs of the disabled, but that it is improving incrementally all the time. Having said that, there's nothing stopping those with disabilities from enjoying this beautiful country to the fullest. Some useful online resources to help achieve this include: European Network for Accessible Tourism (ENAT; www.accessibletourism.org), the US State Department's Traveling with Disabilities section (www.travel. state.gov/content/passports/en/go/disabilities.html), Accessible Journeys (www.disabilitytravel.com/access-network), and the Society for Accessible Travel & Hospitality's list of disability travel websites (www.sath.org/ disability-travel-websites).

E

Eating out

Despite having a rich and tasty legacy of various unique cuisines throughout the country, it's only recently that Colombia began enjoying a reputation as a top global foodie destination. Perhaps this has to do with the new cutting-edge restaurants popping up all over the wealthier neighborhoods in major cities. Regardless, visitors with a healthy appetite will want to experience the traditional regional cuisine that is so much a part of the country's fabric. There's no better way to do this than by taking part in the set lunch specials offered by eateries in most cities and towns. Not only will you be able to sample local fare this way, but you will do so at a steep discount to dinner prices. Set lunch meals usually cost between US$4–6 and typically include a starter, main course, dessert, and juice.

As for the higher-end restaurants, rarely is it necessary to make a reservation, except at the most popular and/or expensive options, such as Andres Carne de Res in Bogotá, and walk-ins are usually welcome. Also, while Colombians are polite, meal etiquette isn't particularly strict. Colombians like to eat with family and friends in a more relaxed atmosphere, so join in and have fun.

Electricity

Colombia's voltage is 110V–120V, which is the same as in the US and Canada. Primary socket types are

North American grounded or non-grounded (two/three-pin plugs). European plugs will require a plug adapter; 220–240V appliances will require a transformer.

Embassies and consulates

Some principal embassies for English-speaking countries in include:
United States: Calle 24, no. 48–50, Bogotá; tel: 1-275 2000; https://bogota. usembassy.gov; Mon–Fri 8am–noon
Colombian embassy in United States: 1724 Massachusetts Avenue NW, Washington, DC 20036; tel: 202-387 8338; www.colombiaemb.org; Mon–Fri 8.30am–2.30pm
Canada: Carrera 7, no. 114–33 14th floor; Bogotá; tel: 1-657 9800; www. canadainternational.gc.ca; Mon–Thu 8am–12.30pm, 1.30–5pm, Fri 8am–1.30pm
Colombian embassy in Canada: 360 Albert Street, 1002, Ottawa ON1 K1R 7X7; tel: 613 230 3760; http:// ottawa.consulado.gov.co/en; Mon–Fri 9am–1pm
UK: Carrera 9, no. 76–49 8th floor; Bogotá; tel: 1-326 8300; www.gov.uk; Mon, Tue, Thu, Fri 9am–12.30pm
Colombian embassy in UK: 35 Portland Place, W1B 1AE, London, 3rd floor; tel: 020 763 79893; www. londres.consulado.gov.co Mon–Fri 9am–1.30pm; document delivery 3–4.30pm
Australia: Carrera 9, no. 115–06; Bogotá; tel: 1-657 7800; the Australian embassy offers limited consular services; for assistance with visa issues it's best to go through their principal embassy in Santiago, Chile:

Eating out in downtown Bogotá.

www.chile.embassy.gov.au
Colombian embassy in Australia: Suite 2, Level 12, 100 Walker Street, North Sydney NSW 2060; tel: 2-9955 0311; http://sydney.consulado.gov.co; Mon–Fri 7am–1pm, 2–4pm
Colombian embassy in New Zealand: 191 Queen Street, Auckland Central, Auckland City, New Zealand; tel: 09-300 6390; http://auckland.consulado. gov.co; Mon–Fri 9am–1pm, 2–5pm
South Africa: tel: 1-214 0397; www. dirco.gov.za; limited consular services–best to go through the embassy in Caracas, Venezuela: tel: 58 212-952 0026
Colombian embassy in South Africa: 1105 Park Street 3rd Floor, Park Corner Building, Hatfield, Pretoria, South Africa; tel: 12 3623106; http:// pretoria.consulado.gov.co; Mon–Fri 8.30am–12.30pm, 2–4pm
Ireland: Avenue Americas 56-41; Bogotá; tel: 1-432 0695; www.dfa.ie; Mon–Fri 9am–4pm; just an honorary consul; the embassy is in London

For a full list of embassies visit www.cancilleria.gov.co.

Emergency numbers

National police/Red Cross ambulance 24-hour line/fire department: tel: 123; civil defense: tel: 1-700 6465 (Bogotá), tel: 123 rest of country; tourist police: tel: 1-337 4413 (Bogotá).

Etiquette

Colombians are notably relaxed where it concerns formalities. Aside from church (where the general rules of decorum and quiet are practiced), you'll find that no matter the city or town, locals don't make a big to-do about etiquette. If a person or family invites you to their home for a meal – a common occurrence as Colombians are famously hospitable – you'll find that arrival times aren't particularly strict and there's no real dress code. Often it's the foreigners who are thrown off the most, especially when they bring notions of etiquette from their home country. Remember that Colombians place enjoyment and fellowship above rules; go with the flow and you'll have a great, stress-free time.

F

Festivals

Colombians love a party, and as proof of this there are more official festivals in each municipality than there are days in the calendar year. Here's a list of the most famous.

January
Feria de Manizales. (www.feriade manizales.gov.co) In early January the coffee-producing city of Manizales throws a diverse party featuring parades, costumes, live music, tango dancing, stunt shows, and beauty queens.
Hay Festival Cartagena. (www.hay festival.com/cartagena) This is the Cartagena de India branch of the UK's Hay Festival, which takes place at the end of January and focuses on literature, art, cinema, music, geopolitics, and the environment. The purpose is to promote culture and social responsibility.
Carnival de Pasto. (www.carnavalde pasto.org) The southwestern city of Pasto has its own carnival, which takes place at the end of January or around the beginning of February. Face painting with black grease and white flour signifies the emancipation of slaves, and there are floats and processions.

February and March
Barranquilla Carnival. This is one of the biggest carnival celebrations in South America. People flock to downtown Barranquilla where, four days before Ash Wednesday, parades and dancing lead to copious amounts of partying

March and April

Semana Santa. The traditional Holy Week is a big event throughout the country. Most cities and towns will feature processions, but the pageantry is particularly notable in places like Popayán.

April

Fiesta Leyenda Vallenata. (www.valledupar.com/festival) The city of Valledupar explodes every year in late April with a four-day party celebrating locally invented vallenato music. During the day crowds gather in Plaza Alfonso Lopez, while at night tens of thousands pack the concert area by the river for more revelry. The festival culminates in an award for best musician.

June

Festival Folclórico y Reinado Nacional de Bambuco. From mid-June to early July the biggest festival in Huila Department takes place in Neiva. There's live music, floats, traditional dances, and many eye-catching dresses and costumes.

August

Feria de Flores. (www.feriadelasflores medellin.gov.co) In the 'City of Eternal Spring,' flowers are always in bloom. Medellín celebrates this every year during the first two weeks of August, when harvesters line the streets carrying great floral displays on their backs. There are also horse shows, concerts, and street parties.
Festival del Viento y de los Cometas. Whatever the windiest August weekend is in Villa de Leyva, that's when the town holds its famous kite festival. For three days everyone packs the central plaza to display their aerial prowess. Contest involve, among other things, best handmade kite and best practitioner in the kids' division.

September

Jazz al Parque. (www.jazzalparque.gov.co) For a weekend in early to mid-September, local and international musicians descend on Bogotá's parks and treat audience members to various types of jazz, including instrumental and big band.
Fiesta de San Pacho. (http://sanpacho bendito.org) Every year in September Chocó Department holds their own carnivalesque celebration, which usually lasts for a couple weeks or more.

November

Independence in Cartagena. The first two weeks in Cartagena see parties celebrating the city being the first to achieve independence from Spain. The event is now linked to the national beauty pageant, which, as the official information states, is held to "unite Colombian regions around the beauty of Colombian women."
Festival Pirarucú de Oro. This festival has been going on since 1987, and takes place in mid-November. It celebrates Amazonian popular music, which has influences in Brazil and Peru as well. Live music and dance is the order of the day.

December

Festival de Luces. On the 7th, 8th, and 9th of December, Villa de Leyva's sprawling central square is lit up with fireworks in order to celebrate the impending Christmas.
Feria de Cali. (www.feriadecali.com). From the 25th to 30th of December, Cali reminds the world why it's synonymous with salsa. There are live music concerts, Paso Fino horse parades, revelry, and, of course, much dancing.

For more information on Colombian festivals, see: www.colombia.travel/en/fairs-and-festivals.

Gay and lesbian travelers

For a predominantly Catholic country, Colombia is fairly progressive where it concerns gay rights. It may not have been the first South American country to legalize gay marriage (that honor goes to Argentina), but in 2016 it did become the fourth after a constitutional court extended marriage rights beyond mere civil partnerships. The country's capital city even has a thriving gay neighborhood, Chapinero, with an official LGBT community center (Calle 66, no. 9a–28; tel: 1-249 0049; http://ccdlgbt.blogspot.com.co).

Aside from progressive laws and pockets of gay neighborhoods in major cities, the general culture of Colombia still errs on the traditional side. Homosexuality often isn't as accepted in the smaller towns as it is in the big cities. LGBTQ travelers should be aware of these sensibilities and, although it isn't the ideal scenario, act with prudence. That said, visitors will find most Colombians to be accepting of all kinds of people, sexual orientation aside.

Health and medical care

Before you go

It's recommended that anyone planning a trip to Colombia see his or her healthcare provider at least six weeks before arriving in the country. It's also helpful to check www.nc.cdc.gov/travel/destinations/traveler/none/Colombia for up-to-date information regarding vaccinations and health concerns in Colombia. Try to get a dental check-up before leaving and if you have chronic health concerns you may want to consider getting a medical ID (www.medicalert.org).

Vaccinations and health risks

Travelers should be up-to-date on routine vaccinations, which include measles, diphtheria, polio, chicken pox, and a yearly flu shot. Anyone planning a trip to the Amazon will want to get a yellow fever vaccination, and these are offered free of charge at the clinic in the Bogotá bus terminal.

Most visitors to Colombia rarely experience any health issues. However, traveler's diarrhoea caused by contaminated food can be an issue, as can swimming in polluted water. Typically tap water in the big cities is safe, but many travelers opt for bottled water regardless. Altitude sickness can be a problem for those arriving in the capital, in which case the best prescription is to take it easy and drink plenty of water. Malaria isn't typically a problem in Colombia, however there is a minor risk. Consult your physician in regards to malaria tablets or taking a round of doxycycline.

Insurance

Visitors from the UK and Europe might be surprised to learn that there is no functioning public health system in Colombia, while visitors from the United States will find a system similar to theirs back home. Most of Colombia's healthcare is privatized. However, there is subsidized insurance for locals living at or below the poverty line. What this means for visitors, however, is that if you get in an accident and need medical care in a clinic or hospital, you will have to pay.

Therefore all visitors to Colombia should buy travel insurance before arriving. One helpful resource that can cut through much of the noise and help you to find a good option quick is www.toptenreviews.com/services/insurance/best-travel-insurance/. Make sure the insurance covers all activities you may be partaking in upon arrival, including and especially adventure sports, trekking, and mountaineering. Ensure that your coverage includes air-ambulance service and emergency flights home.

Those who end up in hospital without health insurance will be faced with exorbitant fees. Be sure to get itemized receipts for any medical services you receive.

Pharmacies and hospitals

Pharmacies are common in every city and town in Colombia. Like in many Latin American countries, pharmacists are allowed to dispense basic, non-opioid medications without a prescription. That means visitors suffering from common afflictions (earache, sore throat, traveler's diarrhoea, etc) should be able to consult a pharmacist and receive the appropriate medication without paying for a doctor's visit. One large pharmacy chain in the country is **Drogas La Rebaja** (www.larebajavirtual.com; tel: 01-8000 93 9900; look for the yellow and red-striped sign). In the capital, many of these pharmacies are open until 8pm or 10pm, but a few are open 24 hours. There's a **La Rebaja Plus** in Chapinero (Calle 57, no. 09–75) and another 24-hour option in the northwest (La Esperanza, no. 43a–11).

As for hospitals, Colombia boasts some of the best on the continent. Travelers' insurance should cover stays in these facilities, and some standout options in the capital include: **Clinica del Country** (Carrera 16, no. 82–5; tel: 1-530 0470; www.clinicadelcountry.com) and **Fundación Santa Fe de Bogotá** (Carrera 7, no. 117–15; tel: 1-603 0303; www.fsfb.org.co). Another useful health resource besides www.cdc.gov is the **British Travel Health Association** (www.btha.org).

I

Internet

Most hotels and hostels in Colombia have Wi-Fi access. Even many *hospedajes* and other family-run lodgings have wireless internet. The speed of such service depends on how remote the town or city you're staying in is. Internet will always be faster in major metropolitan areas than in rural areas. Internet cafés are abundant in major cities, and many can be found in the downtown areas.

L

Left luggage

Most airport hubs and major bus terminals have left-luggage amenities. Prices vary, but you can expect to pay about US$0.50–1 per hour.

Lost property

Most airports and bus terminals have some version of a lost and found, usually for wayward bags. If you've experienced theft of any kind, be sure to file a police report for your insurance records. If your passport has been lost or stolen, file a police report in the jurisdiction where the loss or theft occurred, and report it right away to your embassy.

M

Maps

Almost all official tourist information points in the country will have free maps available for visitors. Tourist offices in many of the big cities not only offer maps of the municipality, but also of the public transportation routes.

Media

Magazines and newspapers

One of the best Spanish-language publications is *Semana* (www.semana.com). For English-language, Bogotá's *The City Paper* is hard to beat. It provides great info and equally good reporting.

The main newspapers in major cities mostly focus on regional issues. Some principal newspapers include:

In Bogotá: *El Tiempo*, www.eltiempo.com, *El Espectador*, www.elespectador.com, *La República*, www.larepublica.com.co.
Cali: *El País*, www.elpais.com.co, *El Pueblo*, www.elpueblo.com.co.
Medellín: *El Mundo*, www.elmundo.com, *El Colombiano*, www.elcolombiano.com.

Radio

There are plenty of terrestrial radio stations, as well as digital options in major cities like Bogotá. For news (and a variety of music), try **W Radio** (www.wradio.com.co). It can be found online or at frequency 690 kHz 99.9 MHz. **Caracol Radio** also has sports and news (www.caracol.com.co; 810 kHz 100.9 MHz).

Television stations

Colombia has around 20 TV stations varying in size and influence from region to region. The two biggest stations are the state-owned **RCN** (www.canalrcn.com) and the private **Caracol** (www.caracoltv.com), both of which are predominantly entertainment channels (lots of *telenovelas* – Colombian soap operas). **NTN24** (www.ntn24.com) delivers 24-hour news coverage; CNN is available in hotels/hostels with satellite TV.

Money

Colombia's official currency is the Colombian peso (COL$). Notes are available in denominations of COL$2,000, COL$5,000, COL$10,000, COL$20,000, COL$50,000 and COL$100,000; the most common coins are the COL$100, COL$200, COL$500 and COL$1,000. Prices given in this book are in US$; at the time of writing, May 2017, US$1 is worth roughly COL$3,000.

Most ATMs accept international debit and credit cards. Those who want to avoid multiple bank fees and international charges should take out as much money as possible at any given time. Banco de Bogotá (www.bancodebogota.com) is a standard ATM that gives out larger amounts (around COL$600,000 per transaction).

Also, EMV (Europay, MasterCard, and Visa) chip technology means it's more secure than ever to use your

Manizales Cathedral.

card when paying for goods and services in Colombia. Be sure to keep reserves of local currency on hand when traveling throughout the country as remote areas of Colombia often have shortages of ATMs.

Tipping

A 10 percent gratuity is expected at most sit-down restaurants and cafés. About half of all eateries in Colombia will automatically add a 10-percent gratuity to the bill. Be sure to ask your server before paying if *servicio* is included in the bill or not.

N

Nightlife

Colombia's nightlife is as varied as it is raucous. This is a culture that likes to party and imbibe. The younger generation in the cities and big towns often prefer the rage-all-night discos. Many, in places like Cali, will opt for a *salsoteca* where they can swing their hips until the wee hours of the morning. However, salsa dance knows no age limit, and revelers young and old, male and female, pack the near limitless salsa clubs found throughout the country in order to court one another or just let off some steam after a long workday. Beer is a staple of the bars and clubs and (depending on the department you happen to be in) rum or *aguardiente* will also be flowing freely. There's no shortage of tropical cocktails along the coast either. The legal

drinking age is 18, and in certain areas the police are cracking down on underage drinking. Be prepared to show ID at many hotspot doors, even if you look well over 18.

O

Opening hours

Business hours in Colombia are often 8am–noon, 2–5pm (or 6pm), with slightly shorter hours on weekends. The two-hour gap is reserved for the siesta, which is practiced in many establishments (although not all of them in the major cities). Banks are typically open Mon–Fri from 9am–3pm or 4pm. Many establishments will be closed on the biggest of public holidays.

P

Photography

It's rarely prohibited to take photos in museums or at tourist attractions. However, when touring indigenous areas with members of the community, be sure to ask permission for any photos you wish to take. Some indigenous do find it rude to take their picture without permission.

Postal services

There are two major postal services in Colombia: **Deprisa** (tel: 01-8000 519393; www.deprisa.com), which is run by the national air carrier

Avianca and offers cargo shipping, and **4–72** (tel: 01-8000 111210; www.4-72.com.co). Deprisa can be found at major hubs, but 4-72 has offices in many more locations including most cities and towns. It costs around US\$0.75–1 to send an international postcard and around US\$1–2 to send a letter up to 20 grams via regular mail. DHL and FedEx also operate in Colombia.

Public holidays

Holidays typically fall on a Monday in Colombia, and if the exact date falls outside of that, the holiday is moved up to the following Monday. Public holidays are known as *puentes* (bridges), because they connect the weekend and working days.

1st January: New Year's Day
Early January: Día de los Reyes Magos (Three King's Day), or the Epiphany
19th March: Saint Joseph's Day
Holy Week: Semana Santa (Easter)
1st May: Labor Day
May: Ascension Day (occurs 29 days after Easter Sunday)
May/ June: Corpus Christi (around two months after Easter Sunday)
29 June: Saint Peter and Saint Paul
June/ July: Sacred Heart (occurs 10 weeks and one day after Easter Sunday)
20 July: Independence Day
7 August: Battle of Boyacá
15 August: Assumption
12 October: Columbus' arrival in America
1 November: All Saints' Day
11 November: Independence of Cartagena
8 December: Immaculate Conception
25 December: Christmas Day

R

Religious services

Roman Catholicism is the dominant religion in Colombia, and it is a pronounced part of the country's culture. However, while most Colombians are Catholic, they are not entirely beholden to Rome: around 75 percent of the population are nominal Catholics, but only 25 percent identify as practicing Catholics. That means there's a great deal of tolerance for other ideas and lifestyles, with most

Colombians adopting a live-and-let-live attitude. In general Colombians observe most religious holidays.

Restrooms

Most restrooms in Colombia are of the standard variety. You'll find that, aside from some of the highest-end hotels, you're required to dispose of toilet paper in a bin as opposed to flushing it. If you're not a patron, budget restaurants will often let you use their restrooms for a price, around US$0.20 or so. Most bus terminals charge to use the restrooms.

S

Shopping

In the major cities of Colombia you'll find explosions of commerce in the form of *centro comerciales*. In Medellín, for example, you can barely throw a rock without hitting a shopping mall of some sort. The downtown areas of the biggest cities tend to offer the best deals, while the zona rosas typically have an abundance of chic boutiques and upscale retailers.

In more recent times travelers with an eye for fashion have come to the country on the hunt for knitted purses. The most authentic are typically crafted in indigenous communities, often outside of Valledupar or in Guajira. The quality of these goods is beyond reproach; the elegant method of knitting them has been passed down through generations of indigenous women for hundreds of years. For them it's as much a spiritual act as it is one of crafting. The bags typically range between US$25–30, and this is one time you don't want to haggle. Just pay the asking price and be happy in the knowledge you're getting a quality product for about 75 percent less than what it would cost in a boutique back home.

Smoking

Colombia, like most Latin American countries, has more or less kept up with global trends where it concerns smoking cigarettes. That means there are few areas anymore where you're free to smoke around

others. Smoking has been banned indoors and in restaurants, and this goes for the smallest of provincial, family-run eateries as well. Smoking is often allowed on restaurant patios, but not in enclosed public spaces. It goes without saying that if you are invited into someone's home, you should ask before lighting up.

Student travelers

Full-time students should take advantage of the International Student Identity Card (ISIC; www.isic.org), available in 70 countries. Possessing one may just entitle you to discounts on transportation and other services and goods. To be honest, though, redeeming these savings may prove difficult, since ISIC isn't exactly on par with American Express in Colombia. Still, teachers can get in on the action by requesting an ITIC (International Teacher Identity Card), also available from ISIC's website.

T

Tax

As of early 2017 the airport departure tax from Colombia is US$37, and this is not included in your airline ticket. Value Added Tax (VAT) in Colombia is 16 percent. In theory foreigners shouldn't have to pay it, but some more expensive hotels add it on anyway. You can request an official VAT report on your bill from hotels that do add the tax.

Telephone

Most cities and towns have an abundance of telecommunications offices where you can enter a *cabina* (cabin) and make local or international calls, paying by the minute. A screen on the phone often displays the price, and these can vary from location to location. Street vendors with signs marked *minutos* will also allow you to make a call for a charge. You can buy a pay-as-you-go SIM card (around US$2) for your mobile if you choose to make calls within the country, and the main telecommunications carriers are Claro and Movistar. However, these days most

Colombians use the cellphone app WhatsApp (www.whatsapp.com) to communicate with one another. It's free and allows you to send texts where you are without the need to change SIM cards. Often hotels, *hospedajes,* and hostels will have a WhatsApp number. For making calls, if outside the area you are calling, dial the one-digit area code followed by the seven-digit number.

Time zone

GMT-5 throughout the year – meaning it's always five hours earlier than Greenwich Mean Time, one hour behind New York City, and two hours ahead of Los Angeles.

Tourist information

You'll find contact information for the principal tourist offices in each town or city throughout the text. Not every town or city has a functional tourist office, but with tourism on the rise in Colombia, expect this to change in the coming years. The main tourist office in Bogotá is in Plaza Bolívar at Carrera 8, no. 9–83, Mon–Sat 8am–6pm, Sun 8am–4pm.

Helpful websites

www.colombianhostels.com.co Extensive network of backpackers hostels in Colombia. A great resource.
www.clubhaciendasdelcafe.com List of coffee fincas that offer tours/ lodging in the Zona Cafetera.
www.despegar.com Booking site for cheap flights within Latin America.
www.gobiernoenlinea.gov.co Government website featuring up-to-date information on new laws and citizens' rights (in Spanish and English).
www.procolombia.co Information on investing, business, and tourism in Colombia (in English and Spanish)
www.ideam.gov.co For weather and climate information (In Spanish).
www.igac.gov.co For maps of the country.
www.presidencia.gov.co Government website.

Tour operators

UK and Australia

Insight Guides tel: 020 7403 0284
www.insightguides.com
Exodus Travels tel: 0203 131 5501
www.exodus.co.uk
Intrepid Travel tel: 1-510 285 0640
www.intrepidtravel.com

Dragoman tel: 1-855 273 0866 www.dragoman.co.uk
STA Travel tel: 800-781 4040 www.statravel.com

You can find an even more extensive list of UK providers at the Latin American Travel Association (LATA) Tel: 203 713 6688 www.lata.org

North America

4&5 South America Travel tel: 1-800 747 4540 www.southamerica.travel
Passport: South America www.passportsouthamerica.com (company offering curated trips to Colombia as well as other SA destinations).
Gap Adventures tel: 1-800 553 8701 www.seecolombia.travel

South America

Colombian Highland Tours/Passport: South America tel: 310-552 9079 www.colombianhighlands.com, www.passportsouthamerica.com (joint venture offering tailor-made tours throughout all parts of Colombia, as well as other South American countries).

V

Visas and passports

Colombia typically offers a standard 90-day tourist visa upon arrival. Passports are stamped upon entering the country and you must receive an exit stamp before leaving. If crossing the border overland know that the larger towns and cities often have a Migracion Colombia office, but the smaller ones may not. It's best to get all your requisite passport stamps in the largest city closest to your exit point. Those who are required to apply for a visa before arrival into Colombia include nationals of Bulgaria, Russia, and the Middle East (excluding Israel), Asian countries (excluding Japan, South Korea, Philippines, Indonesia, and Singapore), Haiti, Nicaragua, and all African countries. The visa process is similar from nation to nation: present multiple photos over white background and a completed application form; allow two weeks for processing. If you're in doubt about the visa requirements concerning your home country, check regulations.

You can request a 90-day visa extension, a *salvoconducto*, at any Migracion Colombia office (typically only Mon–Fri). The price, as of early 2017, is US$23. This will typically be processed on the spot or within 24 hours. Don't apply for the extension any later than 2–3 days before your visa expires. If you do overstay your visa you will incur a fine of around US$133, which only increases the longer you stay. You may be able to get a visa extension before even arriving in Colombia by consulting the embassy in your country of residence, but typically you need a compelling reason, such as medical treatment.

You can't study or volunteer on a tourist visa, so you will need a student visa. If you have already contacted a language institute or volunteer organization, they may well sponsor your visa. You can get a student visa in Colombia, and it lasts six months. They may ask you to provide proof of funds (showing that you have US$400–600 is often sufficient). You can only obtain Colombian business visas outside of the country at the appropriate embassy. The **Ministerio de Relaciones Exteriores** (Calle 10, no 5–51, Palacio de San Carlos, tel: 01-800-097 9899 or 382 6999, www.cancilleria.gov.co, Mon–Fri 7.30am–4pm), in Bogotá, processes student and some work visas. You must register your business or student visa at Migracion Colombia within 15 days of obtaining it or you will be fined. Visa requirements change frequently so check with your consulate before your trip.

Overland border crossings into Ecuador don't require a visa. However, US residents should know that it is now required to obtain a visa before entering Venezuela. You can only apply for one of these 'friendship' visas at one of the very few Venezuelan embassies in the US. It's possible that when attempting to cross overland a border guard might ask for a bribe to waive the visa requirement. Obviously this course of action is not recommended.

For security reasons, copy your passport and keep it with you always. It can present legal problems if police request a copy of your passport and you can't provide one. However, a copy probably won't work as a form of identification when making a payment in a store or restaurant. Drivers' licenses and state-issued ID cards from your home country will typically suffice for this purpose. If your passport does get lost or stolen, file a police report and request a new one at your embassy (see Embassies).

W

Weights and measures

Colombia is on the metric system, but uses US gallons for gasoline

Women travelers

Solo women travelers should feel safe in Colombia. People are friendly, and if you spend time around families they will likely feel protective of you and take you in as one of their own. As with many countries, foreign women can be the object of unwanted attention from local men, but most Colombian males behave, and catcalls and aggressive flirting are the exception rather than the rule. Still, it's best to always err on the side of caution and never go walking anywhere alone after dark. If you do go out alone, make sure a contact has the details about your location and what time you should return. Feel free to wear a wedding ring, or keep a photograph of a supposed significant other that you can produce when you'd like to rebuff unwanted advances. You can show the photo with a simple *mi marido*, (my husband) or *mi novio* (my boyfriend) and that should diffuse the situation. Knowing at least some Spanish will go a long way to avoiding danger and risky scenarios.

Passport checking.

Traveling to Colombia is an enriching experience, no matter your level of Spanish. However, the more you do understand of the language the easer your time in the country will be. Not only that, but being able to communicate with locals on a conversational level will make your Colombian getaway more rewarding than you could ever imagine. Obviously it's not realistic to expect those with little or no prior knowledge of Spanish to learn in a short time. However, using some language tapes and/or taking some classes before your trip is highly recommended. Even just knowing the basics can mean the difference between a pleasant experience and a frustrating one. Be aware that if you intend to take formal classes at an accredited learning institution in the country, you will need to obtain a student visa. Some helpful language-learning resources include:

Amerispan (1334 Walnut St, 6th floor, Philadelphia, PA 19107, USA; tel: 215-531 7917/1-800-511 0179; www.amerispan.com; Mon–Thu 8am–2pm, Fri 7am–1pm EST) offers Spanish immersion and volunteer programs throughout Latin America, including in Bogotá, Cartagena, and Medellín.

Cactus Language Travel Holidays (tel: 0845-130 4775 (UK); tel: 44-1273 830 960; www.cactuslanguage.com) offers Spanish language courses often combined with activities such as salsa or gastronomy in different parts of Colombia, including Bogotá, Cartagena, and Leticia.

LANGUAGE: AN OVERVIEW

The official language of Colombia is Spanish, which is spoken by the majority of the population. However, there are some 60 other dialects spoken by the myriad indigenous communities throughout the country. Those who travel to San Andres and Providencia will find that many locals speak Creole English. Many locals often speak some English, especially the younger generation, but the farther you get from the tourist areas, the scarcer English becomes.

Colombian Spanish, at least the type spoken outside of the coast, is known as a more neutral Spanish than you'll hear in many other countries. It also reflects Colombians' natural politeness. People are deferential here, and when traveling through the interior of the country it is common to hear phrases like *a la orden* (at your service), *que esté bien* (may you be well), *con mucho gusto* (with pleasure). Occasionally people may even regard you as *su merced* (your mercy). One uniquely common phrase that Colombians use when they're feeling more relaxed and less formal is *que chevere!* (so cool). This is one you'll definitely want to learn and remember.

PRONUNCIATION

If your Spanish is limited, it can be intimidating arriving in country like Colombia and hearing how locals pronounce words in their language. Just the idea of rolling of the 'R' can seem like an impossible talent to mimic for many visitors. Those coming from near Europe will find that Colombians don't speak in the Castillian manner, which often substitutes a *th* sound instead of an S. Likewise, those traveling here from the North America will find this to be a more neutral pronunciation when compared to the Spanish of the Mexican culture. While these rules aren't exactly the same throughout the country, here are some guidelines that should help you to understand Colombian pronunciation.

A is pronounced like *car*
E is pronounced like *best*
I is pronounced as *EE*, like *feet*
O is pronounced like *oh*
U is pronounced like *food*
AI is pronounced like *ride*
EI is pronounced like *they*
OI is pronounced like *toy*

CONSONANTS

These are much easier to follow, as they are often pronounced the same way in English. Some exceptions include:

G is used like J if it comes before E or I
H is silent unless it is formed with CH, like *chair*
J sounds like H
LL has a Y sound
Ñ sounds like the first N in *onion*
RR is trilled expertly
X is pronounced s

BASICS

Yes *Sí*
No *No*
Thank you *Gracias*
You're welcome *De nada/por nada*
Okay *Está bien*
Please *Por favor*
Excuse me (to get attention) *Perdón/por favor!*
Excuse me (to get through a crowd) *Permiso*
Excuse me (sorry) *Perdóneme*
Wait a minute! *Un momento*
Please help me (formal) *Por favor, ayúdame*
Certainly *Claro/Claro que sí/Por cierto!*
Can I help you? (formal) *Puedo ayudarle?*
Can you show me...? *Puede mostrarme...?*

I'm lost *Estoy perdido(a)*
I'm sorry *Lo siento*
I don't know *No sé*
I don't understand *No entiendo*
Do you speak English/French/German? (formal) *Habla Inglés/Francés/Alemán?*
Could you speak more slowly, please? *Puede hablar más despacio, por favor?*
Could you repeat that, please? *Puede repetirlo, por favor?*
here/there *aquí (place where), acá (motion to)/allí, allá, ahí (near you)*
What? *Qué? Cómo?*
When? *Cuándo?*
Why? *Por qué?*
Where? *Dónde?*
Who? *Quién(es)?*
How? *Cómo?*
Which? *Cuál?*
How much/how many? *Cuánto?/cuántos?*
Do you have...? *Hay...?*
How long? *Cuanto tiempo?*
Big, bigger *Grande, más grande*
Small, smaller *Chico, mas chico*
I want.../I would like.../I need... *Quiero.../quisiera.../necesito...*
Where is the restroom (men's/women's)? *Dónde está el baño (de caballeros/de damas)?*
Which way is it to...? *Como se va a...?*

GREETINGS

Hello! *Hola!*
Hello *Buenos días*
Good afternoon/night *Buenas tardes/noches*
Goodbye/see you later *Chau/adios/hasta luego*
My name is... *Me llamo...*
What is your name? (formal) *Cómo se llama usted?*
Mr/Miss/Mrs *Señor/señorita/señora*
Pleased to meet you *Encantado(a)/mucho gusto*
I am English/American/Canadian/Irish/Scottish/Australian *Soy Inglés(a)/Norte Americano(a)/Canadiense/Irlandés(a)/Escocés(a)/Australiano(a)*
Do you speak English? (formal) *Habla inglés?*
How are you? (formal/informal) *Cómo está? Qué mas?*
Fine, thanks *Muy bien, gracias*
Take care (informal) *Cuidate*

TELEPHONE CALLS

May I use your telephone to make a local call? *Puedo usar su teléfono para hacer una llamada local?*

Hello (on the phone) *Hola*
May I speak to...? *Puedo hablar con... (name), por favor?*
Sorry, he/she isn't here *Lo siento, no se encuentra*
Can he/she call you back? *Puede devolver la llamada?*
Yes, he/she can reach me at... *Sí, él/ella puede llamarme a [number]*
I'll try again later *Voy a intentar más tarde*
Can I leave a message? *Puedo dejar un mensaje?*
Please tell him/her I called *Por favor avisarle que llamé*
Hold on *Un momento, por favor*
Can you speak up, please? *Puede hablar más fuerte, por favor?*

IN THE HOTEL

Do you have a vacant room? *¿Tiene una habitación disponible?*
I have a reservation *Tengo una reserva*
I'd like... *Quisiera...*
a single/double (with double bed)/a room with two beds *una habitación individual (sencilla)/una habitación matrimonial /una habitación doble*
for one night/two nights *por una noche/dos noches*
first floor/top floor room *una habitación en el primer piso /en el último piso*
with a sea view *con vista al mar*
How much is it? *Cuánto cuesta?/cuánto sale?*
Do you accept credit cards/travelers' checks/dollars? *Se aceptan tarjetas de crédito/cheques de viajeros/dólares?*
What time is breakfast/lunch/dinner? *A qué hora es el desayuno/almuerzo/la cena?*
Come in! *Pase adelante!*
bath/bathroom *el baño*
dining room *el comedor*
elevator *el ascensor*
key *la llave*
push/pull *empuje/tire*
safety deposit box *la caja de seguridad*
soap *el jabón*
shampoo *el champú*
shower *la ducha*
toilet paper *el papel higiénico*
towel *la toalla*

IN THE RESTAURANT

I'd like to reserve a table *Quisiera reservar una mesa, por favor*
Do you have a table for...? *Tiene una mesa para...?*

I have a reservation *Tengo una reserva*
breakfast/lunch/dinner *desayuno/almuerzo/cena*
I'm a vegetarian *Soy vegetariano(a)*
May we have the menu? *¿Puede traernos la carta (or el menú)?*
wine list *la carta de vinos*
What would you recommend? *Qué recomienda?*
special of the day *plato del día/sugerencia del chef*
main course *segundo/plato principal*
coffee... *un café*
with milk *con leche*
strong *fuerte/cargado*
small/large *pequeño/grande*
tea... *té*
with lemon/milk *con limón/leche*
hot chocolate *chocolate*
fresh juice *jugo natural*
soft drink *gaseosa*
mineral water (still/carbonated) *agua mineral (sin gas/con gas)*
with/without ice *con/sin hielo*
cover charge *precio del cubierto*
a bottle/half a bottle *una botella/media botella*
a glass of red/white/rosé wine *una copa de vino tinto/rosado/blanco*
beer *una cerveza*
I need a receipt, please *Necesito un recibo, por favor*
Keep the change *Está bien/quédese con el vuelto*
Cheers! *Salud!*

La carne (Meat)

crudo *raw*
jugoso(a) *rare*
a punto *medium*
bien hecho *well done*
a la brasa/a la parrilla *charcoal grilled*
a la plancha *grilled*
al horno *baked*
ahumado(a) *smoked*
albóndigas *meat balls*
asado(a)/horneado(a) *roasted*
aves *poultry*
cabra *goat*
cerdo/chancho/puerco *pork*
chicharrón *fried pork belly*
chorizo *Spanish-style sausage*
conejo *rabbit*
frito(a) *fried*
hamburguesa *hamburger*
jamón *ham*
lengua *tongue*
lomito *tenderloin*
milanesa *breaded and fried thin cut of meat*
morcilla *blood sausage*
pato *duck*
pavo *turkey*
pechuga *breast*

piernas *legs*
pollo *chicken*
riñones *kidneys*
salchichas/perros *sausages or hot dogs*
ternera *veal*

Pescado/mariscos (Fish/seafood)

almejas *clams*
anchoa *anchovy*
atún *tuna*
bagre *catfish*
calamares *squid*
camarones *shrimp*
langosta *lobster*
langostinos *prawns*
lenguado *sole or flounder*
mariscos *shellfish*
mejillones *mussels*
ostras *oysters*
pulpo *octopus*
salmón *salmon*
sardinas *sardines*
trucha *trout*
vieiras *scallops*

Vegetales (Vegetables)

ajo *garlic*
alcaucil *artichoke*
arvejas *peas*
batata *sweet potato*
berenjena *eggplant/aubergine*
brócoli *broccoli*
calabaza *pumpkin or yellow squash*
cebolla *onion*
chauchas *green beans*
coliflor *cauliflower*
ensalada mixta *mixed salad*
espárrago *asparagus*
frijoles, frisoles *red beans*
hongos, champiñones *mushrooms*
lechuga *lettuce*
maize *corn*
papa *potato*
pepino *cucumber*
porotos *beans*
puerro *leeks*
remolacha *beets/beetroot*
repollo *cabbage*
yucca *cassava*
zanahorias *carrots*
zapallo *yellow squash*
zapallito *green squash*
zapallito largo *zucchini/courgette*

Frutas (Fruit)

aguacate *avocado*
banana *banana*
carambolo *starfruit*
cereza *cherry*
ciruela *plum*

dátil *date*
durazno *peach*
frambuesa *raspberry*
fresa *strawberry*
guayaba *guava*
higo *fig*
lima *lime*
limón *lemon*
mandarina *tangerine*
mango *mango*
manzana *apple*
maracuyá *passion fruit*
mora *blackberry*
naranja *orange*
papaya *papaya*
pera *pear*
piña *pineapple*
pitaya *dragon fruit*
pomelo *grapefruit*
sandía *watermelon*
uvas *grapes*

Miscellaneous

arroz *rice*
azúcar *sugar*
caldo *soup*
cazuela *casserole*
empanada *savory turnover*
fideos *spaghetti*
helado *ice cream*
huevos (revueltos/fritos/hervidos) *eggs (scrambled/fried/boiled)*
mantequilla *butter*
mermelada *jam*
mostaza *mustard*
pan *bread*
pan integral *wholewheat bread*
pan tostado/tostadas *toast*
pimienta negra *black pepper*
queso *cheese*
sal *salt*
sancocho *stew*
salsa picante/salsa ahi *spicy sauce*
sandwich *sandwich*

aguas termales *hot springs*
artesanía *handicrafts*
capilla *chapel*
catedral *cathedral*
cervecería *beer hall/pub*
convento *convent*
disco/discoteca *disco or club*
galería *gallery*
glaciar *glacier*
iglesia *church*
isla *island*
lago *lake*
laguna *lagoon*
mar *sea*
mercado *market*

mirador *viewpoint*
montaña *mountain*
monumento *monument*
oficina de turismo *tourist office*
parque *park*
pileta *swimming pool*
playa *beach*
plaza *town square*
puente *bridge*
río *river*
torre *tower*

autopista *freeway*
carretera *highway, road*
despacio *slow*
entrada prohibida *no entry*
estacionamiento *parking lot*
fuera de servicio *not in service*
gomería *tire repair shop*
no estacione/prohibido estacionar *no parking*
no pare *no stopping here*
¡ojo! *watch out!*
ruta *highway*
salida *exit*
semáforo *traffic light*
sin salida *no exit*

Where can I rent a car? *Dónde puedo alquiler un coche?*
Is mileage included? *Está incluido el kilometraje?*
comprehensive insurance *seguros comprensivos*
How do I get to...? *Cómo se llega a...?*
Turn right/left *Cruzar (or girar, doblar) hacia la derecha/izquierda*
at the next corner/street *en la próxima esquina/calle*
Go straight ahead *Siga derecho*
Where can I find...? *Dónde hay...?*
Where is the nearest...? *Dónde está el/la... más cerca?*
driver's license *licencia de conducir/manejar*
service/gasoline station *estación de servicio*
My car won't start *Mi coche no arranca*
My car is overheating *Mi coche está recalentando*
My car has broken down *Mi coche se rompió/no anda*

airline *línea aérea*
airport *aeropuerto*

arrivals/departures llegadas/salidas
bus (urban) bus colectivo
bus (long-distance) bus micro/omnibus
bus stop parada (de colectivo/micro)
bus terminal terminal de pasajeros
car coche/automóvil
car rental alquiler de coche
ferry ferry
first class/second class primera clase/segunda clase, clase de turista
flight vuelo
luggage, bag(s) equipaje, valija(s)
Next stop please (for buses) La próxima parada, por favor
one-way ticket boleto de ida
platform el andén
ship barco
subway Metro/subterráneo/subte
taxi taxi

TERMS FOR DIRECTIONS

a la derecha on the right
a la izquierda on the left
abajo de under
adelante de in front of
al lado de beside
alrededor de around
arriba/abajo above/below
atrás de behind
avenida/carrera avenue
calle street
cerca de near
cruce con/con at the junction of (two streets)
cruce hacia la izquierda/la derecha turn to the left/right
derecho straight ahead
edificio (Edif) building
en in, on, at
en la parte de atrás in the rear area (as in behind a building)
encima de on top of
entre between
esquina corner
una cuadra a block

AIRPORT OR TRAVEL AGENCY

customs and immigration aduana y migraciones
travel/tour agency agencia de viajes/de turismo
ticket boleto pasaje
I would like to purchase a ticket for... Quisiera comprar un boleto (pasaje) para...
When is the next/last flight/departure for...? ¿Cuándo es el próximo/último vuelo/para...?
What time does the plane/bus/boat/ferry [leave/return?] A qué hora [sale/regresa] el avión/el autobús/la lancha/el ferry?
What time do I have to be at the airport? A qué hora tengo que estar en el aeropuerto?
Is the tax included? Se incluye el impuesto?
What is included in the price? Qué está incluido en el precio?
departure tax el impuesto de salida
I would like a seat in first class/business class/tourist class Quisiera un asiento en primera clase/ejecutivo/clase de turista
lost-luggage office oficina de reclamos
on time a tiempo
late atrasado
I need to change my ticket Necesito cambiar mi boleto
How long is the flight? Cuánto tiempo dura el vuelo?
Is this seat taken? Está ocupado este asiento?
Is this the stop for...? Es ésta la parada para...?

EMERGENCIES

Help! Socorro!
Stop! Pare!
Watch out! Cuidado Ojo!
I've had an accident He tenido un accidente/sufrí un accidente
Call a doctor Llame a un médico
Call an ambulance Llame una ambulancia
Call the... Llame a...
...police la policía (for minor accidents)
...transit police la policía de tránsito (for traffic accidents)
...the fire department los bomberos
This is an emergency, where is a telephone? Esto es una emergencia, dónde hay un teléfono?
Where is the nearest hospital? Dónde queda el hospital más cercano?
I want to report an assault/a robbery Quisiera reportar un asalto/un robo
Thank you very much for your help Muchísimas gracias por su ayuda

HEALTH

shift duty pharmacy farmacia de turno
hospital/clinic hospital/clínica
I need a doctor/dentist Necesito un médico/dentista (odontólogo)
I don't feel well Me siento mal
I am sick Estoy enfermo(a)
It hurts here Duele aquí
I have a headache/stomach ache/cramps Tengo dolor de cabeza/de estómago/de vientre
I feel dizzy Me siento mareado(a)
Do you have [something for]...? Tiene (algo para)...?
a cold/flu resfrío/gripe
diarrhea diarrea
constipation estreñimiento
fever fiebre
aspirin aspirina
heartburn acidez
insect/mosquito bites picaduras de insectos/mosquitos

SHOPPING

What time do you open/close? A qué hora abre/cierra?
Open/closed Abierto/cerrado
I'd like... Quisiera...
I'm just looking Sólo estoy mirando, gracias
How much does it cost? Cuánto cuesta/sale?
It doesn't fit No queda bien
Do you have it in another color? Tiene en otro color?
Do you have it in another size? Tiene en otro talle?
smaller/larger más chico/más grande

SHOPS AND SERVICES

antiques shop antigüedades
bakery panadería
bank banco
barber shop peluquería
bookstore librería
butcher shop carnicería
cake shop pastelería
currency exchange bureau casa de cambio
delicatessen delicatessen
department store tienda por departamentos
fish shop pescadería
florist florista
fruit shop frutería
jeweler joyería
laundromat lavadero
library biblioteca
market mercado
newsstand kiosco
post office correos
shoe repair shop/shoe store zapatero/zapatería
shopping mall centro commercial/shoppings
small grocery store almacén
stationer papelería
supermarket supermercado, autoservicio

toy store *juguetería*
vegetable shop *verdulería*

COLORS

light/dark *claro/oscuro*
red *rojo/colorado*
yellow *amarillo*
blue *azul*
brown *marrón*
black *negro*
white *blanco*
cream *crema*
beige *beige*
green *verde*
wine *bordó*
gray *gris*
orange *naranja*
pink *rosa*

NUMBERS

1 *uno*
2 *dos*
3 *tres*
4 *cuatro*
5 *cinco*
6 *seis*
7 *siete*
8 *ocho*
9 *nueve*
10 *diez*
11 *once*
12 *doce*
13 *trece*
14 *catorce*
15 *quince*
16 *dieciséis*
17 *diecisiete*
18 *dieciocho*
19 *diecinueve*
20 *veinte*
21 *veintiuno*
22 *veintidos*
25 *veinticinco*
30 *treinta*
40 *cuarenta*
50 *cincuenta*
60 *sesenta*
70 *setenta*
80 *ochenta*
90 *noventa*
100 *cien*
101 *ciento uno*
102 *ciento dos*
200 *doscientos*
300 *trescientos*
400 *cuatrocientos*
500 *quinientos*
600 *seiscientos*
700 *setecientos*
800 *ochocientos*
900 *novecientos*

1,000 *mil*
2,000 *dos mil*
10,000 *diez mil*
100,000 *cien mil*
1,000,000 *un millón*

DAYS AND DATES

morning *la mañana*
afternoon *la tarde*
late afternoon *la tardecita*
evening *la noche*
last night *anoche*
yesterday *ayer*
today *hoy*
tonight *esta noche*
tomorrow *mañana*
now *ahora*
early *temprano*
late *tarde*
a minute *un minuto*
an hour *una hora*
a half hour *media hora*
a day *un día*
a week *una semana*
a month *un mes*
a year *un año*
weekend *fin de semana*
holiday *día feriado*

MONTHS

January *Enero*
February *Febrero*
March *Marzo*
April *Abril*
May *Mayo*
June *Junio*
July *Julio*
August *Agosto*
September *Septiembre*
October *Octubre*
November *Noviembre*
December *Diciembre*

DAYS OF THE WEEK

Monday *Lunes*
Tuesday *Martes*
Wednesday *Miércoles*
Thursday *Jueves*
Friday *Viernes*
Saturday *Sábado*
Sunday *Domingo*

SEASONS

spring *primavera*
summer *verano*
fall/autumn *otoño*
winter *invierno*

TIME

at nine o'clock *a las nueve*
at a quarter after ten *a las diez y cuarto*
at one thirty *a la una y media*
at a quarter before two *a las dos menos cuarto*
at midday/noon *a mediodía*
at midnight *a medianoche*
Note: Times are usually followed by *de la mañana* (in the morning) or *de la tarde* (in the afternoon). Transportation schedules are usually given using the 24-hour clock.

FURTHER READING

Colombia has a rich artistic heritage that not only includes canvas and sculpture, but extends to the written word as well. It's no surprise this country has produced some of the world's most interesting authors, as the land and culture of Colombia are nothing if not fascinating. Of course Gabriel García Márquez is the literary lion of the fiction world here, but he doesn't eclipse the country's other fine authors. Moreover, a new generation of writers are emerging throughout Colombia, young and brazen enough to charge forward into new territories, forging a path that doesn't look back to magical realism but searches for the storytelling of the future.

So, for those who are interested in learning more about this country through the written word here are some further reading suggestions that contain both fiction and non-fiction works.

One Hundred Years of Solitude – Gabriel García Márquez. This is the classic that kicked off the closest thing the literary world had to a true revolution in the latter half of the 20th century. Marquez's epic tale of the Buendia family and their ever-evolving town of Macondo captured readers imaginations due to its blending of the real and the fantastic. 50 years on, it is still an incredible read.

Love in the Time of Cholera – Gabriel García Márquez. It makes perfect sense that the writer of *the* epic family drama should try his hand at epic romance. *Love in the Time of Cholera* follows the trials and tribulations of a Costeño, Florentino Ariza, as he spends decades trying to win the hand of Fermina Daza, whose unrequited love has that unmistakable bitter-almond smell of death by cyanide.

Chronical of a Death Foretold – Gabriel García Márquez. This short novel from García Marquez deconstructs the murder of a notable resident of a small town in Caribbean Colombia. The story is told in the non-linear style and features an unreliable narrator as well as colorful townsfolk with their own dubious recollections of how events unfolded.

No One Writes to the Colonel – Gabriel García Márquez. This novella is a notable work in the canon of Marquez in that was written in 1961 and it predates *One Hundred Years of Solitude*. It tells the story of an impoverished colonel hoping to receive his pension. Interestingly, the novel is set during the tumultuous period in Colombia known as *La Violencia*.

⊘ Send Us Your Thoughts

We do our best to ensure the information in our books is as accurate and up-to-date as possible. The books are updated on a regular basis using local contacts, who painstakingly add, amend and correct as required. However, some details (such as telephone numbers and opening times) are liable to change, and we are ultimately reliant on our readers to put us in the picture.

We welcome your feedback, especially your experience of using the book "on the road". Maybe we recommended a hotel that you liked (or another that you didn't), or you came across a great bar or new attraction we missed.

We will acknowledge all contributions, and we'll offer an Insight Guide to the best letters received.

Please write to us at:
Insight Guides
PO Box 7910
London SE1 1WE
Or email us at:
hello@insightguides.com

Oblivion – Héctor Abad. This memoir tells of the assassination of Abad's father by paramilitary groups. It's a first-hand account of the how violence was capable of touching anyone in Colombia at any time.

La Voragine – Jose Eustasio Rivera. *The Vortex*, as it's known in English, written in 1924, follows the exploits of Bogatano José as he relocates to the Amazon during the rubber boom. The novel is striking for its descriptions of the natural beauty of the area, as well as the appalling conditions under which the rubber workers lived.

Maria – Jorge Isaacs. Those who want to read an example of works written during the late 19th century should give this one a shot. It's part of the Spanish romantic movement and follows two central characters from the Valle de Cauca.

The Sound of Things Falling – Juan Gabriel Vasquez. Colombia wasn't always the happy tourist destination it has become in recent years. Narco violence of the 1980s and 90s brought the country to its knees, and few books offer a better glimpse of this turmoil than this one. It looks at the Colombian drug trade through interconnected narratives in Bogotá in the 1990s. It's a well-written tale that has rightfully won many awards.

Delirium – Laura Restrepo. Laura Restrepo is one of Colombia's most famous authors. In this effort she spins a tale of violence and the drug trade in the 1980s, told through multiple perspectives. It's gritty and honest look at a very challenging time.

One River: Explorations and Discoveries in the Amazon Rainforest – Wade Davis. This biographical work details the time a professor, Richard Evans Shultes, spent in Colombia's Amazon studying biology and botany. It provides plenty of anthropological information as well as an account of the ways Colombia has changed in recent times.

Bolívar: American Liberator – Maria Arana. There's a reason there's at least one plaza in every city and town in Colombia named after Simón Bolívar. For the uninitiated, this book is a good introduction to the life of the Liberator.

Birdwatching in Colombia – Jurgen Beckers and Pablo Florez. There are some 1,900 bird species within Colombia's borders. Those thinking about giving birding a shot in the country should have this title as a handy guide.

CREDITS

Alamy 59, 68, 76, 80, 82, 87, 90/91T, 91ML, 91BR, 91TR, 92, 95, 101, 129, 199, 203, 239, 249, 255, 259
Amarildo Ariza 215, 216
Ariana Cubillos/AP/REX/ Shutterstock 44
AWL Images 66, 71, 89, 108, 211ML
Carlos Gonzalez/AP/REX/ Shutterstock 43
Christian Escobar Mora/Epa/REX/ Shutterstock 57, 236/237
Christof Sonderegger/4Corners Images 12/13
Courtesy of ProColombia 7BR, 17T, 212, 213, 214
ddp USA/REX/Shutterstock 61
Fernando Vergara/AP/REX/ Shutterstock 45, 64, 77
FLPA 78BR, 79BR
Getty Images 6MR, 7ML, 8B, 10/11, 21, 24T, 24B, 25, 29, 35, 36, 37, 38, 40, 50, 53, 65, 67, 75, 78/79T, 81, 84, 85, 90BR,

90BL, 91BL, 93, 96, 99, 100, 104/105, 106/107, 115, 124, 134, 135, 139, 141, 142, 154, 165, 166, 167, 171, 180, 181, 186, 187, 188, 191, 193ML, 193BL, 193BR, 194, 200, 201, 204, 205, 208, 210/211T, 257, 262, 263, 267, 268, 269, 270, 272, 273, 274
iStock 6BL, 9BR, 9ML, 17B, 20, 58, 70, 79TR, 94, 109T, 109B, 114, 116, 117, 119, 121, 123T, 125, 127, 130, 131, 133, 137, 161, 163, 173, 174, 184, 185, 189, 192/193T, 192BR, 193TR, 195, 209, 231, 245, 246, 252, 260, 278, 279, 282, 288, 296
Mario Carvajal 211BL
Mary Evans Picture Library 33, 34
Oliver Gerhard/imageBROKER/REX/ Shutterstock 153
PA Images 39, 46
Pedro Felipe 128
Photoshot 242/243
Public domain 28, 30, 31, 62

Robert Harding 4, 18, 98, 155, 159, 177, 210BR
Shutterstock 1, 6MR, 27, 51, 88, 120, 122, 123B, 138, 143, 145, 146, 148, 149T, 149B, 150, 152, 157, 158, 160, 162, 168, 169, 172, 175, 190, 192BL, 202, 207, 210BL, 211BR, 211TR, 218, 220, 222, 224, 226, 227, 228, 229, 230, 232, 233, 234/235, 238, 247, 248, 250, 251, 253, 271, 281, 285, 290, 290/291
Sipa Press/REX/Shutterstock 42, 47, 256, 275
SuperStock 6ML, 7TR, 7MR, 7ML, 7TL, 8T, 9TR, 14/15, 16, 19, 22/23, 26, 48/49, 52, 54, 55, 56, 60, 63, 69, 72, 73, 74, 78BL, 79ML, 79BL, 83, 86, 97, 102/103, 140, 151, 176, 178/179, 182, 183, 206, 217, 219, 223, 225, 244, 254, 261, 264, 265, 276
TopFoto 32
Universidad Nacional de Colombia 41

Front cover: Guatape *Shutterstock*
Back cover: Horse and carriage in Cartegena *iStock*
Front flap: (from top) Cartegena

Shutterstock; Carnival of Barranquilla *iStock*; Paragliding in Bucaramanga *iStock*; Tayrona National Park *iStock*
Back flap: Bogota street *iStock*

INSIGHT GUIDE CREDITS

Distribution
UK, Ireland and Europe
Apa Publications (UK) Ltd;
sales@insightguides.com
United States and Canada
Ingram Publisher Services;
ips@ingramcontent.com
Australia and New Zealand
Woodslane; info@woodslane.com.au
Southeast Asia
Apa Publications (SN) Pte;
singaporeoffice@insightguides.com
Hong Kong, Taiwan and China
Apa Publications (HK) Ltd;
hongkongoffice@insightguides.com
Worldwide
Apa Publications (UK) Ltd;
sales@insightguides.com
Special Sales, Content Licensing and CoPublishing
Insight Guides can be purchased in bulk quantities at discounted prices. We can create special editions, personalised jackets and corporate imprints tailored to your needs.
sales@insightguides.com
www.insightguides.biz

Printed in China by CTPS

All Rights Reserved
© 2017 Apa Digital (CH) AG and
Apa Publications (UK) Ltd

First Edition 2017

No part of this book may be reproduced, stored in a retrieval system or transmitted in any form or means electronic, mechanical, photocopying, recording or otherwise, without prior written permission from Apa Publications.

Every effort has been made to provide accurate information in this publication, but changes are inevitable. The publisher cannot be responsible for any resulting loss, inconvenience or injury. We would appreciate it if readers would call our attention to any errors or outdated information. We also welcome your suggestions; please contact us at:
hello@insightguides.com

www.insightguides.com

Editor: Tom Fleming
Author: Chris Wallace
Head of Production: Rebeka Davies
Update Production: Apa Digital
Picture Editor: Tom Smyth
Cartography: Carte

CONTRIBUTORS

This brand new title was written by **Chris Wallace**, an American travel writer who has been living and working in Colombia since 2005. The project was planned, commissioned and edited by **Tom Fleming**, from Insight Guides' London office. **Penny Phenix** proofread and indexed this title.

ABOUT INSIGHT GUIDES

Insight Guides have more than 45 years' experience of publishing high-quality, visual travel guides. We produce 400 full-colour titles, in both print and digital form, covering more than 200 destinations across the globe, in a variety of formats to meet your different needs.

Insight Guides are written by local authors, whose expertise is evident in the extensive historical and cultural background features. Each destination is carefully researched by regional experts to ensure our guides provide the very latest information. All the reviews in **Insight Guides** are independent; we strive to maintain an impartial view. Our reviews are carefully selected to guide you to the best places to eat, go out and shop, so you can be confident that when we say a place is special, we really mean it.

Legend

City maps

	Freeway/Highway/Motorway
	Divided Highway
	Main Roads
	Minor Roads
	Pedestrian Roads
	Steps
	Footpath
	Railway
	Funicular Railway
	Cable Car
	Tunnel
	City Wall
	Important Building
	Built Up Area
	Other Land
	Transport Hub
	Park
	Pedestrian Area
	Bus Station
	Tourist Information
	Main Post Office
	Cathedral/Church
	Mosque
	Synagogue
	Statue/Monument
	Beach
	Airport

Regional maps

	Freeway/Highway/Motorway (with junction)
	Freeway/Highway/Motorway (under construction)
	Divided Highway
	Main Road
	Secondary Road
	Minor Road
	Track
	Footpath
	International Boundary
	State/Province Boundary
	National Park/Reserve
	Marine Park
	Ferry Route
	Marshland/Swamp
	Glacier Salt Lake
	Airport/Airfield
	Ancient Site
	Border Control
	Cable Car
	Castle/Castle Ruins
	Cave
	Chateau/Stately Home
	Church/Church Ruins
	Crater
	Lighthouse
	Mountain Peak
	Place of Interest
	Viewpoint

INDEX

MAIN REFERENCES ARE IN BOLD TYPE

INSIGHT ⊙ GUIDES

OFF THE SHELF

Since 1970, **INSIGHT GUIDES** has provided a unique perspective on the world's best travel destinations by using specially commissioned photography and illuminating text written by local authors.

Whether you're planning a city break, a walking tour or the journey of a lifetime, our superb range of guidebooks and phrasebooks will inspire you to discover more about your chosen destination.

INSIGHT GUIDES

offer a unique combination of stunning photos, absorbing narrative and detailed maps, providing all the inspiration and information you need.

PHRASEBOOKS & DICTIONARIES

help users to feel at home, when away. Pocket-sized with a free app to download, they go where you do.

CITY GUIDES

pack hundreds of great photos into a smaller format with detailed practical information, so you can navigate the world's top cities with confidence.

EXPLORE GUIDES

feature easy-to-follow walks and itineraries in the world's most exciting destinations, with our choice of the best places to eat and drink along the way.

POCKET GUIDES

combine concise information on where to go and what to do in a handy compact format, ideal on the ground. Includes a full-colour, fold-out map.

EXPERIENCE GUIDES

feature offbeat perspectives and secret gems for experienced travellers, with a collection of over 100 ideas for a memorable stay in a city.

www.insightguides.com

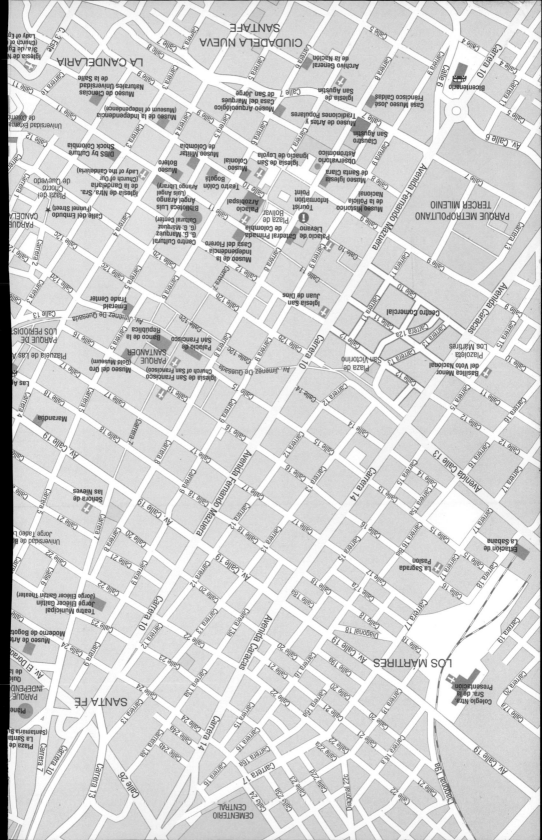